An Overview of the History of the Motorcycle in America

ISBN 978-0-692-13400-9

An Overview of the History of the Motorcycle in America

With a Topical and Social Narrative

by

Mark H. Bayer

Chapter Headings

Acknowledgments

I don't think that people realize the impact that they may have on others. One sentence from someone that you hardly know could potentially have a great influence on the direction in your life. This may have occurred while being totally unknown to the person making the comment. Some fleeting experience might have set a course in your life that lasts decades, though at the time it occurred, it seemed relatively insignificant.

I have experienced many of these occurrences, large and small, and many a great insight came when it was least expected. I do not want to forget the impact of the smallest contributor to my thinking processes and certainly do not want to slight those who have had a major impact either.

I have worked with, received from, and have been guided by so many great people. This is certainly true when it comes to my experience with motorcycles. I will list a few: Jack Barkley, Jean Bayer, Randy Baxter, John Bender, Robert Blaksley, Jim Boughn, Russ Briggs, Bill Brown, Sean Carrigan, Claude Chafin, Harley Eldreth, John Elscott, Darwin Fest, Michael Fitterling, Bob Guisinger, Dave Harris, John Healey, James Herr, Joe Huffman, Hal Johnson, Mike Judy, Jerry Juenemman, Mike Kackley, Curtis Karnes, Jim Koenig, Gary Kuzmich, Wally LaFond, Gary and Wanda Lantz, Jack Larson, Jim Lettellier, Clifford Miller, Dale Miller, Russ Morgan, Lyle Penner, Fred Reynolds, Calvin Roberts, Doug Rollert, Randy Sams, Jerry Semler, Frank Sereno, Jose Settle, Bill Silvers, Peter Slatcoff, Jim Sneegas, Stephen Spencer, Brian Studdard, Jim Sutcliff, Darren Traub, Bob Walker, Stephen Wright, Buzz Walneck, Drew Walter, Mark Wamboldt, Ralph Wayne, Bill Wilson, Jay Wilson, and Steve Young. I am truly sorry if I missed a name or two, but I have really appreciated my involvement with so many great people. I would also like to thank the people involved in publishing this work. Only those people who have worked on such a project know the hours of dedicated effort it takes to compile the information and get it in the necessary order. Hopefully, I will not forget to add last minute names which will come up later. It is my desire to recognize everyone who has been a help. If this did not occur in a specific situation, I apologize, I certainly did not want to leave anyone out.

Foreword

I have been involved in motorcycling for well over half a century. My addiction began when I rented a little Japanese two-stroke from a gas station back in 1964. I drove that bike like an idiot, weaving around cars and riding around town in a really unsafe manner. I make that comment because I did ride that way as a teenager, but I do not recommend unsafe riding practices in any form. Please ride safely. Within a year after renting that bike I purchased a used Honda 50 Cub, the model with an electric starter. Several friends also bought Honda 50 Cubs, and we rode around together like a Cub motorcycle gang.

I don't think we intimidated many people on those little Honda 50s.

I was thoroughly immersed in two-wheeled travel by that time. Within a year I moved up to a Honda CB160. and my best friend at that time bought a Honda CA150 Dream. I still have strong memories of riding that 160cc bike with what seemed to have a lot of power. Back in 1965 it actually seemed like a big bike.

Like a lot of new riders in the late 1960s, we rode our bikes everywhere and whenever we could. I loved riding off road. I had a number of street scramblers back then: a Honda 305, a 350, and a 450 as well.

*My '67 Honda Scrambler, From the
author's collection*

My brother and I owned a
first edition Yamaha DT 1. Several friends and I would just
ride the unpaved gravel back
roads and occasionally open a
farmer's gate and ride wherever
the trail would take us. I don't
ever remember running out of
gas.

Around 1968 or 1969 I
owned half of a 1959 Triumph
Thunderbird with a friend. It
had a stripped first gear, so
we had to start in second gear,
which could be hard to do on
a hill. Riding the 650 Triumph
did make me feel like a real
biker.

At that time I began to
understand the importance of
image. My Honda 450 would
smoke the Triumph in regards
to acceleration and would even
outperform it in regards to top
speed; however, the Triumph
had a persona which surpassed that of the Honda. The
Triumph had street credibility,
while the Honda just never did.
The bathtub panels had been
removed from the Triumph,
so it looked like a Triumph
Tiger. Americans never liked

the bodywork, and bikes with
them were quickly stripped of
those parts.

About the same time, I
purchased an old military Harley-Davidson Knucklehead
with another friend (John),
and we spent a winter customizing it in a building owned
by his dad. We ordered a set
of fork "extenders" that fit on
the springer front end, making it look like a chopper. They
just slipped on and had to be
welded to the forks at the top.
I am sure now that they were
probably unsafe. We used a
front wheel from a small Japanese bike with the brake removed. Imagine a 700-pound
motorcycle with one brake in
the back. The back brake was a
single shoe unit, so when you
wanted to stop you had to plan
a half a block ahead. What a
dangerous machine.

On its maiden voyage the
rider was using the bobbed
back fender as a seat, which
consisted of a folded rag over a
piece of wood sitting on top of
the fender. After hitting a bump
in the road, the fender bracket
failed, causing the fender to be
pushed against the back wheel,
causing the fender to flip under
the bike and then up in the air,
ripping part of the rider's jeans
off. I was riding behind the
bike and could see it all.

It looked really funny but
was actually very dangerous. I
laughed so hard I was weaving
all over the road. What stupid

things people do when they are young and are unaware of how unsafe their practices are.

I got married to my wife, Jean, in 1970 and continued riding. For a number of years I gave up riding because of work, children, and a limited budget. I still followed motorcycling and occasionally had a chance to ride a friend's or relative's motorcycle.

One summer I was at a family picnic, and my brother had his Yamaha 360 dirt bike there. I took it for a ride and thought I would make a grand jump over a small hill. I was not used to the bike and was going a bit fast and allowed the front wheel to come down first, causing me and the machine to go down. I remember sliding on the ground with my mouth getting filled with dirt like a shovel. People in the area saw me, and I am sure I looked re-

ally uncoordinated instead of the professional moto-crosser I was attempting to look like.

In the late 1980s I purchased two BSA 250 Starfire motorcycles. One was a street model and the other one was a stripped down version built for off road riding. At that time, I loved the British bikes for their history and for their good looks. Most British bike companies were gone by then, except for Triumph. They were rarely seen and were already being collected or put in garages and stored. I sold the stripped-down bike for a measly $200 and within several years sold the street bike. I really liked the remaining motorcycle, but because it always had some minor mechanical problem, I chose to sell it. It was broken more than it was in good running condition.

My 1969 BSA Starfiure, From the author's collection

I replaced the BSA with a Honda, which was on the opposite end of the spectrum in terms of reliability. The Japanese motorcycles were much more reliable. From that time on, I just stuck with bikes I could count on to start and run with minimal or no problems. I still loved the old British bikes and still do.

Sometime by the end of the 1980s I began having an interest in vintage motorcycles and began collecting books and magazines. That's when my interest in motorcycle history began to grow.

I casually studied motorcycle history but also started several types of motorcycle riding clubs. One group was called the "Honda Enthusiasts." We typically had around five to ten riders and, on rare occasions, had up to twenty bikes and riders. We would ride interesting routes of a hundred miles or less. It was rare to go over 150 miles, though we occasionally did.

Another group was called the "Midwest Cruisers." We used this name because many people in the group did not ride Honda motorcycles and we did not want people to think that only Honda motorcycles were welcome.

For several years I made two identical ride schedules using both group names. I finally gave up the riding clubs because I was the only one who made, scheduled, and led the rides. It was rare that anyone else would lead rides, so I finally got tired of doing all the planning. I am not complaining; I was just doing something which was not inspiring any growth or involvement by others. We typically had a dozen rides a year and often connected with other riding groups.

I started another club called "VCME" (Vintage and Custom Motorcycle Enthusiasts). This group was really small, never growing beyond half a dozen people, but we did have several shows, which were fun.

Donnell's Event, From the author's collection

The largest VCME show we had featured over a hundred motorcycles, but most events were much smaller. We actually had few vintage or custom motorcycles ever show up; most were just street bikes.

VCME turned into "The Cowtown Rockers" around 2012, and this group did several events called the "Mods VS Rockers" rallies. These shows were really fun, but because of a few people who got out of control and who were not members of our club, we lost our event location. This was a huge loss, because it was a great place for events. The last Cowtown Rocker event was called "Bikes, Bands, & BBQ" and was held in 2016. I occasionally run across some of those people who were a part of those early groups.

I also helped start a group called "Grand Classic Events" in 2004, which primarily did car shows. We would typically have motorcycles at our shows, but usually not many. I was unable to get much of a car show going until a guy by the name of Harley Eldereth got involved. After Harley began leading, our events grew significantly. With most groups in which I was involved, I would also make a dedicated web site. After several years, I was managing over fifteen sites. Many were still in operation at the time of this writing. Just type

in "Mark Bayer motorcycles" and see what comes up. A show that I organized during those early years might have twenty to forty cars with half a dozen bikes. When Harley built the shows they would grew to typically 200 vehicles, but some had over 600 cars and motorcycles. Grand Classic Events sponsored a number of shows at different locations, including a show for Gladstone, Missouri. Our group helped a past mayor of Gladstone do that show, which grew into a substantial event. It grew from around eighty vehicles to over 350.

Another primary event was a show for a large church, Vineyard Church of Kansas City. This show has still continued after a dozen years, and typically has several hundred cars and a dozen or so motorcycles on display. I really appreciate Mark Wamboldt, Joe Huffman, and others who always made me feel a part of the event long after the original group discontinued organizing the event. Thanks a lot, Mark and Joe.

The Grand Classic Events web site was up from 2005 until 2017, but after around 2013 the domain was used by Dave Harris. Dave was a founding member of the Grand Classic group and used the site to promote his personal car-related activities. He even hosted a car corral for awhile.

One of my greatest pleasures has been my involvement with the VJMC (Vintage Japanese Motorcycle Club). Since 2011, Frank Sereno and I, along with many other great people, have seen the Kansas City chapter of the VJMC grow into one of the largest VJMC clubs in the US. Hopefully this growth can continue as the years pass. It is rare that groups can maintain healthy growth because of group dissention among members, which is sadly the norm. Perhaps we can defy what is typical of motorcycle clubs.

Our events began in the early years with around twenty bikes, and years later might host as many as 175. We can almost always count on more than a hundred bikes at our events, unless the weather is bad. Our shows have became the largest vintage Japanese motorcycle events in the entire Midwest. We started off by having one yearly event. This number has grown to six within five years, if you count an annual two-stroke show.

Event Photo, From the author's collection

I ended up writing dozens of articles for the VJMC's magazine, *Vintage Japanese Motorcycle Magazine*, a few articles for web-based papers, and several for the other related magazines. The years with this group has been more fun than can be described.

I actually began doing small motorcycle events in 2004. The first one was called "Bike Day." Bike Day was held in a small coffee shop parking lot. From that first event, which included cars, motorcycles, and three bands, I have been involved in well over a hundred car and motorcycle shows between 2004 and 2017. Many were individual events, some were events held monthly, and many were events in which

I just helped organize, promote, and manage. Events have been done in grocery store parking lots, miscellaneous business locations, an airport hanger and parking area, church parking lots, motorcycle dealership lots, public parks, at restaurants, and even in a mall parking lot. A number of large events were done at the Kansas City downtown market area, which was a really nice venue.

The largest event in which I have ever been involved was at a large city park area in Parkville, Missouri. The Grand Classics Events group started the event (around 2008), which grew to somewhere above 600 vehicles located in several large public parking lots. It was held monthly, as long as the weather was accommodating. I think the event is still going on.

Without a doubt, my life has been intertwined with motorcycle-related activities. I just love the sport. From casual riding to occasional long distance rides, I have put tens of thousands of miles on the seat of a motorcycle. At the time of this writing, I have been riding motorcycles for over fifty years. Being involved in shows or events came out of my love for motorcycles, and the more I engaged in developing events, the more I wanted to be an active part of seeing more of them happen. My natural tendency to understand things led me into studying the history of the motorcycle.

Starting in the mid-1980s I began making notes on the history of the motorcycle, which continues to this day. I have put together over fifty notebooks of various sizes covering many topics. One topic has been that of collecting sales data information. For at least a decade, whenever I come across a relevant figure I make a note of it in a book. I have notebooks on people, events, movements, racing, brands, stages of motorcycle development, and many other related topics. I love the obscure topics and the traditional historical topics as well.

As I have studied I have also acquired many books and other miscellaneous materials. As I write this, I have several hundred motorcycle history-related books and, I am sure, thousands of miscellaneous pieces of material related to the sport of motorcycling. The focus of my collection is usable information, not that of owning valuable or collectible books. I say that because many of my most prized books are books few would find valuable in terms of collectability. My book collection has little value but great breadth.

I started teaching a motorcycle history class at the University of Missouri in Kansas City (through the Communiversity program) sometime after 2012 and have continued to do so several times a year.

My experience in the world of motorcycling has been a great experience, which has allowed me to know so many great people. I would not change this part of my life for anything.

Event Photo, From the author's collection

Event Flier, From the author's collection

Introduction

Auto Era Cycle, Courtesy of Motorcycle Illustrated

The motorcycle has been in existence for around 150 years, though it has only been a recognized category of transportation for a little over 117 years. I pulled into an event years ago on a Honda Gold Wing, and several motorcyclists on well known American brands of machines noted loud enough so I could hear, "Honda doesn't really make motorcycles, but some of their bikes are close."

There should not really be any confusion about what constitutes a motorcycle. A motorcycle is simply a two-wheeled vehicle which is self-powered. A scooter is typically different in that they, generally but not always, have smaller wheels and the rider sits on the machine like a chair (feet in front of them on a floorboard). A moped is just a small motorized machine with an engine and pedals. A minibike is just a little motorcycle. Many of the early motorcycles had pedals because they were just a few steps away from the bicycles which preceded them.

Moto in Latin simply means "to drive" or "to move." *Cycle* simply means to "orbit, to turn, or move in a circular manner." In its most basic definition, a motorcycle is just a machine which moves by its own power. All of these terms are primarily culturally understood. I make the comment above because the history of the motorcycle includes so much more than just developmental facts about how the motorcycle evolved over time.

The motorcycle community is filled with social groups, special interest groups, people with strong biases, brand-dedicated people, loosely organized clubs, highly organized clubs, and so much more which could only be understood by those having spent time in the community at large. Many members of the motorcycle community know little more about motorcycles than the values their subgroup holds. Giving an easily understood overview of the motorcycle and its history has been a driving force behind the writing of this book.

The origins of the motorcycle, or self-powered vehicles, really go back to an earlier time when industrious and innovative men were trying to find better ways to travel. People have always had an interest in going places. Looking far back to ancient times, floating things down a river was one of the first forms of transportation, probably preceding the development of the wheel. There were actually experimental carts moved along crude trails by boat-type sails, there were crude bicycles which were coasted because they had no pedals, there were "skateboard"-type devices pulled behind an animal, and many other things used to make transportation easier. All of these devices were developed to make travel easier and faster.

It was actually the development of steam power in the late 1600s which catapulted the development of self-powered transportation forward. America didn't see much interest or development in steam power until the late

1830s. It seems hard to understand today, but one of the big innovations which allowed steam power to develop was making a workable piston. It was hard to get a round piston in a round sleeve with close enough tolerances to actually work well. Without this issue being resolved, the internal combustion engine would have never been able to be developed. There was no equipment available to make efficient pistons and barrels, and furthermore, the development of lubricants was so archaic that allowing the rubbing of metals together was a significant hurdle apart from piston development.

As steam power was developed and steam engines became more common, the internal combustion engine became a potential reality because more people experimented with various forms of industrial power. It was not until the mid-1880s that a petroleum-based fuel replaced coal, especially in small steam power plants.

As petroleum-based fuels became available, more efficient power plants were designed that allowed for the internal combustion engine to mature. These new engines were at the edge of technology. Even after early petroleum-based engines were built, compression, carbure-

tion, ignition systems, cooling, weight, and lubrication issues still made engines low in power, short in lifespan, and high in maintenance.

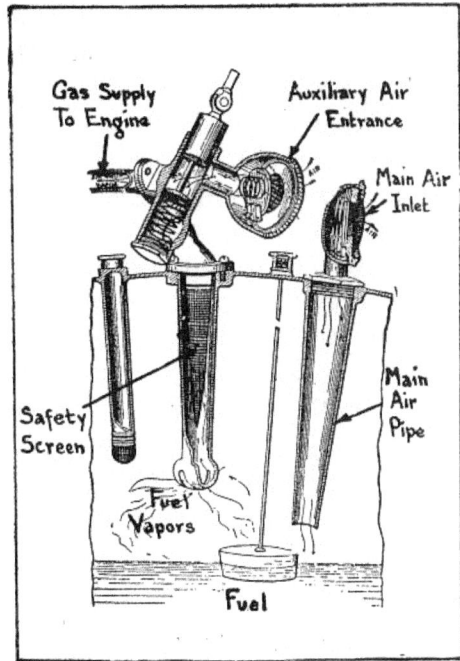

Improvements from the vapor carburetor to the float type was a huge advancement. The vapor unit pictured is from the pre-1900 period. Courtesy of Motorcycle Illustrated

Fuel delivery was a huge area needing development. The first carburetors simply used gas vapors being funneled into the engine. These vapor devices were originally called "surface carburetors" in that fuel was simply mixed with air as the air was swept over a gasoline-filled chamber or through a wick. Air simply wafted over fuel being held in a reservoir and into the engine. These carburetors were inefficient, inaccurately metered, and unsafe, but that was the nature of these early engines.

Better wick systems were developed later, followed by various float and nozzle systems. Afterwards, various spray devices were used until a relatively usable carburetor was developed. Carburetors were generally developed separately from engine manufacturing in that the developmental technology needed to advance fuel delivery was in a field by itself.

One of the early issues with automotive or motorcycle carburetors, compared to stationary engines used for pumps or other industrial purposes, was the fact that these vehicles moved and jolted around. Motorcycles would also turn at angles or fall completely over. A vehicle would also be required to accelerate and decelerate, while a service pump would essentially be stationary. It is just hard for the modern enthusiast to understand how crude and volatile these early engines were when compared to the high-tech fuel injected or turbocharged machines of today.

Engine development was just one of the big issues. Brakes, lighting, tires, chain or belt development, wheel bearings, and oiling systems were also crude and unreliable in the early years. Metals were poor, and the development of the engine often followed the development of better metals.

As mechanical and reliability issues were advanced, the community of manufacturers, motorcycle businesses, and motorcycle enthusiasts grew by leaps and bounds. From being a new type of machine and having to compete with the automobile, the motorcycle had found its way into modern life as a clearly defined mode of transportation.

The US produced its first motorcycles by the tail end of the 1890s, which were heavily influenced by European machines. France and Germany were approximately ten years ahead of the US in engine development. There were imports as early as the teens, though very few. Between the wars (WW I and WW II) there were also low numbers of imported motorcycles.

Motorcycle sales remained low because the US market was very small. It was after the end of the 1940s that imported motorcycles began to come across onto our shores in larger numbers. What seemed to be a growth market in the 1950s became a rush during the early to late 1960s. The Japanese motorcycle invasion led to exponential growth in motorcycle sales never seen before or since. Even when motorcycle sales would have a great year in more recent decades they never came close to the motorcycle to population ratios of the late 1960s to the early '70s.

The development of the motorcycle generally paralleled that of automotive developments until the 1950s. One exception is engine design. American cars were mostly using flathead engines until the early 1950s, while most motorcycle engines moved to OHV designs by the end of the 1930s—Indian being one of the exceptions.

Hot rod culture, a southern California phenomenon, was primarily made up of automobiles. This culture did include some motorcycles, though few in numbers, but it was desert racing which caused motorcycling in southern California to grow by leaps and bounds after the late 1950s.

KCVJMC Picnic, From the author's collection

The automobile "club" defined the rebel racers from the 1930s. The "rebel" motorcyclists didn't fully evolve until the 1950s. The motorcycle community has been relatively different from the car community since the 1920s and continues to be so even today. The motorcycle has generally been a poor man's sport, while the automobile has encompassed a more elite crowd.

Since the 21st century, the motorcycling community has continued seeing its own dedicated followers maintain a strong community presence.

New motorcycles are more advanced than ever before. Vintage motorcycle have become a very popular pastime, and a few new brands occasionally pop up to be offered to the public. Old brand names are being resurrected, and advanced technology is still being copied by competitors. There has defiantly been a motorcycle renaissance since the early 21st century; it's just been a smaller, more confined group of enthusiasts compared to those in the field of automotive development.

This book is about motorcycle history and the development of motorcycles over the decades. Information discussed will primarily relate to the American motorcycle experience. The book will begin with an historical study of general motorcycle history, then cover important topics which define the sport, primarily within our geographic boundaries.

This will not be an exhaustive study, just the important stuff. I have spent years putting together lists, which never seem to end. I guess you have to set some boundaries, as this topic covers so much territory that there has to be a primary focus.

Years ago I recognized that a great many riders know very little about the history of motorcycling and determined that most would benefit from knowing more. If you read and study this book, your general knowledge of the motorcycle should be much greater than it was before you started. Furthermore, if you desire to do additional research, the topics in this book should be a guide to doing further study as it interests you.

Please enjoy the book and enjoy the sport of motorcycling; we have such a great and diverse community of enthusiasts.

Chapter 1

The Earliest Years of Motorcycle Development

From the 1860s to around 1900

The history of the motorcycle begins with the invention and development of the bicycle. The bicycle, or "running machine" was developed in 1817 by Karl Von Drais, a German engineer. "The Draisine," as his contraption was called, allowed a person to travel from point A to point B more quickly and with greater excitement.

From the 1820s until the end of the century, bicycling grew in popularity, coming to the United States around 1865. There were many developments as the bicycle matured, but the ideal "bicycle" was one which could move under its own power. Sylvester Roper, an American living in Boston, was the first known individual to create a functional self-powered bicycle.

There were a number of experimental machines prior to Roper's steam motorcycle, however, some had three wheels. These early machines did not make enough power to propel a bicycle fast enough to allow the rider to balance it. There may have actually been a steam bicycle as early as 1818 in France and a British tricycle in 1831. Through the years, I have occasionally come across a notation about an early experimental steam bike or tricycle, but there is generally little detail in the information given about them.

Roper, a steam technology buff, tinkered with steam engines, so he ultimately designed and built a small steam engine and attached it to a bicycle. Roper's steam bike, along with a steam-powered four-wheeler, were marvels in his day.

Roper Steam Cycle, Taken at Barber Vintage Motorsport Museum

Roper could also be considered to be the first "rebel" biker. In 1869 he raced some bicyclists in Cambridge, Massachusetts, and his machine began to wobble at around forty mph, which was incredibly fast for that time. He crashed and died. His death was claimed to be from a heart attack associated with the speed he traveled, rather than the result of the crash.

Lucius Copeland, another American, followed Roper and built his own steam bicycle around 1884. Copeland also started the first American motorcycle company, the Motor-Cycle Manufacturing Company of Philadelphia. The term "moto-cycle" was born. Copeland's bicycle was configured the opposite as the large-wheeled bicycles of the time, which had the larger wheel in front. Copeland placed the larger wheel in back as the drive wheel with the steam boiler in front of the wheel.

As bicyclists were riding greater distances, having a power source allowed the rider to go farther with less effort. There were numerous other attempts at developing a steam-powered bicycle but with no significant developments which made such a machine popular or practical. The steam-powered bicycle was to remain a novelty without real sales potential or mass popularity.

Gottlieb Daimler, courtesy Barber Vintage Motorsport Museum

Realistically, these early developments were merely experiments, rather than attempts at developing an entirely new field of transportation. Because there was little context for self-powered vehicles, these experiments were probably more about novelty and uniqueness. Furthermore, the effort to heat the boiler, keep the water tank full, adjust the steam level, and operate such a machine on bad roads was enough effort in itself that steam power on a bicycle was never common nor commercially viable.

Usually credited as the first true motorcycle because it was powered by an internal combustion engine, was the German Gottlieb-Daimler of 1885. The Gottlieb-Daimler was powered by an engine design and developed by Nikolaus Otto in the late 1870s. This two-wheeler, with two side wheels to balance the bike, produced around a half horsepower and would travel up to five mph. Actually, five mph was considered moving at a good pace in the 1880s. Most motorcycle history books begin with this machine, although it really had four wheels and was just the foundation on which to experiment with the engine.

The builders went on to build four-wheeled vehicles, never again to attempt to build on a two-wheeled platform. In 1889, Daimler also designed the first V-twin engine.

The Gottlieb-Daimler was an experiment, while the Hildebrand-Wolfmuller was designed and built to be the first motorcycle available for sale to the public. The Hildebrand-Wolfmuller, another German machine, was sold after 1894 and was powered by a water-cooled 1500cc flat, forward-facing twin-cylinder engine. Estimates are that from 800 to 2,000 machines were ever built and sold.

Hildebrand-Wolfmuller

The basic design, a semi-bicycle type frame with an engine at the forward end of the frame, was to become the basic format for the motorcycle. I cannot confirm my resource, but I understand that the first experimental machines may have been steam-powered. The battery-operated ignition system was the major failure of this machine, leading to its unreliable operation. The motorcycles were deemed unreliable and hard to operate, so buyers quickly lost interest and the business quickly ceased. It was Frederick Simms and, later, Robert Bosch who developed a self-generating electrical system, which greatly advanced the potential of the internal combustion engine and allowed for further motorcycle development.

The French-designed De Dion Buton single-cylinder engine of 1896 was to spark the future development of the motorcycle engine. This little 138cc, half horsepower, IOE engine (inlet over exhaust) was the design which was used to power many brands of motorcycles built after 1899. Others, such as the Orient (1899), the Holley (1900), the Indian (1901), the Royal (1901), then the Merkel (1902), as well as dozens of other manufacturers, generally copied the De Dion-Buton engine design for their first motors.

De Dion 3-wheeler with engine visible. Courtesy of Motorcycle Illustrated.

The list of early American motorcycles probably exceeds 180 brands. The Orient-Astor, built in Waltham, Massachusetts, and the Holley, built in Pennsylvania, are considered

by some to be the first commercially produced and sold American motorcycles which used this engine.

In the beginning, some manufacturers   purchased the little engines, then later contracted to build them, then built their own versions. The fact is the De Dion-Buton engine was the backbone of many early motorcycles because of its simplicity, reliability, low build cost, and light weight.

As would be expected, every so often a new brand of motorcycle will pop up as being the "first" American motorcycle. With this in mind, there are several other potential American motorcycles to consider when looking for the earliest development.

One   such   motorcycle would come from the work of Edward J. Pennington. Pennington was quite an inventor, drawing up plans for airships, motorcycles, automobiles, ignition systems, and a variety of other mechanical things. Some have claimed that he first designed a motorcycle in 1895, but it did not run. It is alleged that, long after that date, he was sued for selling plans which did not work.

Some call him a genius, others a swindler, but the fact is that he had numerous ideas which later became significant. I have never done much research on him because of conflicting information and because many historians discount his work.

The next potential study is on the work of Robert Keating, a onetime professional baseball player. Keating is also claimed to have invented the rubber home plate (2005-2015, Society for American Baseball Research, Daniel E. Ginsburg).

Again, there is little information on Keating other than the assertion that he began inventing things after 1862, which included a better bicycle wheel sometime around 1898. One source claims he built a motorcycle during that time period. In Jerry Hatfield's book, *The Standard Catalogue of American Motorcycles* (p.366), Keating's motorcycle is mentioned as being built in 1901 or 1902. Hatfield's book is one of the best resources for information on American motorcycles.

Another potential American "first" is the Marks motorcycle. Stan Dishong, a California motorcycle legend in his own right (deceased 2008), restored a Marks Motorbike claiming to have been originally built in San Francisco in 1896. There is almost no information corroborating Mr. Dishong's claims; however, the motorcycle is certainly very old and could easily meet those standards. The Marks is like the other early motorcycles, with an engine which appears to be much like the De Dion-Buton attached to a bicycle frame. The final motorcycle to be discussed as potentially one of the earliest US motorcycles is the O. J. Plummer, which will be covered at the end of this chapter.

O. J. Plummer Motorcycle, Courtesy of the Kansas City Museum

O. J Plummer, From the author's collection

O. J. Plummer, Courtesy of the Kansas City Museum

As a mode of transportation, however, they were essentially unknown, except to a very few people. The horse and train still reigned as the dominant forms of transportation. The interest in building the motorcycle needs a little more discussion.

Stepping back a bit, let's take a few paragraphs to look at why the motorcycle was built in the first place.

The progressive and mechanical side of the development of the motorcycle is fairly straightforward. Small versions of steam-powered engines were built and placed on carts, buggy's, and bicycles. Steam power led to gasoline-powered engines, which were placed on a variety of vehicles as well.

As efficient and reliable engines were developed, they were copied and used by more people experimenting with different modes of transportation. Success bred success, and more people entered this new arena of building vehicles, which grew exponentially as a marketable product. This could only occur because there was a growing interest in mechanical things and the belief that this new form of transportation would someday have significant benefits.

The reality is that there were many people experimenting with these new machines, and they all typically looked very similar and used many very similar parts. Because they were primarily engines on a bicycle, the core engineering elements were not original to the builders (none created the wheel or bicycle frame), so the issue is bragging rights, rather than significant or genuine innovation. By 1900, several people had built bicycles with engines, and many more were on the way.

There were many in opposition to challenging the horse as the primary means of power, and many did not believe

13

that these new machines could change the horse's position, however, as machines grew more reliable, moved faster, and could work harder than the horse, more people developed new forms of machinery. Furthermore, as people were bicycling farther distances on typically very bad roads, some form of power was greatly desired. An engine on a bicycle could go farther, faster, and with less effort, especially up hills.

As the world approached the turn of the century, there were great expectations placed on mechanical inventions. The steam engine had changed the way people traveled after the 1830s, and then the internal combustion engine using crude gasoline was about to make even greater changes after the 1890s. Between 1880 and 1900, the men, the vision, and the basic foundational design elements had been set for a revolutionary new breed of engineering to take place. The first innovations came from Europe through Daimler, Simms, De Dion-Buton, Minerva, Phelon & Moore, Scott, Werner, the Collier Brothers, Bianchi, Klement, and many others.

From the end of the 1880s to 1900, there was at least one electric bike, quite a number of steam contraptions, a "spring" powered bicycle, but many petroleum-powered machines. After 1900, America quickly followed suit and, within a decade, was a major contributor to the new motorcycle engineering.

After the turn of the century, the internal combustion engine was the dominant source of power for all two-wheeled vehicles, though few were sold. It was these earliest developments, discussed above, which paved the way for the practical and exponential use of the internal combustion engine. The same was true for the automobile. In 1900, there were about an equal number of electric, steam, and petroleum-powered vehicles, but by the early 1900s, nearly all were gone but the gasoline engine.

In an article dated June 2, 1900 in *The School Journal*, page 632, there is an interest in the new "single motor" bicycle. The article states that there is a demand for these machines because they will go faster and farther, causing less fatigue. In the eighth paragraph, there is a note stating that a specific motor-cycle "is distinctly an automobile" because it has no "pedals."

At this early stage, the term *motorcycle* was a generic term as was the term *automobile*. It should be noted that in 1895 there was a "motorcycle" race put on by a Chicago newspaper, and all the vehicles had four wheels, none had two. The four-wheeled vehicles were called *motorcycles.* Some people have attempted to make an issue as to who originated the term *motorcycle,* but in reality, there was no frame of reference other than simply generic terms generally understood by people. I have a copy of a Barnum & Bailey ad dated 1896 which promotes a Horseless Carriage show, and the ad calls these four-wheeled vehicles *motorcycles.* As noted above, what we call an *automobile* today had been called a *motorcycle* by some and a *motorcycle* had been referenced as an *automobile* before 1900. All of these terms were generally sorted out a little before 1910.

There were very few cars, trucks, or any self-powered vehicles at all in this early time period. Beginning around 1895 there was a new energy behind the technology of self-powered vehicles. Even by 1900 there were few who were aware of the huge advances in technology in this arena. The truck, the automobile, and the motorcycle developed down somewhat different tracks. The truck came first as a steam- or battery-powered vehicle. Gasoline power came later. After some success, the same technology was placed on the buggy. The self-propelled buggy was to become the template for the automobile after the 1890s. The motorcycle came through the bicycle.

The original goal for the gas engine on a bicycle was to allow the bike to go farther, easier, and to go up hills better. I have seen vintage ads dating from the very early 1900s which promote engines on a bicycle as a way to travel with greater ease.

In these early years, many people were afraid of these vehicles. The noise, the exhaust fumes, the speed, and the way they would scare horses caused much concern. The sheer lack of knowledge about them made them questionable vehicles.

There is an interesting story that goes like this: Sometime in the early 1900s a farmer had heard that there was an automobile in town. He quickly rode his horse to town to see the vehicle, as he had never seen one before. He looked it over and rode home. That evening he told his family that many people were confused about these new machines. He stated, they are "not automobiles," as many have been told, they are "Oldsmobiles."

Another story told as true goes this way: A farmer sees a loud, thumping, smoking, beast carrying a man down the road close to his farm. He grabs his shotgun and shoots the beast to save the man, only to find out it was a motorcycle.

The engineering development of the motorcycle up until around 1900 was simple, crude, and was being done in a very limited number of places around the world. France, Germany, and the US were the dominant locations of research. The work done was monumental, setting the stage for what was to come after 1900. The motorcycle was to see expansive development after the turn of the century and within a decade and a half would establish its own identity around most of the developed world. This was also true in America. The structural form would be finalized, as would be its primary markets.

Shortly after the early 1900s, the bicycle lost much ground to the motorcycle.

Before moving to the next chapter, the O. J. Plummer motorcycle will be discussed. Plummer claimed to be one of the first American motorcycle builders but the Plummer was most likely just one of the very earliest machines to be built. The study of the Plummer will transition the discussion from 1900 to the post 1900 time period, as that machine was a transitional motorcycle.

Was the first Kansas City motorcycle and one of the first American motorcycles made, the O. J. Plummer? While doing research for a book on the early motorcycle community in the Kansas City area, I came across an article in the *Kansas City Star* dated June of 1950. The article was titled "Kansas City's

First Motorcycle." I anxiously pulled the article up to view the contents. It was an interview with Oscar J. Plummer about a motorcycle he stated that he had built around 1898. At the time of the article Plummer was around seventy-two years of age. Plummer identified himself as an "avid bicycle rider" in the 1890s who had seen a picture of a French racing tandem used to lead bicycle races back in that time period.

He claimed that he had never seen a motorcycle at that time, but with the desire to go faster, Plummer determined to build his own motorcycle. Plummer stated that "without drawing on any of the construction knowledge compiled from the eastern manufacturers," he built his own motor-driven bicycle. Furthermore, this was claimed to have been done when Plummer was but twenty years old. Plummer stated that it took him two years to build the original machine, then additional time was taken to rebuild and perfect the bike to his liking. If this were true, the motorcycle would have been completed in 1900.

Plummer goes on to say that the bike would go sixty mph, could get thrity-five miles per gallon, and was very reliable. Of most interest to me was the assertion that this motorcycle was "the oldest in Kansas City" and was the "first to be seen on Kansas City streets." These claims make this motorcycle a very significant machine indeed.

After reading this article, I called every person listed in the phone book in the Kansas City area with the name of Plummer in hopes of finding a relative who might be able to substantiate the information in the *Kansas City Star* article. I also understood that over sixty years had passed since the newspaper article had been written. People either had no knowledge of an Oscar J. Plummer or questioned my intentions for wanting information.

I discussed my findings with another avid motorcycle historian and friend, Jay Wilson. Wilson immediately responded that he had seen the bike several decades earlier in a museum located in an old mansion known as the Kansas City Museum. When he had made that statement, I remembered the museum, and motorcycle as well. Back in the late 1970s or early 1980s, when my children were young, I had taken them to this museum and remembered the bike was displayed in a corner next to a large staircase. At that time, I had an interest in motorcycles, but primarily newer ones. The bike had not been on display for at least several decades, and this por-

tion of the museum had also been closed for several years while remodeling was being done. I made several calls to the museum, and those who answered the phone were not aware of a motorcycle in their collection. I was finally able to get in touch with Lisa, one of the Curatorial Specialists, who confirmed that the motorcycle was in storage.

I set up a date for a few knowledgeable people to go to the warehouse and actually see the bike. On March 15th, 2011, about ten interested motorcycle enthusiasts were given a viewing. Along with myself and Jay Wilson, were Ralph Wayne, Jack Larson, Earl Mustard, Jack Benson, Tim Thoele, Dan Holman, Jim Lepisto, Mike Judy, and Jerry Similer.

We spent about two hours combing over the machine, and here were the original findings: First, the bike was certainly an early model, but no one felt like it had been built before the 1900s. Most placed the machine between 1900 and 1905.

The engine was clearly modeled after the French De Dion Buton motor, which became the model for most early motorcycle engines. Mr. Plummer had his name, "O. J. Plummer", cast into the top of the crankcase and "K.C.Mo." cast at the bottom of the crankcase. Jack Larson, an engine builder, guessed that the bore would be around three inches and the stroke around three-and-a-half inches, making the engine about 400cc in capacity. The cylinder head looked like it had been professionally cast, possibly for an early car, motorcycle, or utility engine. The barrel appeared to be cast with cooling holes drilled from the top to the bottom of the cylinder. The oil feed was manufactured by Lunkenheimer and had been copyrighted in 1902.

Tim Thoele identified the carburetor as possibly a Longuemare, though no markings were found. The frame was clearly derived from a bicycle design but was much heavier in construction than a typical bicycle frame. The front forks had two lower fork blades on each side of the wheel supporting the tire, and the back had doubled up struts. The belt sheave was nearly as large as the back wheel, and there was no pulley or belt tensioner to tighten the drive strap to limit slippage.

The real proof of its old age were the wood wheel rims with the older type canvas tires. These were wooden rims with wrapped canvas tires with vulcanized rubber over the outside edge. These predate clincher rims with pneumatic tires found on early motorcycles. Clincher-type rims are generally dated after 1905, as they are made of steel.

When I had first seen the picture of the motorcycle in the 1950 newspaper article, I thought it looked much like an Orient. The Orient motorcycles were built from 1899 to 1905 by the Waltham Bicycle Company in Waltham Massachusetts. Orient was one of the first companies to build velocipedes to lead bicycle races. Some experts have called the Orient the first manufactured and marketed motorcycle offered in the US. It was the squared-off tank above the back wheel with battery container hanging below the frame backbone just in front of the rider's seat which gave me that impression. I had commented to Jay and others of my observations. Several days later, Jay called me with some additional confirming thoughts. The position of the gas tank, placement of the tank filler cap, placement of the battery box, position of the engine, size of the engine, placement of the carburetor, and shape of the frame, all indicated that the machine was heavily influenced by the Orient.

Did Plummer buy an Orient and alter it, rebuild an Orient to his liking, buy various Orient parts and build it, copy the design of the Orient and fabricate it himself, or was it some other derivative of these possibilities?

The bottom line is this; Plummer's motorcycle is far too close to an early Orient motorcycle to be an accident. The origin of the double blade front forks still remains a mystery.

Several years after my initial study of the Plummer, I was able to compare the Plummer with an actual Orient. The Orient was a much smaller motorcycle, and there appeared to be no interchangeable parts, however, the core design was certainly similar. The Orient and the Plummer are different motorcycles but similar in looks.

What can be determined is this; the O. J. Plummer machine is an example of a very early motorcycle. Everything about its construction points to a build date of 1903 to 1904. Jay Wilson places a probable build date of 1902 or 1903 because of the construction of the crankcase. He stated that later crankcases were split vertically. The crude canvas-wrapped tires with a vulcanized rubber tread then glued to wooden rims are very old and could easily date earlier than 1900. This type of tire and rim were generally not seen after 1905. The tires and rims indicate that the motorcycle would be from the 1898 to 1905 time period.

From another newspaper article dated February 1908, Plummer is noted as a member of arguably the earliest motorcycle club in Kansas City. He was also associated with many of the earliest motorcycle enthusiasts and dealers in Kansas City, confirming that the motorcycle is what it is claimed to be.

What can be surmised is this: The O. J. Plummer is most likely the first motorcycle to run on the streets of Kansas City, just as he stated in the 1950 newspaper interview. The bike is not an altered Orient, nor is it made of various Orient parts. Nonetheless, the Plummer motorcycle is a very significant find and is, without a doubt, one of the earliest examples of an American motorcycle. It would also be true to say that there would be only a very few known American motorcycles which would date earlier than the Plummer.

Now onto the next chapter.

Chapter 2

The Motorcycle From 1900 to around 1917 (to WW I)

By the end of the century a mechanical revolution had started without a doubt. Certainly there were many innovations that went back for more than a century which were the backbone behind the more modern mechanical developments. Now, however, there was not only greater focus but a new energy behind these new developments in a more singular and direct path focused on this new form of transportation. These inventors now had moving machines that had a practical application.

There was also a market for these machines, even if just a small one. The last chapter leads us up until developments were growing so fast that few could keep up with the latest innovations. The foundation had been set, but now hundreds of additional people were getting very much involved in this new field as interest was heating up.

From 1898 to 1905 activity had begun, with little shops and garages popping up by the dozens. In 1901 it was estimated that fewer than ten machines had sold, but by1905 sales had grown to approximately 2,200 machines. Between 1906 and 1915 estimated sales grew from a little under 3,800 machines being sold in 1906 to over 19,300 machines in 1910. By the end of this period (1915), motorcycle sales were estimated to be a little under 64,000 machines being sold by the major builders.

For the sake of comparison, in 1899-1900 there were around 2,500 automobiles sold in the US compared to the ten or fewer motorcycles sold (using the estimated 1900 figures). In 1910 there were approximately 459,000 cars sold compared to 19,300 motorcycles sold. In 1915 there were an estimated 717,000 automobiles sold to an estimated 64,000 motorcycles. As the years progressed car sales continued to outnumber motorcycle sales by huge percentage points until the 1970s, but that discussion is for another time.

All of the sales numbers used above are estimates from numbers which have been collected over the past decade and are for general comparison only. The point is this; the automobile outsold the motorcycle by huge margins from the very beginning of the industry. If you added trucks, cabs, and delivery vehicles, the motorcycle figures would be even further reduced in terms of percentage points.

The growth of motorcycle manufacturers was primarily in the eastern and northeastern states. By the end of the time period being discussed, there were approximately fifty-two motorcycle brands in New York, forty in Illinois, twenty-nine in Massachusetts, twenty-six in California, twenty-five in Ohio, twenty-two in Wisconsin, twenty in Pennsylvania, and around fifty others in other northern and northeastern states. These figures should be fairly accurate, as I counted up manufacturers in the noted states from a dozen or so motorcycle history books.

There were at least two early builders of motorcycles in Missouri. First was O. J. Plummer, the builder of the Kansas City Plummer motorcycle. He did not appear as though he was planning on manufacturing a motorcycle, but he was certainly a man very involved in this new technology. In St. Louis, however, Harry R. Geer was a manufacturer of motorcycles and also claimed to be the largest parts distributor in the Midwest. It might be more accurate to call him an "assembler" of machines. His three products were called the "Green Egg," the "Blue Bird," and the "Model 4." Apparently, the Green Egg was made from a Hercules motorcycle, the Blue Bird was derived from a Mitchell motorcycle, and the Model 4 was derived from a Reliance motorcycle. Little can be substantiated about these motorcycles because there is possibly only one of his motorcycles which still exists today.

In 1907, Geer claimed that he had "the largest line of new and used Motor cycles," appearing in a sales ad in the *Cycle and Automobile Trade Journal*. Geer operated in St. Louis from around 1901 to 1911 and appeared to be more of a parts distributor than a motorcycle builder.

Most of these builders were very small companies, and with some, it might be a stretch to even call some of them manufacturers. Some brands have no machines which still exist, and some brands have no sales numbers available at all. Some brands consist of just drawings, with the claim that machines had been built at one time. The purpose in stating the figures noted above, however, is to indicate the progression of activity in this new arena and the new interest in these machines.

This was a new category of transportation developing, which was driven by this new interest in mechanical things. The fledgling motorcycle market was to continue and to take on its own personality as time and development went forward.

Within a decade and a half, after the turn of the century, there were hundreds of new upstart manufacturers of motorcycles. The United States had over a hundred of their own builders, such as Ace, AMC (not the British AMC), Arrow, Apache, Bailey, Black Diamond, Black Hawk, Briggs, Cleveland, Columbia, Comet, Crawford, Crouch, Curtiss, Cyclone, Dayton, Eagle, Emblem, Excelsior, Flanders, Geer, Greyhound, Harley-Davidson, Henderson, Hoffman, Hudson, Indian, Iver Johnson, Keating, Keystone, Marmon, Miami, Mitchell, Monarch, Ner-A-Car (same as European motorcycle), Orient, Pope, and Thoroughbred, just to name a few.

As noted before, there were possibly more than a hundred builders of motorcycles in the US, though many were very small builders as Floyd Clymer mentions in his classic book, *A Treasury of Motorcycles of the World* (p.166-167). Here is a short list of thirty-nine major brands being manufactured during the pre-WWI time period. These are just the larger manufacturers.

AMC	1912-1915
American	1911-1914
Apache	1907-1911
Auto-Bi	1902-1912
Bayley Flier	1913-1917
Champion	1911-1913
Columbia	1900-1905
Curtiss	1902-1910
Cyclone	1913-1920
Excelsior	1908-1911
Emblem	1909-1925
Erie	1905-1915
Flanders	1911-1914
Geer	1905-1909
Greyhound	1907-1913
Harley-Davidson	from 1903
Holley	1902-1910
Indian	1901-1953
Iver-Johnson	1907-1915
Marsh	1901-1920
Merkel	1902-1922
Miami	1905-1923
Militaire	1911-1920
Minneapolis	1901-1915
Mitchell	1901-1910
Monarch	1912-1915
Orient	1900-1910
Pierce	1909-1913
Pope	1908-1916
Reading Standard	1903-1922
Schickel	1912-1915
Sears	1912-1916
Shaw	1907-1912
Spacke	1911-1914
Steffey	1902-1905
Thiem	1903-1914
Thor	1903-1916
Wagner	1901-1914
Yale	1902-1915

This is an incomplete list of many of the early manufacturers, many of which built bicycles.

As can be seen, many were also short-lived. Many had a lifespan of ten years or less. Limited markets, poor dealership commitment and development, the inability to remain competitive, and the escalation of automobile sales made it hard to market motorcycles. Furthermore, marketing in those early days was primarily regional in nature.

The first motorcycles shared many basic similarities. Sometime around 1898 what has been called "motor tandems" were built. These were elongated bicycles with motors used to ride in front of racing bicycles. These machines would go thirty to thrty-five mph, leaving a draft, which allowed bicycles behind the tandem to go faster.

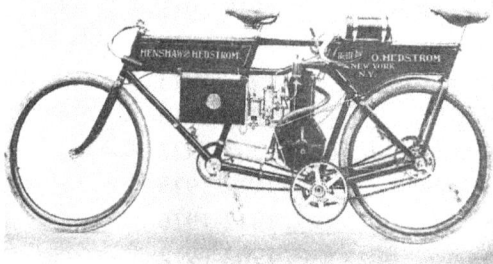

Hedstrom Bicycle Racer

These exhibitions were popular and drew large crowds. Most tandems were unreliable and often broke down. What encouraged George Hendee, the founder of Indian Motorcycles, to check out a particular tandem in New York City was the fact that it was known to be very reliable. The machine had been operated by Oscar Hedstrom.

Hendee, a well known and very successful one time bicycle racer, was now building what was called the "Silver King" safety bicycle. He contacted Hedstrom and paid him to design a self-powered bicycle which was easy to use, reliable, and marketable.

Hedstrom made a reliable machine for Hendee, and the rest is history. Because the machine was so new and Hendee didn't want to build a factory up front, he contracted the Aurora Automatic Machinery Company to build the engine and many of the other parts. Aurora copied Hendee's Indian and made several motorcycles, which were direct copies.

The Aurora Machine Company was responsible for at least four other brands of motorcycles, which were basically copies of the Indian. This was a typical story of how many of the early brands got their start. This was also true with Colonel Pope. Pope built at least eight brands of bicycles. He just sold his motorcycles through his bicycle dealers by simply putting a different name on the tank.

Early Indian Camelback

What is important to understand is that most of these

24

early companies were building a product to sell, rather than attempting to build a "brand." In the very beginning, because there was no specific transportation category for the "motorcycle," enterprising people were just building something to sell. Once the motorcycle became a specific commodity in a specific class of transportation then the brand became a marketable selling product.

Another early bicycle manufacturer who made motorcycles was Orient. The Orient motorcycle was built by Waltham Manufacturing in Waltham, Massachusetts, and sold early De Dion Buton engines on bicycle pacers. They built pacers as early as 1898, but the motorcycle was not available until 1899 or 1900.

By 1905 Waltham discontinued building motorcycles and began building automobiles. During the first five or six years, nearly all of the new motorcycles had a bicycle-type frame. These frames were often called a diamond frame because of the basic shape. The machines also included pedals, a leather belt- or chain-drive, and the engine.

As the engines grew more powerful, pedals were no longer needed to get the bike up a hill or through mud. Nearly all were single-speed machines until around 1908. After 1908 two-speed transmissions with the gears often in the rear hub were offered, and later three-

speed transmissions became common.

Single-speed, belt-drive motorcycles continued to be built for another decade and slowly disappeared from the market as the cheap models. Ariel, a British motorcycle, did have a three-speed transmission as early as 1904, but that was a rarity. A few models had two speeds available if the rider would stop the bike and switch the drive belt from the larger rim to a smaller one.

At first, there were no brakes. To stop, the rider had to stop the engine of the motorcycle, then start it up again when he wanted to proceed. Rear brakes were nonexistent in the earliest bikes but slowly emerged as a necessity. By 1905 all motorcycles had some form of brake on the rear wheel only.

Engines had to be manually oiled by the rider until the 1920s. A rider could tell by the bluing of the exhaust header or by the color of smoke coming out of the exhaust pipe when to give the engine a squirt of oil. One early rider noted that as his engine heated up he would slow down. When he "oiled it," he would again get up to the desired speed.

As could be expected, motorcycles required a great deal of maintenance and were still unreliable. An article written around 1905 noted that a rider was able to travel nearly twenty miles between maintenance stops.

One author noted that somewhere around 1915 usability and reliability greatly increased, making motorcycles much more practical and attractive. In his book titled *Early Motorcycles,* written by Victor Page in 1914, he suggests that the motorcycle engine should be rebuilt about every 750 miles. Page also noted that because of the limited power of many of the early engines, the rider had to use his pedals to help get the bike up steeper hills.

If you look at the previous chart, you'll see that many of the early manufacturers were out of business by 1915, or even before. There are several basic reasons for this. First, because many of the builders used primarily bolt-on parts, manufacturers who spent money on developing their own machines quickly surpassed the ones who did not develop their products. Secondly, because the automobile quickly outsold the motorcycle, the motorcycle market remained very limited. Thirdly, many early motorcycle builders were not able to build a dealership network but were tied to small local markets, which kept production costs high and growth potential small. Finally, primarily because of the Model T, a motorcycle often cost nearly as much as a new Ford. In the years after WWI the number of motorcycle manufacturers was cut in half.

Motorcycles were used in WWI but in numbers much less than what was used in WWII. The motorcycle was used primarily as a means of relay communication. Motorcycles were much easier to use than the horse. The horse required feeding, housing, stable maintenance, saddle storage, and medical attention. The horse also required lots of space when not being used, while motorcycles could be stacked side by side.

The advantage of the horse was that nearly all of the young men were familiar with them. Motorcycles were very new, few had ever operated one or knew anything about maintenance.

The military clearly saw the usefulness of the motorcycle, and after the first great war, the motorcycle had nearly replaced the horse. By WWII the horse was nearly gone while the motorcycle was used by the tens of thousands on and off the battlefield.

The war helped the institution of the motorcycle in several big ways.

First, the motorcycle was shown to be faster than the typical horse—especially on paved roads. Secondly, the military picked the machines with the best engineering and the greatest reliability. This encouraged manufacturers to continue development and production of only the most reliable and usable machines.

Next, the motorcycle could be stored without requiring any ongoing maintenance. Motorcycles could be stored in large groups and left alone until needed, even for years if necessary.

Fourth, they could be easily hidden and made no noise unless they were running. They could also be moved much easier than the horse.

Finally, the motorcycle could use the same fuel as other military vehicles, and there was no longer the need to store horse feed or large amounts of water. The motorcycle helped bring the military into the next century.

The first motorcycles commercially sold typically had less than two hp. By 1905 power was up to three or four hp; by 1910, five or six hp;, and by 1915, up to fifteen hp. Race bikes like the 1916 Cyclone had twenty-two to twenty-five hp, but that was a high performance machine.

The single-cylinder motorcycle dominated motorcycle production in the early years. Europe continued primarily with single-cylinder engines while America went to the V-twin. America wanted big bikes, while European countries typically wanted smaller machines.

Late teens Reading Standard, Period advertisement

When more power was needed, manufacturers just added another cylinder. The single-cylinder engine was followed by the V-twin almost universally—especially in America.

Other configurations like the five-cylinder Megola (the cylinders circled the front or back wheel), the early in-line four like the Belgian FM (1904), the American Pierce or early Henderson (a design which was to re-surface later), and oddities like the Werner V-8 (an airplane engine on a motorcycle frame) were generally very rare and short lived.

Henderson 4

Before 1905, the engines were located in several places. The early Raleigh had the engine above the front wheel, the Shaw placed the engine above the pedals, the Lawson placed the engine behind the back wheel, and the Singer had a model with the engine above the rear hub.

FN 4 from arund 1914

As noted before, the early Werner became the model which led the way with the engine, gas tank, seat, and pegs (pedals on early bikes) in the current configuration.

Competition has always followed the development of the motorcycle. The earliest races were simply reliability tests to show that the self-powered machines were usable.

The first documented race dates back to 1895. This was a race sponsored by a Chicago newspaper with a $2,000 purse (around $50,000 in today's money). The race included two-, three-, and four-wheeled vehicles, all called "moto-cycles". Over eighty vehicles were to race, however, when the actual date came, there were fewer than eight vehicles prepared to race. The fifty-four mile race from Chicago to Evanston, Illinois, concluded with only one vehicle finishing.

There was a one-mile motorcycle race held at a Los Angeles horse racing track in 1901, followed by numerous miscellaneous speed oriented races held in various parts of the country prior to 1907.

The first recognized races in the US which were popular were oval track races held on wood circuits designed originally for bicycles. The first tracks opened in 1909. These wood tracks evolved directly from bicycle "Velodrome" racing.

At first, the motorcycle just led the bicycles until the bicycle races began. It wasn't long until the races were between motorcycles alone. The tracks grew larger and the motorcycles went faster until the events included numerous serious accidents.

Gruesome accidents caused the demise of the sport by the early 1930s. You must understand that this was well before television and radio was popular, so it was one of the few major attractions, which generated a great deal of excitement. Some called board racing a "blood sport." Tracks opened in many large market areas with crowds from twenty to thirty thousand people.

During this time the larger manufacturers, especially Indian, Harley-Davidson, and Excelsior, spent a great deal of money building and promoting race bikes. Racing has always been the dominant way manufacturers developed the engineering of their machines. Motorcycle racing was seen as a major way to promote a specific brand of motorcycle and certainly a way to show how good a specific brand was engineered.

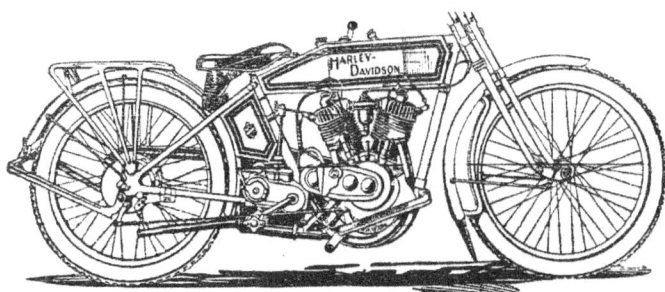

1915 Harley-Davidson

11-Horsepower, GUARANTEED 3-Speed Sliding Gear Transmission, Automatic Mechanical Oil Pump, Step-Starter and 66 Refinemnts.

-- $275.00 --

The 1915 Harley-Davidson three-speed twin is the first motorcycle to climb a sixty per cent grade. It has taken a sidecar and passenger up a forty-five per cent grade without a murmur.
1915 CATALOG ON REQUEST.

Early Harley-Davidson, Period advertisement

Motorcycle racing grew to include several basic platforms, including paved roads and unpaved surfaces. Various forms of road racing, hill-climbs, and varieties of off-road racing are still the dominant forms of motorcycle competition. In racing, either the riders ability, the machines' speed, handling, or acceleration have been the central objective. There will be more about racing in another chapter.

Indian was the first mass produced motorcycle in the United States. In 1901 Indian built three machines, 143 in 1902, 376 in 1903, and by 1910, 6,137 motorcycles were built.

Harley-Davidson's production numbers were much lower than Indian's until the late teens, at which time Harley-Davidson became the largest manufacturer in the US.

By 1913 US motorcycle sales had reached an estimated 70,000 units yearly (32,000 machines were Indian sales alone), but this was to come to a quick halt because of the huge increase in automobile sales. As with motorcycle production, there were also many automobile manufacturers bidding for their market share. The big change started in 1908 when Henry Ford unveiled his Model T.

When first marketed, the Model T was hand-built like all the other cars, but as mass production techniques were developed, the price went down. Demand for the Model T became so great that the T accounted for nearly forty-five percent of automobile sales. By 1927, nearly 17 million Model Ts had been produced.

As production grew, the price for an automobile, not just the Model T, declined. By the mid-teens, a basic Model T could be purchased for as little as $295. Other manufacturers copied Ford, and the automobile became much more popular.

The automobile was a more practical vehicle than the motorcycle because it could carry more people, did not require advanced riding skills, could carry more cargo, and could be enclosed during poor weather. Also, women were able to drive the automobile much more easily than a motorcycle.

As car prices declined and motorcycle prices remained much the same, the car became much more desirable as a utility and transportation vehicle. This led to a sharp decline in motorcycle sales, and by 1914 motorcycle sales had dropped by nearly a third. Motorcycle sales in the US were not to regain the pre-1914 level until the early 1960s.

This drop in motorcycle sales impacted the sport in several ways. First, many manufacturers went out of business, reducing the number of brands. Secondly, many who used the motorcycle for utility purposes exchanged their machines for automobiles. Thirdly, it established a clear division between the sport and utility rider. The motorcycle was still used by many as a utility vehicle, the numbers were just much smaller. Finally, the motorcycle manufacturers had a much narrower group of people in which to market their machines.

In the late teens the motorcycle business had almost died in the US. Motorcycling was still strong in Europe, where motorcycles were still used as general transportation. The sidecar was also much more popular in Europe than in the US.

The motorcycle was better suited for Europe, especially England, because of the narrow and winding roads. In America there was a vast area of expansive land. England, Germany, France, Spain, and Italy consisted of many small villages with much more of the country being paved than in America.

These European countries also did not require the large machines which were a necessity in the US. Many of the foreign manufacturers built some V-twins, but the single cylinder motorcycle was the staple in those early years.

The V-twin became the standard in America. Most American motorcycles had small singles until around 1911, then there was a general switch to the V-twin engines. Glenn Curtiss built the first V-twin in the US. He was followed by Harry Geer in 1904. Indian built a V-twin racer in 1906 then a street version in 1907. Thor had a V-twin in 1907, and Thiem offered one in 1908. In 1909 a number of motorcycle manufacturers offered V-twins, such as Marsh Metz, Reading Standard, Reliance, Torpedo, and Harley-Davidson. Dozens more had V-twins, especially after 1911, making the V-twin the most common engine type in the US market. Most manufacturers still offered single-cylinder engines as well along with the larger V-twin engines.

The motorcycle during this formative period of development had found its place within the arena of transportation. The core design configuration had been determined, its market found, and its basic social identity established. Let me list some of the developmental highlights of the motorcycle during this period. Note the following:

- **Large numbers of startup manufacturers emerged between 1901 and 1917, but most were gone within the first fifteen years of motorcycle development.**

- **The earliest motorcycles were engines on bicycle frames.**

- **Many early brands sold under multiple names; Columbia, Crescent, Imperial, Monarch, Rambler, Thiem, etc.**

- The Aurora Machine Company of Aurora, Illinois, made engines for the early Indian Motorcycle Company, and many of the same parts were used on other motorcycles, such as Sears, Torpedo, Reading Standard, and a list of smaller companies who just put their name on motorcycles looking just like the Indian (they appeared to be the same).

- Many bicycle companies added motorcycle building to bicycle manufacturing. Examples are Indian, Columbia, Raleigh, Pope, Geer (a big bicycle dealer turning to motorcycles), Schwinn (purchased Excelsior in 1912 and Henderson in 1917), etc.

- The De Dion Buton engine was the backbone of the early motorcycle industry.

- Before 1905, most motorcycles had no brakes. When brakes were added, they were on the rear wheel only.

- Lights were not standard on any of the early motorcycles. Early lamps were typically kerosene or carbide (acetylene) powered. After 1912, lamps became common and standard on motorcycles.

- Indian quickly became the largest US manufacturer, but by the end of the teens Harley-Davidson had taken the lead

- Motorcycles did not have speedometers until the teens.

- Leather belt drive systems were the most common until the mid-teens.

- Three-speed transmissions begin to emerge by the mid-teens.

By the end of this period the motorcycle had come to some maturity. The basic design had been formalized, and primary brands had also been established and were becoming better known. Motorcycles had also become very reliable during this time period.

Excelsior Motorcycle Company purchased Henderson in 1917. This left Indian and Harley-Davidson as the largest manufacturers still in business.

Many engineering innovations had been developed to a vastly greater state than existed in the early years. This set the stage for the motorcycle to create its own niche market during the time period between WWI and WWII.

The best way of putting it would be to say this: Between the years of 1900 and 1917 the level of motorcycle development greatly exceeded the developments of the next fifteen years. The weaker businesses were gone, the sport was clearly established, and the American motorcycle had its own enthusiasts who wanted to ride on two wheels.

MOTORCYCLE ILLUSTRATED

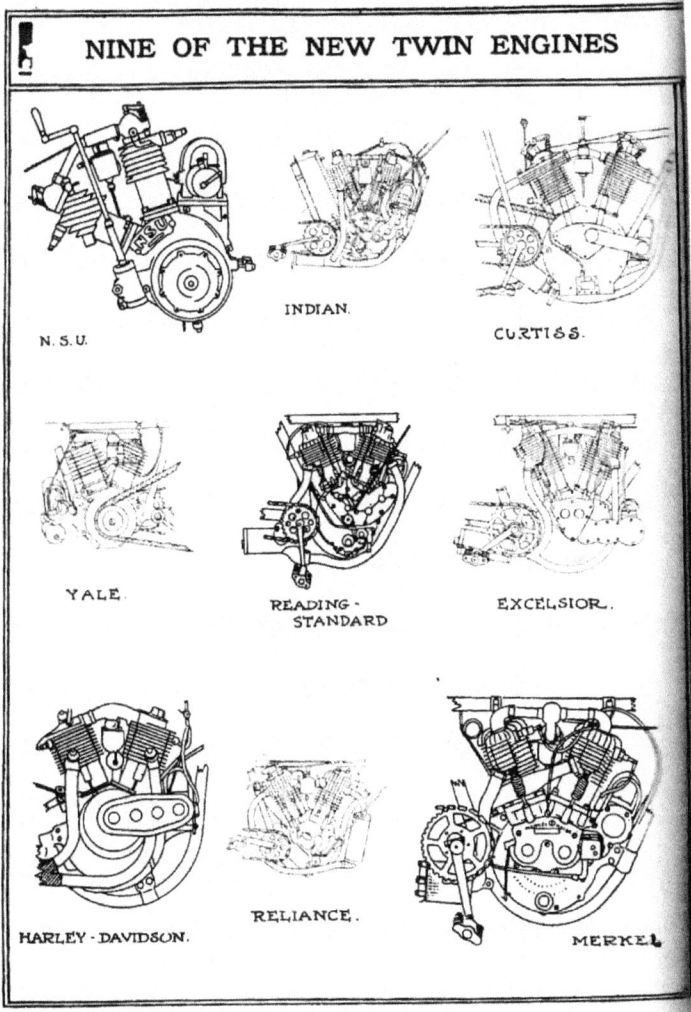

NINE OF THE NEW TWIN ENGINES

N.S.U.

INDIAN.

CURTISS.

YALE.

READING-STANDARD

EXCELSIOR.

HARLEY-DAVIDSON.

RELIANCE.

MERKEL.

Nine New V-Twins, With permission from 1910 Motorcycle Illustrated *reprints.*

Chapter 3

The Motorcycle Between the Wars

From around 1917 to around 1940

Part A—The history of the American and British motorcycle up until the WWII time period.

By 1915, or before the WWI time period, the basic layout of the motorcycle had been firmly established. Much more development was to come, but motorcycles were very usable, reliable, and were much more safe than in the early years. Better clutches were designed, three-speed transmissions were common, better suspensions were under development, and brakes were minimally improved.

Better oiling systems reduced engine failure, and now chain drive was dominant. Motorcycles had moved from oil type lamps to electric lighting, and lighting had become standard, rather than an option. It was not design and engineering factors that most impacted motorcycle development during this time period; it was the huge increases in automobile sales.

Motorcycle Headlight.

Combined Lamp and Generator.

Motorcycle lamps dating around 1910, Courtesy of Motorcycle Illustrated, Volume 5

After WWI America had become a much more dominant world power. Our social structure, political position, military might, and economic growth had made the US a major force in world affairs. America was now investing heavily in transportation, farm equipment, trucks, and automobiles. Mass production was becoming common, which allowed auto sales to soar because of their reduced cost.

The car was outselling the motorcycle by huge numbers, primarily because of the Ford Model T. As motorcycle sales were decreasing, automobile sales were on the increase.

During this inter-war period, many American motorcycle companies went out of business. Note the following list of manufacturers which went out of business before WWII:

Auto-Bi _____	1912
American, Thiem, & Flanders	
_____	1914
Flying Merkel _____	1915
Pope and Thor _____	1916
Dayton _____	1917
Cyclone and Marsh ___	1920
Autoped and Badger __	1921
Reading Standard_____	1922
Miami and Yankee ____	1923
Neracher _____	1926
Ace and Cleveland ____	1929
Excelsior-Henderson __	1931

After 1929, Harley-Davidson, Indian, and Excelsior-Henderson were the only companies remaining—with Excelsior-Henderson stopping production in 1931.

1920s Indian Power Plus, From the author's collection

To be more accurate, there were three additional two-wheeled vehicle manufacturers still operating at the end of this time period, however, they were more utilitarian oriented vehicles, rather than sport machines. The Simplex Servi-Car was built at the end of this time period, as was the Cushman and Powell scooters. All were built in low numbers.

Simplex Servi-Car, Period advertisement

Harley-Davidson and Indian were both struggling in sales by the end of the 1920s as sales seemed to be going down. If it were not for law enforcement sales and huge numbers of military bikes being built, their businesses could have certainly been in greater danger of extinction.

On the other hand, the British motorcycle businesses were not only strong but growing in the number of small manufacturers. The British manufacturers also had a much broader range of motorcycles than the American builders did. As stated before, the large V-twin was the staple of the US companies, while the British companies made a much broader variety of machines. These machines included small utility motorcycles, intermediate-sized bikes, and large machines designed for utility.

British motorcycles were also built for side car use, as well

as for sport. Many new companies emerged during this time period and continued far beyond the WWII period. Examples of these British motorcycle companies are the following:

AJW_____ 1926-1979
Brough Superior 1915-1940
BSA _____ 1910-1973
CTS _____ 1931-1940
DOT _____ 1907-1978
Douglas_____ 1907-1957
Excelsior (British) 1910-1965
Francis Barnett__ 1920-1966
James_____ 1902-1966
Norman _____ 1939-1962
Norton _____ 1902-1978
Panther_____ 1904-1968
Sunbeam_____ 1912-1965
Triumph ___ 1902-1983 (and
  beyond)
Velocette _____ 1905-1971
Vincent _____ 1928-1955

It must be noted, however, the British firms were typically smaller companies and their motorcycles often were built from the parts of various manufacturers working in the British industry at large.

An example would be the generous use of Villiers engines throughout the history of the British motorcycle industry. Best known for making two-strokes, they actually began by producing four-stroke engines. Villiers started in 1912 and continued as an independent engine builder until the end the golden age of the British motorcycle. Well over fifty brands (possibly double that) of motorcycle manufacturers used Villiers engines in their motorcycles over the years, including Vincent in the 1920s.

Not to move too far ahead, but the British companies certainly had their own struggles before and after the WWII era as well. Before the war and because most companies were small, the fluctuation in business was a huge financial burden. After the war, because their manufacturing ability was so limited, many were not able to build enough motorcycles in the quantities necessary without getting the payment for them. They were not able to supply hundreds of motorcycles to dealers without getting the payment for their machines up front. The point is this; many American companies went bankrupt while British companies were generally thriving and expanding. In America the motorcycle was a small market product, while in Britain the motorcycle was sold in much larger quantities.

The American motorcycle was quickly becoming a recreational machine driven by enthusiasts, rather than being a major part of the transportation system used by the general public. The utilitarian part of motorcycling was much larger in England, Germany, and France.

European motorcyclists certainly had their enthusiasts as well, it was just that the service aspect was a much greater part of the motorcycle community overseas. In the United States winter weather made the car a much more practical form of transportation, especially in the northern states. The upper half of the country suffered from cold winters, limiting motorcycle riding for around half the year.

Because the American motorcycle industry did not grow nearly as fast as the automobile industry, there was a manufacturing reversal. In the early years there were hundreds of small motorcycle builders with fewer automobile manufactures. Now there were dozens of growing automobile manufacturers with fewer motorcycle builders bidding for a smaller market.

To bolster sales, motorcycle manufacturers worked on strong exporting programs. One source stated that forty-five to fifty-five percent of US motorcycle production was sent to foreign markets. This lasted a little more than a decade, until the world wide depression further eroded motorcycle sales in all parts of the world.

The Great Depression was especially rough on US manufacturers. As noted earlier, the automobile business was booming in America, while motorcycle sales were in general decline. Note the estimated sales figures:

In 1920, 52,000 motorcycles sold, compared to around 1,450,000 automobiles

In 1924, 29,900 motorcycles sold, compared to 3,180,000 automobiles

In 1928, 31,000 motorcycles sold, compared to 3,160,000 automobiles

In 1932, 12,600 motorcycles sold, compared to 1,100,000 automobiles

In 1936, 14,840 motorcycles sold, compared to an estimated 3,300,000 automobiles

In 1940, 21,800 motorcycles sold, compared to around 2,100,000 automobiles (the motorcycle figures probably include military production bikes)

Because Britain did not have the expansive land and road networks that America had, they were having the growth in the mid-size and smaller motorcycle segments. America was a large country with huge open spaces and long distances between towns. England's land mass could be placed in about two US states, and towns were generally much closer together. Roads were also more narrow in Britain, making travel by smaller machines more practical.

The majority of British motorcycles were 500cc and smaller. The larger machines were often used for sidecar setups with the larger engines needed to pull the additional weight.

The sidecar in England was typically a replacement for the automobile. In America it was a different story. The big V-twin dominated; however, during the latter time period, especially after the late 1920s, both Harley-Davidson, Excelsior, and Indian did offer a limited range of smaller bikes.

The primary American market was for the large V-twin motorcycles. It must be noted that Harley-Davidson built a twenty-one cubic inch motorcycle, often called the "Peashooter." It was a 350cc single built from 1926 to the mid 1930s, and Indian built several smaller bikes called the "Prince" and the "Light Twin" (a flat twin) during a similar time period.

Excelsior also built a two-stroke single early in this time period, which had a sixteen cubic-inch engine, being a little under 300cc in size. According to Jerry Hatfield in his book, *Antique American Motorcycles*, the engine was a copy of the small British Triumph engine of the same time period.

None of these models were big sellers. America was known for its big V-twins, and Europe was best known for smaller and mid-sized bikes. Indian was best known for the Chief and the Scout, both V-twins. Indian also had an in-line four-cylinder engine (front to back) derived from the Henderson motorcycle.

The Chief was originally a 1,000cc V-twin, later a 1,200cc twin, and at the end a 1,300 V-twin. The original Scout was a 600cc V-twin and later had a 750cc brother. After the later 1930s there was a 500cc bike called the "30.50." The in line four was little over 1,200 cc in size.

Harley-Davidson was famous for its 45 (750cc), 61(1,000cc), 74 (1,200cc) and after 1936, its 80 cubic-inch 1300cc V-twins.

Excelsior made 500cc, 750cc, and 1,000cc V-twins, like most other manufacturers. At the end of the model run, Excelsior made a model called the "Super X," which was the performance leader of its day. The Excelsior-Henderson in-line four was about 1,300cc. All the in-line fours from Henderson, Excelsior-Henderson, and Ace sold in small numbers because of the high prices. It was the V-twins which were the sales leaders.

Here is an overview of the connection between the Excelsior, Henderson, Ace, and Indian motorcycle brands. The Excelsior motorcycle brand was built from 1907 to 1931, having been purchased by Schwinn (the bicycle company) in 1912. Excelsior was best known for large V-twin motorcycles, which were some of the most powerful of their day.

The Henderson brand of motorcycle, designed by William Henderson in 1911, was built from 1912 to 1931. The brand was also purchased by Schwinn in 1917. After the Henderson brand was sold to Schwinn, the Excelsior-Henderson brand was created.

Excelsior Super X, Period advertisement

After a dispute, William Henderson split from Schwinn to build a new motorcycle. With outside financial support, William Henderson then founded the new motorcycle company in 1919. Using the name of Ace and with the new motorcycle being much like his previous Henderson motorcycle, another in-line four was created. He did make them enough different in order to avoid any copyright infringements.

After William Henderson had been killed in a motorcycle accident while testing a new model, his right-hand man, Arthur Lemon, continued with the development of the Ace motorcycle. Ace continued in business until 1927 being built in low numbers. Ace was having serious financial problems and was sold to the Indian motorcycle company in 1927 and then was produced from 1927 to 1942. First called "Indian-Ace," than later the name *Ace* was dropped, the model was then known as the Indian Four.

Schwinn dropped the Excelsior-Henderson brand because of the great depression, so the Indian version was the only one to continue in production. The big fours were known for smoothness, power, and prestige. Any of these models mentioned above were quite expensive for their day and are highly collectible today.

In 1936, Harley-Davidson built an OHV engine, called the "Knucklehead," to replace the existing side-valve engines. This engine was built from 1936 to 1948. It was to create a sales advantage over the Indian side-valve engine, which continued to the end of Indian production in 1953.

Harley-Davidson Knucklehead, Period advertisement

An interesting side note is the story of Alfred Rich Child and Harley-Davidson. Rich Child was a Harley-Davidson sales representative for several northern states, who was later sent to represent the motor company in Japan during the mid 1920s. After setting up an import company with extensive parts distribution, he was a part of building a Harley-Davidson factory in Japan. The factory was approved by Harley-Davidson, because the agreement included royalties to be paid to the home company. As war with the West was looming on the horizon in the late 1930s, Rich Child was forced to sell out his assets and was quickly sent back to America. The Japanese Harley-Davidson became the Rikuo, which continued in production with many changes until the end of the 1950s. Upon his return to the states, motorcycle sales volume was so low that his employment with the motor company was discontinued. After WWII, Rich Child ultimately became a BSA and Sunbeam motorcycle distributor.

1955 Rikuo (Japanese Harley-Davidson), Courtesy of Yesterday's Antique and Classic Motorcycles

Indian had been the dominant American motorcycle producer until around 1920. During the teens, Indian built nearly half of all motorcycles sold in the US. When the original founders stepped down from leadership by 1917, mismanagement quickly followed. The new leadership at Indian was looking only for profits. As internal theft grew, inventory issues became apparent and expensive, and growing overhead expenses began crippling the company. As Indian struggled, Harley-Davidson forged ahead and became the dominant US motorcycle manufacturer.

Indian continued to struggle until the depression of 1929. During 1930 Indian built fewer than 4,000 motorcycles. The prospect of bankruptcy became a real possibility when Indian sales had dropped significantly and the company had lost nearly three-quarters of a million dollars in one year. At that juncture, E. Paul Du Pont stepped in and took over the reins of the company. Many historians feel that he saved the failing company from extinction. His infusion of capital and business savvy gave the company another two decades of life.

It was through Indian's failures that Harley-Davidson grew much stronger. Harley-Davidson also suffered from huge sales losses, but were affected much less because of its better management and better cost controls. At this time there were just three primary American motorcycle manufacturers which still existed. Harley-Davidson had now become the dominant sales leader. along with Indian in a distant second place, with Excelsior-Henderson trailing in third and being discontinued in 1931.

In 1927 small numbers of foreign motorcycles began trickling into the States by the New York motorcycle dealer Reggie Pink. The AMA, in their tribute to him, referred to him as the "first" to import British motorcycles into the US. Pink imported Norton, Douglas, Triumph, Velocette, and Ariel motorcycles in small numbers. Pink was also known to race a BSA.

Some British motorcycles may even have come across the Canadian border into the States because there were numerous British living in Canada who were loyal to the home country and wanted to help their home manufactur-

ers. There were some who have stated that there were a few British motorcycles brought to the States by individual enthusiasts as well, but in very small numbers.

Even though there were no developing dealerships beyond Pink's agency, this practice was seen as a serious potential threat to the American manufacturers, who wanted a closed market as a means of protecting their business.

1938 Triumph Speed Twin, From the author's collection

The Great Depression hit America in late 1929. By early 1930, and especially after 1931, world markets became further depressed than ever. From the mid-1930s until WWII there were modest gains in motorcycle sales as Harley-Davidson and Indian continued to revise and perfect old and new models.

A new threat was to concern Harley and Indian during this post-depression time period through a new British motorcycle importer. In 1938 Johnson Motors, in Los Angeles, opened a Triumph, Ariel, and Indian dealership. Originally called "British and American Motors," this was to become the trend in a big way after the war. The fear was that the smaller, lighter, less expensive, and more reliable British motorcycles would easily outsell the American brands if allowed to compete on an equal basis.

Various forms of motorcycle racing continued to develop between the wars and grew in popularity faster than did motorcycle sales. Board track racing was most popular from 1919 to the mid 1920s but continued into the early 1930s.

Vintage Board Track Racer, Courtesy of Russ Briggs

Vintage Board Track Racer, Courtesy Barber Vintage Motorsports Museum

Because board tracks were seen as costly to maintain, as well as unsafe, racing moved to dirt tracks.

Horse racing had at one time been a major sports attraction but was now being circumvented by motorcycle racing. The financially struggling AMA was slowly organizing motorcycle racing into specific categories.

Hill-climbing was growing in popularity as well. Hill-climbing in the early days was more about the potential of the motorcycle to go up steep grades (its ability to actually climb steep hills). Later hill-climbs were about the elapsed time it took to go up a steep hill (how long it took to go up a hill, rather than how extreme the incline was). Then, as is the case today, the difficulty of the hill itself became the greatest challenge. Steeper hills with more powerful motorcycles were making the sport more appealing; however, the hill-climbs before WWII were nothing when compared to the hill-climbs of the past several decades.

The motorcycle had found its niche as an industry. It was just a much smaller segment and more confined group than that of the automobile. I have had numerous old timers explain to me that in the early 1950s the motorcycle community was not only much smaller than what we have today but more of a community of people who knew each other. I would imagine that this statement defined the community of motorcyclists of the late 1920s and 1930s; a small select group of enthusiasts who were much smaller in number but connected through the motorcycle.

To look at the key development in the motorcycles of this time period, note the following:

The Indian motorcycle brand made significant commitments to produce military motorcycles for WWI. By doing this, they did not keep their dealership network strong. After the war they suffered, while Harley-Davidson did the opposite. By working to keep their dealers better supplied and organized, they suffered less after the war than Indian.

As a review of this time period"

Twist throttles, foot clutches, electric lighting, and rear drum brakes become the norm. By the end of the 1920s, front brakes become more common.

Brakes were still generally very poor.

Tire size becomes larger, with front and rear tires being the same size as a cost saving factor. Because of tire size, fenders also become larger.

Harley-Davidson offers a flathead in 1921.

Frames are strengthened, because engines become larger

and more powerful; motorcycles no longer look like an engine on a bicycle frame.

Better roads demand more reliable motorcycles because people are riding farther than they ever did before.

Engine oil pumps become common, no longer requiring hand pumps to be used. The pump is often driven by the throttle, more gas for more speed = more oil injected into the engine.

Gas tanks become larger and go over the frame backbone, rather being placed inside frame members.

Going into the 1930s better metals are used.

Chrome plating becomes common, as does brighter and fancier painting designs.

The Cushman scooter emerges in 1936.

Over 120 Miles To The Gallon
More Than 30 Miles Per Hour

USHMAN MOTOR WORKS, LINCOLN, NEBR

1936 Cushman Scooter, Period advertisement

The American motorcycle market was being reduced in size and was enjoyed by a limited group of enthusiasts which was to change after WWII.

The growth of the automobile greatly impacted the motorcycle. By the end of the teens, an automobile, most likely a ford Model T, could be purchased for less than some motorcycles. From this time on, until the pre-WWII era, motorcycle sales were in general and significant decline. The demand for larger and more reliable motorcycles was the dominant force behind motorcycle development.

American manufacturers went from dozens of manufacturers to just two dominant ones—Harley-Davidson and Indian.

The AMA struggled because of the low volume of motorcycle sales as certainly did the manufacturers.

Few foreign bikes were imported because the market was low. On the other hand, the British manufacturers were having a renaissance in market and growth. The development of the British motorcycle was to reach such a high level that the basic designs remained the same until the 1970s. Triumph unveils its 500cc Speed Twin in 1937, which was to become the foundation for most of the British motorcycle industry going forward.

Not quickly at first, but by the mid-1950s, the motorcycle in America was to see significant changes, which were to only increase as the decades continued. Huge changes were about ready to impact the

American motorcycle community in ways not experienced before. The American brands found themselves confronted with very capable opponents.

Part B—The development of the Japanese motorcycle up until the WWII time period.

At this juncture, I will cover the history and development of the early Japanese motorcycle industry, from the early years until the WWII time period. Most of the Japanese motorcycle history covers the post-1950s era but the beginnings go way back before WWII. The Japanese had little impact on the motorcycle industry prior to WWII, but after the war, and especially after the early 1960s, the influence of the Japanese industry was huge. It could be said that post-WWII Japanese motorcycle development literally transformed the areas of technology, manufacturing, sales, and design for all of motorcycling around the world. I want to cover this topic before the next chapter to set a foundation for the big changes which were to come.

Japan had shown a limited interest in the motorcycle as early as 1903, although the first motorcycle was seen in Japan before 1900. As in America, Europe, and other parts of the world, the bicycle was also the precursor to the Japanese motorcycle. As is commonly understood, the bicycle had become a popular form of transportation in the West, and its evolution led directly to the development of the motorcycle.

In Japan, however, most of the country was largely rural, and the majority of people were poor, so the motorcycle developed only in areas with larger populations. Being a mountainous country was also a factor, which created many pockets of isolated farmers, most of whom remained in the dark ages of transportation development. The dominant forms of transportation in Japan were carts or wagons drawn by horses or oxen. The rickshaw was also popular. Japan also had a public rail system, which grew exponentially from the 1880s to WWII.

The popular Japanese bicycles of the day had big front wheels like those in America and Europe, but after the early 1900s the safety bicycle became dominant in Japan, as in the West. The safety bicycle allowed for an engine to be easily attached somewhere on the frame.

When the internal combustion engines became comparatively reliable they were placed on anything which worked better with a power source. It was the De Dion Bouton engine, like with the American motorcycle, which first caught on as the ideal power source.

Within just a few years, nearly everyone interested in powered transportation had made a similar copy of this engine, as noted in an earlier chapter. There were other engines which had been built, such as the Butler, the Millet, and the Hildebrand & Wolfmuller, but none of these had nearly the influence as the De Dion Buton motor. In England the Holden, AJS, Norton, OK Supreme, Triumph, and Werner motorcycles emerged along with many other brands. In France, Belgium, and Holland the Hildebrand & Wolfmuller, Buchet, Clement, and Peugeot emerged. There were dozens of other brands of motorcycles as well which could be mentioned, but are not important to this article. The American brands have already been covered. Some engines were nearly identical, some were marginally different, but all were using the basic De Dion Buton template as their foundation.

From 1894 to 1903 there were dozens of experimental motorcycles from America and Europe which were built and marketed on a limited basis in Japan and were not only very similar but were basically engines on a bicycle.

The Japanese motorcycle industry started in a similar fashion, with one major difference. After the early 1900s, the first Japanese motorcycles copied existing American and European machines primarily as an attempt to copy the West. Japan's interest was not to necessarily create a popular new form of public transportation but was an effort to emulate the technology of the West so as to not become dependent technologically or militarily.

According to an article published under the title "Centennial History of the Japanese Car," the first motorcycle seen in Japan was a Hildebrand & Wolfmuller, which was displayed in Tokyo in 1896 (Alexander, p.24). It was not until around 1901 to 1903 that the motorcycle reappears in Japan and then in very small numbers.

Let's consider the influences which allowed the motorcycle to be developed in pre-WWII Japan. This development is closely connected to the political history and survival needs of the nation. Japanese motorcycle development begins after the Meiji Renewal, dating from around 1868 to 1912.

Japanese leaders, led by Emperor Meiji, recognized that their country was far behind the West in technology and economic development.

They realized that their status and strength as a nation was connected to their modernization and industrialization.

The decision was made to copy the governmental systems of the West, especially the US, Britain, and Germany. Because the Japanese people were poor, having been governed by their former feudalistic system and having a poor educational system, a major transformation was necessary. By heavy investing by the Japanese government, developing a new educational system for the masses, bringing in professionals from many fields to train Japanese artisans, and by allowing the creativity of the masses to explore the development of new businesses, a fast pace national development was sought.

New businesses evolved quickly, and the successful ones were strongly supported by the government, then sold below the cost of their development to committed and capable managers and investors.

By 1900 Japan had caught up with the West in the areas of textiles, metallurgy, railroad systems, and commerce. As Japan entered the twentieth century, the country wanted to copy the West through industrialization, road and transportation developments, and entrepreneurship by capable visionaries.

The years before the turn of the century and until around 1937 (just before WWII) were some of the most tumultuous years of social, industrial, educational, and governmental change for Japan. Nearly everything was rapidly changing. Japan grew from a backwards feudal country to one which had to modernize to survive in the emerging twentieth century world. This fast paced need to develop moved Japan from a "shogun" state (regional rulers established by the emperor) to a centralized nation-state which had become an Imperial power and controlled Korea, Taiwan, and a small part of China.

This extraordinary growth moved Japan from a rural nation of simple farmers to the beginnings of becoming an industrial giant. By the very early 1920s Japanese exports, especially in the textile business, brought new wealth to the masses. This wealth allowed increasing numbers of people to buy cars and motorcycles.

This was also the time when there was a huge increase in the numbers of imported motorcycles. From America, Indian, Harley-Davidson, and Henderson motorcycles were imported. From Great Britain, Matchless, Norton, AJS, and Velocette were imported. From Germany, NSU and BMW were also imported in low numbers. There were probably other brands which made their way into Japan, but the above brands were the most prominent ones.

On September 1, 1923, Japan was struck with the Great Kanto Earthquake, which was devastating to the country. It most impacted the center of Honshu Island (center and coastal area of the mainland) and had its greatest impact in several of the largest cities. Over 143,000 people were killed and another 40,000 were missing, never to be found. Along with the large number of deaths, there was an epidemic of disease along with a forty-foot tsunami which destroyed hundreds of homes, along with massive road destruction. The reconstruction costs which came with the Kanto earthquake stifled the progressive development of the country for decades. As the author of a Smithsonian article stated, the quake put "an end to a period of optimism symbolized by that city. The Kanto earthquake accelerated Japan's drift toward militarism and war" (Joshua Hammer, *Smithsonian Magazine*). Some historians say that it had a continuing financial impact which continued to the WWII era. From this disaster to the WWII period, Japan was even more limited and guarded with its financial resources, and more guarded as a country.

Pre-WWII Japanese motorcycle development could be divided into three basic periods of development. The first was the period from just before 1900 to around 1907. During this first period there were just a few people interested in this new type of two-wheeled vehicle. What interest there was, came from people seeing a Hildebrand & Wolfmuller motorcycle sometime around 1896, along with seeing an American Mitchel in 1901-3.

Several Japanese engineering types, artisans, or machinists attempted to make their own machines, copied from the very limited number of motorcycles which they had seen on Japanese soil. There were no official Japanese manufacturers known to exist during this earliest time period. This was essentially the stage in which the interest for an original Japanese motorcycle first emerged.

The second stage came between 1908 to around 1916. By this time, Japan had moved from a backwards nation to one with much stronger industrial and military strength. Along with automobiles, utility vehicles and motorcycles were being developed for utilitarian purposes. Japanese motorcycle builders were hard at work copying the west, and at this point in time, were not attempting to surpass current machines in technical developments. Because the industry was new, and because they thought that the west already had the most advanced machinery, just getting reliable and competent working vehicles was their primary goal. Japan's engineering potential was beginning to materialize.

The third period begins in the late teens to the start of WWII. Japan's economy grew at a fast pace; however, during this time period a large portion of the national resources went to support the growth of the military. Large amounts of money went to manufacturers to build equipment which would bolster Japan's military strength, and little was spent on products to benefit the needs or interests of the masses.

During this period of time there was an effort to surpass the West in technology; however, western models were still heavily copied. Because there was government money being invested in the development of various types of transportation, factories began to spring up. Before the Kanto earthquake, government money was available to the innovator. After the great earthquake, money was funneled to rebuild the damaged nation. After much rebuilding had been done, money was heavily directed toward military goals.

Noted below are four lists of Japanese motorcycle manufacturers which were in operation from 1900 to the beginning of the Second World War period. Some names come up

on all four lists, such as Miyata and Meguro, while Toyo is found on three. All the lists note at least ten manufacturers from the 1900 to late 1930s period, while the longest lists include twenty-six brands. Many manufacturers did not make complete motorcycles, and some brands may reflect a mixture of parts from various companies. Furthermore, some names may reflect models of motorcycles, rather than specific brands of motorcycles.

Four lists of Japanese motorcycles built from 1900 to the WWII period are recorded from different sources:

I

Pre-WWI Motorcycles
NS Shimazu _____ 1908-1909

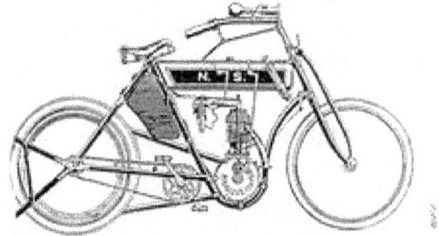

Japanese NS Motorcycle

Hino _____ 1910
NMC _____ 1912-1962
  (Nippon Motor Corp.)
Asshi _____ 1912-1964
  (Miyata Works)
Miyata _____ 1912-1964
  (Miyata Works)
Toyo _____ 1920-1960
  (Mazda)
Thunder _____ 1921
Mushashino _____ 1923
  (Kogyo Mfg.)
Giant _____ 1924-1954
  (Wasp)
Komine _____ 1924-1956
Meguro _____ 1924-1961

(Meguro Mfg.)	Showa _____ 1939-1960)
Aero Fast_____ 1925-1927	(Showa Works)
(Nippon Motors)	Yamaguchi _____ 1941-1964
Thunder _____ 1925-1938	(Yamaguchi-Hodaka)
(Watanabe Takeshi)	Emuro_____ 1945-1961
Lion_____ 1926-1933	(Health Motor Co.)
(Osaka Bicycle)	Health _____ 1945-1961
Yamato _____ 1927-1958	(Health Motor Co.)
(Yamato/Lucky)	Bis Motor _____ 1946
JAC _____ 1928-1934	Mitsubishi _____ 1946-1965
(Japan Automobile Co.)	(Mitsubishi Heavy Industries)
New Era _____ 1928-1937	Fuji _____ 1946-1968
(Nippon Jidosha)	(Fuji Heavy Industries)
SSD _____ 1930-1935	Honda_____1946-current
(Shishido Brothers)	(Honda Motor Company)
Abe Star_____ 1930-1959	IMC_____ 1947-1961
Daihatsu _____ 1930-1979	(Itoh Motor Co.)
(Daihatsu Kogyo)	Toyo _____ 1947-1961
HMC _____ 1931	(Toyo Motor Co.)
(Hyogo Motors)	Maruichi_____ 1948-1959
Ideal Real Car_____ 1931	(Maruichi Bicycle Co.)
(Yokoyama)	Tohatsu _____ 1948-1966
Tsubasa _____ 1931-1960	(Tokyo Hatsudoki Co.)
(Tsubasa Industries)	Lilac (_____ 1948-1967
Cabton _____ 1932-1958	Marusho Motorcycle Co.)
(Mizubo Jidosha)	
Aikoku_____ 1933-1958	
Rikuo _____ 1935-1962	Derived from: A Century of Japa-
(Rikuo Aristone)	nese Motorcycles; Ganneau. Page
Post WWII Motorcycles	192

II

Pre-WWII Motorcycles

Lizuka Trading...1899.. self-powered 2-wheeler, no other information

Torao Yamba...1908.. engine in a bicycle frame

Narazo Shimazu...1909.. 400cc belt-driven motorcycle

Miyata ..1913.. 175cc two-stroke (Asahi)

...1921.. OHV engine built, no manufacturer noted

Shimazu ..1927.. 250cc motorcycle engine built

JAC (Meguro)...1928.. 250cc motorcycle becomes available

Miyata...1933.. two-stroke Asahi returns to production

Cabton...1934.. 350 single built

Rikuo...1935 . builds Harley-Davidson motorcycles under contract

Meguro...1937.. 500cc motorcycle built, first complete bike

1945 First Post WWII Motorcycles Built

127 Total Units, No Manufacturers Listed

Miyata ..1946.. resumes motorcycle production

Honda ..1947.. Honda begins selling bicycles with engines

Meguro... 1948...resumes motorcycle production, 1962 joins Kawasaki

Kawasaki...1949.. begins production of 125cc motorcycle

Derived from: 100 Years Of Japanese Motorcycles; Pavey. Page 2

III

Maruyama...1895-1940s ....Bicycles to motorized bicycles to motorcy-
cles
Miyata ...1900-1940s... bicycles to motorcycles
Shimazu ...1907-1929
Nihon (NMC) ...1908.............. from Shimazu
Toyo (Mazda) ...1920s-1940s
Meguro ...1924-1940s... continues after WWII
Showa ...1924-1940s... continues after WWII
Abe ...1928-1931 .... joins Meguro in 1931
Japan Mo. Co. ...1929.............. from NMC, dating back to 1908
Riuko ...1933-1940s... copies Harley-Davidson motorcycles un-
der contract
Tokyo ..1934 .... produces Aikoku motorcycles (called the
"Patriot")
Muzucho ...1934.............. produces the Cabton motorcycle
Miyata ...1935.............. builds Asahi motorcycle
Sankyo ...1935.............. builds H-Ds under contract, name be-
comes Rikuo in 1936
Ritsurin ...1936
Meguro ...1937
All of these are pre-WWII manufacturers
(from: Japan's Motorcycle Wars; *Alexander pages 22- 50)*

IV

Miyata ...1909-64 .... Japan
Kurogane ...1930-40s....... Japan
Tokyo Kurogane Motor Company
...1930-40s....... Japan
Meguro ...1937-64 .... Japan

1958 Meguro, Thailand Motorcycle Forum

Tohatsu ...1935-66 .... Japan
Sankyo (Rikyuo) ...1935-62 .... Japan
Suzuki ...1936- .... Japan
Taiyo ...19??- .... Japan

Yamatargo ...1929-? .... Japan
Yamaguchi ...1941-64 .... Japan
Dividing line between WWII and post WWII motorcycles

Rabbit ...1946-68 .... Japan
Pointer ...1946-62 .... Japan
Honda ...1948- .... Japan
Abe-Star ...1949-1955 .... Japan
Toyo Motor ...1949-Early 1960s
.... Japan
Kawasaki ...1949- .... Japan
Derived from; Classic Motorcycles web page: www.classicmotorcycles.com.

This list has been adjusted to reflect the first years of Japanese motorcycle production to the later years of production.

These lists range from eleven listings to twenty-six. Note the following listings related to the period of Japanese motorcycle development mentioned above:

	1896 to 1906	1908 to 1916	1917 to 1941	(pre-WWII)
I	1	4	21	(26 total)
II	1	3	7	(11 total)
III	3	1	12	(16 listed)
IV	0	1	9	(10 listed)

As is evident from the above figures, motorcycle development was exponential in growth as the years progressed. In the early years there were very few builders, but after the late teens the numbers of companies more than doubled. The accuracy of the above figures is not known, but what can be seen is that the numbers of people or companies involved in motorcycle manufacturing or development more than doubled as Japan moved toward the WWII period. This was to again transform into exponential growth after the war. As a comparison, I will list American manufacturers from the same time period. Note the following from Floyd Clymers *A Treasury of American Motorcycles* pages 166-7:

(1899 to 1907)	(1908 - 1916)	(1917 - 1940)
28	42	9

This is a total of seventy-nine American manufacturers making machines before WWII. As can be seen, America had a large number of manufacturers early on, with the numbers dropping more than two-thirds after the late teens. The sales of the inexpensive Ford Model T automobile, and the Great Depression after 1929 killed the motorcycle industry in the US. Furthermore, these numbers do not reflect the one-off machines, or numerous manufacturers which never produced bikes to sell.

After WWII America was left with Indian and Harley-Davidson as the only two motorcycle brands commercially available, along with a handful of scooters, like the Whizzer, Cushman, Powell, and Simplex. In Europe (including the UK) the numbers are so much larger that it would take an independent study to even begin to calculate the numbers. England alone had well over a hundred brands of motorcycles built before 1910, and well over another 150 between the teens and the WWII era. It was recorded that England has had as many as 685 (one book lists 1,100) brands of motorcycles in their long history.

The same is true of other European countries. France, Germany, and Italy have had at least 1,000 total brands since 1900. To put these figures in perspective, most were small companies. These are actually conservative figures.

The US and Europe mushroomed with different brands of motorcycles before WWII, but the numbers radically decreased after the First World War (www.ozebook.com, the "A-Z of motorcycles"). Because this section is concerned with pre-WWII Japanese motorcycles, post-WWII developments will not be covered with any detail. To sum up, Japan started very slow and grew in motorcycle development until WWII.

The US and Europe did the opposite. Their numbers were large from 1900 to the 1940s, but motorcycle production nearly disappeared after WWII. The US was different, as before WWII nearly all brands had already disappeared there. Since WWII Japan has become the world's largest manufacturer of motorcycles, and the US and Europe have significantly decreased in volume (the US and Europe have produced many small specialty brands, which were produced in very small numbers). The point in the lists and numbers noted above is that Japan was growing in the numbers of companies which were building motorcycles, while America had a burst of new companies which began to die after the mid-teens. Before WWII Japan had seen a huge growth in the motorcycle industry, while America had seen a significant decline. England and Europe maintained their industry until the First World War (England, in particular, had large numbers of low volume manufacturers), then huge decreases in technological developments and production numbers occurred within several decades after WWII.

The following can be said of these early Japanese motorcycle builders:

First, nearly all the early Japanese motorcycles were built in crude shops until the later teens. Little government money was spent on motorcycle development, except when it was for military or governmental purposes. Most of the efforts by these early builders was to make a reliable and functional national motorcycle, rather than to build motorcycles which could compete in the international marketplace. Japanese-made motorcycles were primarily engineering studies, rather than attempts at making competitive machines.

It was not that Japanese builders did not want to compete in national markets; it was just that the international market place was struggling. This was especially true in the US. A greater goal was that

of becoming self-sustainable, rather than making competitive and marketable machines. I found no manufacturers during this early period which built motorcycles as a primary business. These early builders thought that American and European motorcycles were the best, so the Japanese efforts were geared toward matching existing technology. Japanese motorcycles remained crude copies of foreign motorcycles until the 1930s, at which time their engineering had advanced to western standards.

Secondly, all types of motorcycles were copies of American, British, or other European brands of motorcycles (the non-British motorcycles were predominantly German). The Harley-Davidson Model J was first sold in Japan in the 1920s, and then manufactured by contract from 1924 until around 1937. It was then copied without a contract until 1958. Several companies manufactured these bikes, including Muraya in 1924, Sankyo in 1933, Meguro in the 1930s, and ending with Rikuo until 1958. I have read several different time-lines for the Japanese Harley-Davidson, but suffice it to say, the bikes were copied by different manufacturers throughout the over thirty years that the motorcycle was manufactured in Japan. Toward the end of its tenure, many changes were made to make it more usable for Japanese motorcyclists. This H-D copy was a favorite for police, governmental, and military use in Japan before WWII.

Apart from the Japanese Harley clone, British brands, such as BSA, Ariel, and Triumph, were commonly the foundation for motorcycles in Japan before WWII. The Japanese builders continued to copy western designs even after WWII. However, by the early 1960s their technology was advancing beyond the US and British standards of practice. They actually continued to copy western brands, because they thought that this was what the customers wanted.

1955 CAD (Norton Copy), Courtesy of Barber Vintage Motorsports Museum

Thirdly, because Japan had very limited natural resources, along with a limited home market, motorcycle manufacturers were small and few. The Japanese Harley was certainly an exception. Different numbers have been published, but somewhere around 18,000 Rikuo H-Ds were reported to have been produced before they stopped building them.

The majority of motorcycles operating in Japan were imported. It should be noted, however, that the numbers of bikes imported was very small compared to western standards. This was because Japan is a small country compared to the West. Importation all but stopped after the Kanto earthquake. Most people were poor and would have been unable to purchase or operate a car, scooter, or motorcycle. Noting the three lists of motorcycles above which existed between

1900 and the late 1930s (pre-WWII), Ganneau listed twenty-three names, Pavey lists ten, and Alexander lists sixteen. It should be noted that only five of the names can be found on all three lists. A sixth is found on two lists. Many companies used multiple names, such as Mushashino and Kogyo, Nippon and New Era, and Cabton, Mizubo, and Jidosha. These lists probably include a mixture of manufacturers which worked closely together, using individual parts from different manufacturers to produce specific motorcycles. Lists could also include a model and a maker, which would appear as two brands.

My point is this; in 1913 there were only 1,284 self-propelled machines operating in Japan (motorcycles, scooters, cars, and trucks combined). By 1922 the number rises to 9,992 and by 1934 there were only 70,481 vehicles registered in Japan (Alexander, page 36). Compared to US registration figures, these numbers are very small. According to Harry Sucher, in 1912 there were at least 175,000 motorcycles alone registered in the US (p.22). By the 1920s the number of registered vehicles on the roads rose to the millions in the US, and by 1930, the number is around twenty-seven million registered vehicles. From 1900 to the 1930s the US had over a hundred manufacturers, while

Japan had somewhere between ten and twenty builders. Japan was a small player with a minor market in the field of motorcycle manufacturing during this time period. By the WWII period, their motorcycle industry was building motorcycles comparable to the West.

Fourthly, as Japan grew closer to the WWII period (after 1930), they became more protectionist in practice. As the world markets were suffering, tariffs were applied to their own individual markets to protect their own businesses. Japan did the same.

The problem Japan had was that their population was growing at a pace beyond what their own land could support. Japan responded by determining that they had to be strong militarily to protect themselves as a nation and to protect the alliances they had built with a few other nations. The result was that more money was spent building up the Japanese military, and less went for developing products for the masses. From 1900 to the 1920s the motorcycle was developed as an attempt to match western technology. From the late 1920s to WWII the motorcycle was developed for either military use or for general transportation purposes. The caveat was that as Japan grew more independent as a nation, the motorcycle had to become a self-sustaining entity and independent from the West as well. Japan wanted to build its own motorcycles so as to not be dependent on the West.

Finally, most Japanese motorcycles were smaller displacement machines. Again, the Japanese Harley remains an exception. Motorized bicycles were common, 175, 250, 350, and 400cc motorcycles were the norm. Typically, the largest would be in the 500cc range. Unlike the West, Japanese builders appeared to have a closer working relationship with each other, which is not the norm in the western hemisphere. Being in a smaller world with many living in population centers this would be expected. Larger displacement motorcycles, apart from the Rikuo, did not come until a decade after the war. Even until the end of the pre-WWII period the Japanese motorcycle was considered inferior to those in the West, however, a decade after the war this was to drastically change.

In this next section, I will attempt to condense the best and most current information available about the earliest Japanese motorcycles. Nearly all this information will come from four primary sources, however, there are various other sources mixed in as well. There seems to be some contradictory and confusing data, however. I will do the best I can to make a linear developmental

chart. The most important observations are these: First, the Japanese were quick to copy others and secondly, they produced machines in very small numbers compared to the West. Thirdly, they tended to build newly designed machines rather than to continue developing older machines. Fourthly, the Japanese were much more interdependent than the West. They tended to work towards national goals, rather than to promote individual ambitions. Fifthly, the Japanese motorcycle industry doesn't really get started until after the 1920s. From the early 1920s until WWII the Japanese motorcycle development was on the increase, until the war stopped all production. A decade after the war Japan was well on its way to being the world's largest producer of motorcycles. In America during this time period the automobile begins to far surpass the motorcycle in sales numbers, and after WWII there were only two motorcycle manufacturers left. Finally, the Japanese motorcycle development was much more interrelated than the same industry in either the US or Europe. This was primarily because Japan is a smaller country and had fewer resources. The recessions Japan experienced in the 1920s and the increased government controls placed on businesses during the 1930s stifled the motorcycle industry, except as it related to the military or government needs.

As stated before, the first motorcycle appeared in Japan in 1896. This was a Hildebrand & Wolfmüller, imported by Shinsuke Jomonji, a member of the Japanese House of Representatives, who demonstrated the machine in front of the Hibiya Hotel in Tokyo (the motorcycle was destroyed by the great earthquake in 1923?).

In 1901 (Hiko states this occurred in 1903) a Thomas motorcycle and tricycle were imported, and the motorcycle was ridden extensively through Tokyo, generating considerable press and social interest.

The first motor vehicle race in Japan was allegedly staged between the two Thomas machines and a Gladiator quadricycle on Nov. 3, 1901. The Thomas is generally considered to be the first production motorcycle manufactured in the US, and its appearance in Japan at this early date is considered remarkable. as most Americans would never see a motorcycle until after 1905 or later.

The first actual motorcycle to be produced in Japan was one built by a man named "N. Shimazu" in 1908 (Ganneau, p.9). It looks much like other 1900-1903 motorcycles built around the world. It's basically an engine in a bicycle frame. Mr. Shimazu is to reappear numerous times in early Japanese motorcycle development. A

Wikipedia article titled "Early Japanese Motorcycles" notes: In 1908 Narazo Shimazu created his first two-stroke engine, a 400cc single-cylinder, and used it to propel a bicycle. In 1909 he produced his first four-stroke engine as well as a motorcycle frame to go with it. This is generally thought to be the first motorcycle made in Japan.

"Shimazu produced more than twenty of his NS motorcycles at Nihon Motorcycle Company (NMC) and later produced more than 700 Arrow Fast motorcycles at Japan Motors Manufacturing." The Arrow Fast dates from around 1925 and will be discussed later. Note the drawing in the previous chart which was the first known Japanese motorcycle dating back to around 1908.

Next comes a motorcycle built by a Mister Miyata, a gunsmith. According to Ganneau (p. 9) his motorcycle was a copy of a 550cc British Triumph imported around 1913. Called the "Asahi," it was primarily used by the police and the Japanese Prime Minister (p.10).

It was also noted that the factory closed in 1916, so it was a short-term project. Adrian Pavey notes that a 175cc two-stroke Asahi was also built in 1913; little else is known of this version of the motorcycle (p.2).

Hiko suggests that another bike was built around this same time period (no specific years given) by the Nihon

Motorcycle Company. It was stated to be a 250cc two-stroke machine. Little is known of this machine, except that it was manufactured in very small numbers, fewer than a hundred units. Starting in the early 1920s there were new motorcycles built in Japan.

In 1921 there was a 150cc motorcycle built by an individual identified as Mister Watanabe. This was claimed to be the first overhead-valve engine designed and manufactured in Japan. The engine was later enlarged to 300cc, however, no other information is available.

In 1923 a two-stroke single was built by Musashino Kogyo. The carburetor and transmission was of European origin (Hiko).

In 1924 the Japanese government passed the "Military Vehicle Subsidy Law," which moved the motorcycle industry from back alley garages to large factories. This coincides with the Japanese interest in the Harley-Davidson motorcycle. Alfred Rich Child had become an importer of Harley-Davidson motorcycles to Japan in 1924. After around five years of importing Harleys, Child determined that building them in Japan would be a better plan economically. It was also an idea which Harley liked, because the crash of 1929 was adversely hurting their profits.

Harley-Davidson sent engineers over to Japan in 1931 to build a factory to build both 45 ci (750cc) and 74 ci (1200cc) motorcycles. Things went well until the mid-1930s. As worldwide tensions mounted, Japan was growing more isolationistic. In 1936 Child sold the assets of his businesses to a Japanese investor and quickly left Japan. Japan stopped paying Harley-Davidson royalties and made the motorcycle their own (for more information go to the AMA Motorcycle Hall of Fame).

The Japanese Harley continued in production until 1942, at which time an estimated 18,000 had been built. After the war, they resumed production until 1958, at which time production finally stopped (Wikipedia: Riuko). The Riuko was primarily used for military and government use; however, some were sold domestically. I have come across a few different versions of the Riuko story, but what I have noted is generally correct and is an interesting part of the Japanese motorcycle story.

We can now go back to the 1924 Arrow Fast motorcycle, designed and built by Mister Shimazu. According to Hiko, the first Arrow Fast had a 633cc side-valve engine with a three-speed transmission and a reverse. The next year a 250cc version was built and sold in the hundreds, thus becoming the first mass-produced Japanese motorcycle. Engines were still very poorly made, which meant that most motorcycles were imported. Hiko stated that eighty percent of all motorcycles were imported because of the low quality of Japanese machines.

During the 1930s two companies came together to build the Cabton motorcycle. Mizuhmo and Riuko, both found in the above lists of early Japanese motorcycle manufacturers, came together to build a 500cc motorcycle, which was alleged to be a copy of an Ariel (Hiko). Built from around 1934 to WWII, the motorcycles manufactured by this cooperative were copies of English motorcycles. Another motorcycle, dating back to 1930, was one built by Toyo Kogyo, later known as Mazda. Ganneau notes that only around thirty were made (p.16).

Pavey notes in his book that the 1934 Cabton motorcycle was a 350, rather than a 500. These minor discrepancies are typical (p.2).

The next motorcycle which was developed was built by Nihon Keijidousha Kougyo. Like other early Japanese motorcycles, his bike was a low production machine. Using the initials *NKB*, it was a small displacement machine looking much like its European counterparts. Built around 1937 to 1939, some include an earlier date, the motorcycle was said to have used numerous parts from other companies. The factory was located in Hiroshima so was destroyed during WWII (Hiko).

Probably the most significant older Japanese motorcycle manufacturer was Meguro. Meguro motorcycles were made by Meguro Manufacturing Co. Motorcycle Works, founded by Hobuji Murato and a high ranking naval officer Takaji Suzuki, in 1937. It is one of the oldest Japanese motorcycle companies and became a partner of Kawasaki Heavy Industries, Ltd.

"Named after a district of Tokyo, it had its roots in Murato Iron Works, which was established 1924." I have seen some references to Meguro's date of origin as early as 1930, and the Kawasaki takeover in 1963 or 1964. Ganneau gives the final date that Meguro existed as its own company as 1961 (p.192).

Every book or website I studied which was related to the early Japanese motorcycle included some conflicting information. I am confident that most of the pertinent information currently available can be reconciled so that the basic lines of development are not radically altered. As time progresses and as there is greater interest in the early years of the Japanese motorcycle industry, I am confident that more studies will be made. I plan to continue my research as well.

In Adrian Pavey's book, *100 years of Japanese Motorcycles*, Pavey notes these highlights regarding Japanese motorcycle development:

1908 Torao Yamaba bolts the first Japanese motorcycle engine into a bicycle frame

1909 Torao Shimazu designs and builds a belt-driven 400cc motorcycle

1913 Miyata builds a175cc motorcycle under the NMC name

1921 the first OHV motorcycle engine built

1923 Musashino builds an all Japanese motorcycle

1927 Shimazu builds a 250cc motorcycle engine only

1933 Miyata resumes production of the 2-stroke Asahi motorcycle

1935 Riuko builds the Japanese Harley-Davidson motorcycle

1937 Meguro introduces its first motorcycle with a 500cc motor

1940 Japanese motorcycle production goes over 3000 units per year, an all time high.

Although simple and somewhat incomplete, this outline gives us a valuable Japanese motorcycle development timeline. Probably the best history is provided by Jeffrey Alexander in his book, *Japan's Motorcycle Wars*. The pre-WWII period was a time when the vast majority of vehicles were built for utilitarian purposes, rather than for sport.

Japan was a country which had more times of economic struggle than times of having a booming economy.

Conclusion

Japan essentially copied the motorcycles of other countries until the WWII period. After the 1960s they became significant motorcycle design innovators.

Earlier in this chapter, I referred to three stages of Japanese motorcycle development. The first stage went from around 1900 to around 1907. In this stage, the few motorcycles that were made were copies of foreign bikes built in back alley garages by relatively unskilled, mechanically-oriented artisans. They were poorly made and were unreliable.

The next stage goes to around 1916. In this period, most motorcycles were imported, but a few Japanese manufacturers did begin to emerge. Japanese motorcycles were still considered to be unmarketable outside Japan and remained unreliable.

The final stage goes to the WWII period. In an effort to become independent from the West and because of the growth of the military, the Japanese government began to invest money in the transportation industry, which included the motorcycle sector. Motorcycles were still copies of western machines, but because of larger amounts of money being available, the motorcycle saw significant engineering and manufacturing improvements. Production numbers remained low compared to the West, but the foundation was being set for future growth.

It has been the growth of the industry after WWII that has been astonishing.

The Hosk, built by Yamarin, looks much like a British big single. Still a copy, but it looks much cleaner, more modern, and has the appearance of being well-engineered. The Hosk was never sold outside Japan but shows the progress made after the war (Ganneau p.26-37).

Japan's real problem has been access to natural resources and foreign markets. Once this situation improved, Japan's industries, including the motorcycle industry, rapidly forged ahead. The post-WWII period has been referred to as the Japanese "Economic Miracle."

Directly after the war, Japan struggled to rebuild their industrial base. Companies, such as Toyota, Nissan, Honda, Sony, Nippon, Panasonic, Toshiba, and Kawasaki Heavy Industries (the Kawasaki motorcycle division is dwarfed by the company's other interests) are now some of the largest in the world. A much longer list could easily be made.

Like the big four Japanese motorcycle manufacturers, Yamaha, Honda, Suzuki, and Kawasaki, Japan has become a world leader known for performance, reliability, quality, innovation, and highest sales volumes around the world.

From inferior products copied from the designs of others, to some of the best motorcycles currently made in the world, the early history of the Japanese motorcycle industry is an interesting story worth reading. From the 1908 NS to the Japanese motorcycles built after 1968, there is no greater show of engineering development. The Japanese miracle was a product of necessity. They were a country with few resources and a very limited market within their own borders.

To succeed was required of their people in order to exist beyond a subsistence level. Their livelihood depended upon creating products which would succeed in a world market, while seen at the same time as a less desirable product. They had to produce a better product for less money at a reduced retail price. They did it by discipline and exhibiting less division as a country. In the field of motorcycling, after WWII, they achieved these goals in spades.

We will now move on to the post-WWII era, to what is often called the British motorcycle invasion.

Chapter 4

After WWII to Approximately 1963

The British Motorcycle Invasion

After World War II, as with the period after the First World War, America was to again see some major social and political changes. Directly after the war America suffered from significant financial woes. America not only had a huge war debt, but the thousands of returning veterans had a hard time readjusting to civilian life, as could be expected. These war-torn young men wanted much more than their old way of life. As they married, established families, and had children, America's industrial potential was just about to develop at a level never seen before.

Population growth outside cities and towns, largely attributed to the increases in automobile transportation, created a new suburbia, unknown to America prior to 1950. There was significant highway development connecting the coasts, allowing much more free travel.

Since the mid-1930s there had been continuous road development, but in the early 1950s the Interstate highway system began to take form. It was not until after the Eisenhower Interstate Highway bill was passed that these road systems were to be fully developed, however, roads had been seeing slow, but continual, improvements for several decades prior to that.

More back roads were being paved, more streets were having street lights installed, and more people were beginning to travel much farther than what was common before the war. People wanted to travel in the 1920s and 1930s and certainly did. The drive to see more of America gained significant momentum after the Second World War. The growth during the 1950s was strong and upwards, setting the stage for what was to happen in the next decade. The 1960s was to become known as one of the fastest periods of growth in modern times. This growth was to impact the motorcycle world as well.

Indian Chief, From the author's collection

From the end of the 1940s to the early 1950s there was a growing interest in the motorcycle. Many soldiers had been introduced to the motorcycle during the war, creating interest which had not been there

before. The large cumbersome American motorcycles did not appeal to many of the younger generation. After returning to the States, automobiles were found to be in short supply. Because of this, many began riding motorcycles as basic transportation, since they were readily available. During this same time period, there were many scooter manufacturers emerging in the US, producing commuter vehicles for the masses. As individuals bought scooters, it wasn't long before they wanted more power, and many purchased larger and more powerful motorcycles.

Thrilling Sport and Thrifty Transportation

HARLEY-DAVIDSON *HYDRA-GLIDE*

Every mile is money saved, every moment a thrill... when you ride this swift, smooth "streamliner"! It takes you comfortably to daily work or distant points... at amazingly low cost. It brings you endless good times at race-meets, tours and other exciting motorcycling fun events. With it you can play a vital part in your local defense program. Easy terms. See your dealer. Mail coupon.

HARLEY-DAVIDSON MOTOR CO., Dept. PS, Milwaukee 1, Wisconsin

Name

Address

City   State

DEALERS: Valuable franchises available for the full line of famous Big Twins and the 125 Model. Write today.

80 POPULAR SCIENCE

Harley-Davidson, Period advertisement

Another factor which increased the interest in motorcycles was that during the war many Americans had fought alongside British soldiers. The British military used motorcycles much more than the American armed forces did. Many an American remembered the light and compact British singles, which were as fast as the big American V-twins. Furthermore, they were more agile and were also much easier to operate.

The motorcycle, either American or British, was seen as able to fill basic transportation needs and was generally less expensive. The need for low-cost transportation, the need for a more exciting transportation, the need for another form of transportation beyond the car, and the ability to have an inexpensive machine to ride or race all enhanced the interest and value of the motorcycle.

After the war, both Harley-Davidson and Indian experienced sales growth, though modest. By 1948 many British motorcycles, especially Triumph, BSA, Ariel, Velocette, AJS, and Matchless, were being imported in small but growing numbers. By the early 1950s the numbers were growing significantly—especially on the coasts. As the chain of dealerships selling British motorcycles was increasing, sales numbers also saw growth. This "British Invasion" was to change the face of motorcycling in America and was to set the foundation for the next big jump in growth.

At first, a few dealers were just importing motorcycles for their own shops directly from

England. As a few dealers became distributors, motorcycles were being made available to a broader market. Little dealers began to pop up all over the country in small numbers, selling motorcycles to a much broader market.

Before 1950 American motorcycle sales were in the less than 20,000 per year range. Most of these motorcycles were either Harley-Davidsons or Indians. By the early 1950s the sales numbers had more than doubled, and most of the new growth was with the British bikes. By 1960 US motorcycle sales were around 70,000 motorcycles per year, with around two-thirds being British motorcycles.

Of the British bikes in the early years, Triumph, Matchless, and BSA were the dominant brands. A typical story went like this: A young man would open a repair shop and would work on small engines, lawn mowers, older cars, or anything mechanical needing to be fixed. Motorcycles would be included as something they would work on. At some point, a distributor would contact him and offer to give him a few motorcycles to sell without the dealer having to put money up for them. Because money was tight, no money would change hands until a motorcycle would be sold. He would sell a bike or two and was then a motorcycle dealer. Some businesses would grow, and some would stay small. I have been told of many dealers who worked out of an area no larger than a two-car garage, never getting much larger.

BSA, Period sales brochure

At the end of the 1940s and going into the 1950s, most motorcycle dealers were small and crude compared to modern standards. A typical dealer might only have one or two motorcycles on display. A larger dealer might have a dozen bikes, though that would be a dealer in a larger market area. Large clean and attractive dealerships were definitely in the minority. There were certainly dealers all over the country, but most could be found in areas with larger populations.

1960s Motorcycle Dealer, Motorcycle dealers at this time were smaller than the dealers of today and stocked fewer motorcycles. From the author's collection

Dealers were typically in low-rent areas of town because they did not make enough money to have better facilities. I can remember the tail end of the 1950s, and even the larger dealers were small compared to modern dealerships today. A larger dealer might move from his garage to an old gas station or even an old empty car dealership.

Lowly populated areas would rarely have a motorcycle dealer. I interviewed a man in his mid 90s (in 2015) who could remember the 1940s and 1950s, and he stated that he rarely saw a motorcycle. He might only see one every few months. I have interviewed

many older men who remember the small, greasy, low-volume motorcycle shops of the 1950s. This was the most common type of dealership. It was also the lower income, blue collar worker who purchased motorcycles because individuals with larger incomes would generally purchase an automobile.

As noted in the last chapter, there were several low-volume importers of British motorcycles before WWII. As mentioned, Reggie Pink, whose dealership was in NYC, imported British bikes as early as 1927 and was known to have continued after WWII. I have also read where Pink may have sold motorcycles to a small but growing list of independent dealers, making himself an early distributorship.

1950s Ariel Square Four, From the author's collection

Another East Coast dealer named Rod Coates imported Triumph motorcycles as early as 1937. Coates was later an importer of other British motorcycles just after the war. He imported Triumph, Vincent, Ariel, and other British bikes until he worked with Alfred Rich Child to develop the BSA import business in 1950. Coates finally became the Service Manager for the Triumph Corporation for the entire East Coast.

Also mentioned in the last chapter was the Johnson Motor dealership from 1938. Johnson Motors was to become the Triumph distributor for all the dealers on the west coast after WWII. Johnson Motors was to build their business to servicing well over 300 dealers by the mid-1960s.

Along with this development, other brands from other countries were also on the move. Both CZ and Jawa, Czechoslovakian-made motorcycles, were also imported to the US by the early 1950s. The Berliner Corporation began importing German Zundapps as early as 1951, the Italian Ducati in 1958, Norton in 1961, and Matchless in 1963.

Bikes from around the world began to find their way into the US market in small numbers after WWII. As noted above, a few British motorcycles began coming over before WWII, followed by many other brands after the war. The larger British brands generally came before 1950; however, brands from around the world

including those from Italy, Germany, Spain, and Japan began being imported from the late1950s.

By the early 1960s dozens of new brands of motorcycles were imported to America. Most failed to find a significant market and were gone by the late 1960s. The Spanish and Japanese motorcycles were generally the last to be imported at the end of this time period. Of all the bikes, the Japanese machines were to have the best reception over time, although they had a rough start.

From Germany, NSU, BMW, and Zundapp were the more significant manufacturers. Smaller brands which were imported were Adler and the Maico brands. There were other motorcycle brands shipped over from Germany, however, their numbers were very small. Today, BMW is the best known and the one which has remained the longest.

From Italy, Ducati, Moto Guzzi, and Aermacchi were the primary brands imported. Aermacchi is best known in the US as carrying the Harley-Davidson name. Harley purchased fifty percent of the company in 1961 and sold off their shares in 1978.

The Spanish Bultaco and Montessa motorcycles were imported in very small numbers at the end of this time period and were to become much more important after the mid 1960s.

Both the German and Italian manufacturers were well-known for their advanced designs and exotic engines. The Italian Moto Guzzi raced a supercharged four in the 1930s and raced a V-8 powered motorcycle in the 1950s. Guzzi was a brand well known for its racing exploits in Europe before WWII.

The German NSU was also known for its advanced motorcycle designs. The NSU Max and Supermax machines were a significant influence on Sochiro Honda and his motorcycle development. NSU was one of the early manufacturers who used pressed-steel frames and OHC engines.

NSU Super Max, Period advertisement

BMW was also well known for advanced designs and very high-quality construction. BMW built aircraft engines in the early years but were banned from engine construction after WWI. In response, they built a motorcycle. Some suggest that the BMW flat-twin was a general copy of the British Douglas, as the German manufacturer made engine parts for the British company.

NSU, Courtesy of Yesterday's Antique and Classics Motorcycles

Many of these foreign companies were encouraged to market to the US customer because our country appeared to have an open market, and they were looking for ways to bolster their businesses after WWII.

Of all the brands to begin importing to the US, the ones with the greatest impact were the motorcycles from Japan. Sochiro Honda began his engineering firm in 1947 in a single garage-sized building. Honda was a poor Japanese boy who learned how to repair bicycles through the efforts of his father. By age twenty-two he had his own repair shop. He raced bikes and attended the Hamamatsu School of Technology and was a rebellious but creative student.

After World War II, he purchased several hundred crude single-cylinder engines and attached them to bicycles.

The transportation needs of Japan were so great that he sold all that he could produce. This sounds much like the beginning of motorcycle development discussed in chapter two.

After running out of salvaged motors, he began to build his own. Honda had also refined the piston ring, which was a weak link on many of the earlier engines. He began producing engines which had a reputation for reliability. From there the real story begins. From Honda's innovation to mass production his efforts were to be greatly rewarded. Honda led the pack in innovation, reliability, and consistent progressive development.

He began importing motorcycles to the US in 1959, however, some bikes were brought over earlier for testing. Some were also raced. Not many bikes were imported in 1959, but in 1960 the numbers grew exponentially and continued to grow after that.

Most of the early bikes were small. At the time that Honda began marketing motorcycles in the US, Honda was mass producing thousands of motorcycles monthly and was already building more motorcycles than most of the British companies. Most of his production went around the world, though Honda would aim for the American shores.

When Honda released the 305cc Super Hawk in 1961, a

revolution began. The motorcycle would outperform most of the British 500s and would keep up with many of the 650s. When *Cycle World* tested one in May of 1962, its performance was beyond the belief of many readers. With a tested top speed of 105.2 mph, it was faster than most British 650s. The author of the article noted that the entire staff was "deeply impressed" (*Cycle World*; "On Honda 1962-1967," p.8). A year later they tested another Super Hawk with an aftermarket 350cc kit, which went through the quarter mile in 14.9 seconds (*Cycle World*, October 1963). These figures were truly astonishing for that time period and gave Honda a great deal of respect from the motorcycle community.

1960s Honda Dream, From the author's collection

Beyond sheer performance, Honda motorcycles were proven to be durable as well. I still remember a mechanic telling me back in 1966 that he was sure that Hondas would have tin-can pistons in the engine (meaning the parts would be of low quality). When he finally worked on one he was surprised at the quality and precision of the engineering and parts. Honda was to become the largest motorcycle manufacturer in the world by 1961, setting a standard which was hard for many other manufacturers to meet. What set Honda apart was the ability to create new bikes so fast, make them reliable, and sell them at bargain prices.

Yamaha Industries followed other Japanese corporations into the motorcycle business because of their desire to expand their business through the use of their surplus foundry capacity. Their main products were musical instruments, hence the tuning fork as their logo.

The 1955 Yamaha YA 1 was an improved copy of the older DKW RT125.
From Wikipedia Commons

Starting in 1954, Yamaha copied the German DKW RT125 as a base model. The DKW had been copied by numerous other companies, such as Harley-Davidson and BSA. The 250cc series Yamahas were copied from the German Adler MB200/250 series, as did other Japanese companies. All of the early Yamahas were two-strokes. The first four-stroke was the 1970 XS-1, a refined copy of the Triumph Bonneville.

Yamaha began racing their motorcycles in the mid 1960s and has become one of the most significant racing brands. Yamaha did as other Japanese companies did. They copied the best designs, perfected them, and then made their own technically advanced designs. Cooper Motors is said to have imported a few Yamahas as early as 1958; most were sold after the early 1960s, though. In 1960 Yamaha began importing their motorcycles through their own importing company, which has been the standard for Japanese manufacturers in general.

73

Michio Suzuki began building silk looms in 1909. They were a major business in Japan until WWII bombs destroyed their factory. After the war, the loom business was weak, and the company looked for a new product to develop. Transportation was a major need in Japan, so the Suzuki Corporation designed and built a simple motorized bicycle in 1952. Their next product was a copy of the German DKW RT125, similar to one built by Yamaha. All their early motorcycles were small two-strokes, which were developed slowly.

Suzuki entered racing in 1955 with little success. By the early 1960s, development had allowed them to see some success. They were given a boost in 1961 by East German, Ernst Degner of the MZ motorcycle company, and began winning races at a much faster rate. He was an important figure in turning their mundane engines into high performance ones.

Suzuki was still a very small company at this time, and they looked to exporting motorcycles to the US as a means of growth. The first Suzukis were imported in 1962 in small numbers. Suzuki motorcycles were to be slow sellers until the mid-1960s. It was the 1965 X6 Hustler which put Suzuki on the map. The T20 Super 6, as the Hustler was also called, was faster than many British 650 twins at that time.

Kawasaki Heavy Industries dates back to 1878. Kawasaki was involved in ship-building, building locomotives, and building aircraft. As with other companies, WWII destroyed their manufacturing base. Kawasaki has again regained their status as a huge corporation, doing billions of dollars of business around the world. The motorcycle division is just a drop in the bucked of this massive engineering corporation.

After the war, the company was looking for ways to expand their business and gain industrial momentum. In 1950 they built and sold a 148cc engine kit to fit on a bicycle. Again, this is a common story as to how motorcycles were first built. The light motorcycle/moped division continued building small vehicles until they bought the Maguro company. Maguro was a Japanese motorcycle company dating back to 1924. Kawasaki put their name on the Maguro line of motorcycles and even continued using the Maguro name in Japan.

Kawasaki began exporting motorcycles to the US in 1963. In their first year they offered just two 125cc models. In 1964 and 1965 they added a 250cc single derived from the Maguro brand.

In 1966 Kawasaki jumped from a limited line of machines to a complete line of motorcycles, including 50cc, 85cc, 100cc, 115cc, 125cc, 150cc, 175cc, 250cc, and a 650cc twin. The big bike was a copy of the older BSA A10 series of machines, which Kawasaki had copied earlier and sold in Japan as a 500cc motorcycle. They began as a really small exporter and had a hard fought battle for their market share while Honda, Yamaha, and Suzuki were going full swing.

There were a few other brands of Japanese motorcycles imported by the end of the 1950s to early 1960s, like the Lilac, Marusho, Maguro (Kawasaki), Fuji, and the Tohatsu, but they were to disappear early and had little impact on motorcycling in the US.

Marusho

Bridgestone Tire Company, the company providing most of the tires for the larger Japanese manufacturers, also built a line of advanced two-stroke motorcycles. They were first imported in 1963 under the name of Rockford. Bridgestone discontinued making motorcycles around 1967.

The Japanese motorcycle was to end the dominance of the British motorcycle by the mid-1960s. The other brands of motorcycles from other continents mentioned above were to have a reduced impact as well. It was the Japanese motorcycle that was to bring huge changes to the sport of motorcycling. Honda was to bring the greatest shock to the motorcycle community early on, with the other brands developing later. The fullest impact was yet to come. The reliability, low prices, quality of construction, advanced engineering, and sporty appearance was to make a compelling case for the motorcycles from under the rising sun.

Probably one of the greatest assets of the Japanese companies was their ability to produce new models very quickly. If one model sold well one year, there would be four new models the next. This was an asset in the early years, but later on there were so many new models that one could question whether this was actually a hindrance. More on this later.

By this time period, the great Indian brand had been struggling for decades and finally failed. Indian was in trouble during the 1930s because of the Great Depression and the depressed motorcycle market. In 1930 a majority share of the company was sold to Paul DuPont. The company had mostly bad years and was never fully able to recover and was then sold to Ralph Rogers in 1945.

Rogers brought out two British-styled motorcycles in 1948, a 220cc single and a 440cc twin. They were later increased in size to 250cc and 500cc engines, being more traditional sizes. The engines were not fully tested, and many of the internal parts were not clearly marked, so repair work was complex and troublesome. The bikes proved to be unreliable and costly to repair, but most of all, they severely tarnished the image of Indian. The basic design was good; it was just that the bugs had not been worked out, so the numbers of warranty problems made the model unsustainable.

The Indian Chief remained until 1953, selling in low numbers. After 1953 the name was used on the bikes of other brands. This part of Indian history will be covered next. Most historians end the first stage of Indian motorcycle history in 1953.

Sometime after 1955 the British company Brockhouse Engineering took over the Indian name and tried to revive it. They used British Royal Enfield motorcycles badged as Indians and also made several of their own machines sold as Indians. Indian-badged Royal Enfield motorcycles were built between 1955 and 1959, however, unsold stocks of these motorcycles remained until 1961.

Associated Motorcycles then took over Brockhouse during 1959 and 1960. As the company (Brockhouse) went into liquidation, they (AMC) began selling AJS and Matchless motorcycles through the Indian sales division. They ended up using the Indian dealer network to sell a variety of different British motorcycles, but it just didn't work well. The Royal Enfield-badged and Indian-badged motorcycles (which were Royal Enfield motorcycles re-badged as Indians) were occasionally sold side by side in the same dealerships. This was also a problem because Royal Enfield was a competitor of the AMC brands.

Set the pace

on American roads

with *Indian*

in '55

TRAILBLAZER

Indian Royal Enfield, Period advertisement

The years 1959 to 1962 were tough for AMC and the Indian sales division. They had sold Brockhouse/Royal Enfield/Indians, AJS/Matchless motorcycles, sometimes sold with the Indian name, and other AJS/Matchless-badged motorcycles without the Indian name. Even when the old Indian brand was not used, Indian was often used in the sales ads. It was all very confusing, especially to the customers. I have attempted to put the story together as clearly as is possible, considering that I have records with somewhat different "facts."

What is clear, however, is this was a confusing time for AMC and the marketing of badged Indian motorcycles as they tried to put a broken manufacturing and marketing system into place. They did this while their core business was also failing in sales. With every segment of their business in survival mode, there was little happening that was positive for them. In 1963 Berliner Corporation took over what sales remained, and all production ceased in 1966. One article estimated that between 1955 and 1961 there were approximately 7,000 motorcycles sold with the Indian badge. The Indian name was not to go into extinction yet, but this will be discussed in the next chapter.

Harley-Davidson did much better than Indian during this time period. As the sole remaining American motorcycle manufacturer, they had a stronger hold on the American market than did Indian. Their sales had been consistently larger than those of Indian, and they had a much stronger dealer network in place. By building big V-twin motorcycles consistent with the traditional American market and maintaining a strong hold on their dealerships, Harley-Davidson was able to continue on.

By also continuously developing their motorcycles, keeping parts and service readily available to their buyers, and by promoting the "built in

"America" concept, Harley-Davidson maintained enough rider commitment to sustain their market share.

The British companies, however, were making serious inroads into the American motorcycle business by offering smaller, lighter, faster, and less expensive machines. As noted above, the British took over nearly two-thirds of the American motorcycle business for approximately a decade or more.

In 1951 Harley-Davidson took some of the larger importers of British bikes to court, claiming that there was unfair competition between the two countries. They wanted the tariffs to be raised on the British motorcycles so they could compete in terms of retail price. Harley-Davidson lost the case because the British motorcycles were seen as being in a different market. During the case, the judge wanted to actually see the motorcycles. People representing the British manufacturers rolled their machines on the elevator and took them up to the courtroom. The Harleys would not fit on the elevator without being partially dismantled, clearly showing that their bikes were very different. The British bikes were also much smaller in engine size, even though they often offered higher performance than the Harley-Davidsons. These factors caused the judge to de-

termine that Harley-Davidson was serving another market segment.

To compete, Harley-Davidson built the smaller, lighter Sportster in 1957. The Sportster has become an iconic machine in America, still being a major part of Harley-Davidson's business, even today. Harley-Davidson remained the sole large motorcycle manufacturer in the US for decades.

After WWII, the AMA (American Motorcycle Association) motorcycle clubs grew substantially in number. During the 1930s there were around 620 clubs, but by the mid-1950s there were over 1,600 active AMA clubs across America. Individual clubs sponsored group rides, competitive events, and social activities. A key AMA event, which was made available to all clubs, was called the "Gypsy Tour." These tours dated as far back as 1913 and had become major motorcycle events by the mid-1950s. The primary reason events got larger was that roads were becoming better, and riders could travel greater distances more easily.

Along with productive club activity, there was also a growing number of motorcycle rebels who were not fitting in with the typical friendly atmosphere that prevailed at most events. Most of these early rebels were ex-GIs who had not settled down and who were from larger cities. One of the most famous events which encouraged this rebel movement to grow was the 1947 Hollister, California, Gypsy Tour riot. There are numerous stories which described what happened in Hollister, some tame and some not as mild. What was finally recorded, however, did give motorcycling a bad name. Pictures of drunk bikers racing, fighting, and being aggressive toward the towns people was reported and was a fearful image. Newspaper headlines stating that "Motorcycle Gangs Take Over Town, Many Injured" made the motorcycle an image of fear, rather than a machine of sport.

1947 Hollister Rally

To better understand this, the motorcycle in the 1950s was typically ridden by less cultured people, who were not generally the most refined. Furthermore, for safety reasons, motorcyclists typically wore Army Air Corp-styled leather jackets and western-styled leather chaps. These additions gave them an aggressive look not typical of a more cultured society.

For a decade after the Hollister event there were a number of movies made about the motorcyclist and motorcycle gangs. The image of the young rebel also became a hot topic, and motorcyclists were often placed in this category. Mothers told their daughters to stay away from "bikers." The 1950s' Marlin Brando movie, *The Wild One*, was supposedly based on the Hollister riot.

These images, along with the carefree lifestyle which the motorcycle encouraged, drew a disproportionate number of less sociable people to the sport of motorcycling. By 1957 the AMA had to discontinue the Gypsy Tours because there were too many antisocial bikers mixing with law-abiding riders. Motorcycle clubs became better known as "gangs," which greatly hurt the sport in general.

An AMA spokesperson, in an attempt to protect the sport of motorcycling, allegedly made the comment that ninety-nine percent of motorcyclists were law-abiding enthusiasts, not rabble-rousers. This comment led to some proudly stating that they were part of the one percent who were part

of the "outlaw" category of motorcyclists. The term *one percenter* still defines these rebel groups.

The sport of motorcycling had been growing at a faster pace than during the previous generation, but the rebel aspect of the sport was killing it. Motorcyclists in the 1950s and early 1960s were identified as people generally outside the traditional social core of society. The motorcyclist was generally considered to be a person who courted a more dangerous lifestyle, as well as one considered to be of a lower social class and deserving less esteem.

The Boozefighters motorcycle club formed in 1946, the Market Street Commandos (who later joined the Hells Angels) formed in 1947, the Hells Angels formed in 1953, the Pagans formed in 1959, the Bandidos formed in 1966, and the Mongols formed in 1969. These were the big groups; there were also many other smaller one-percent gangs that formed in various areas of the country from the late 1950s and into the 1960s. These groups far too often defined what larger society thought motorcycling was.

The image of the motorcycle as the machine for the tough guy and the rebel kept many people from engaging in the sport. But it was also the catalyst which drew others to it. These polemics still exist strongly today; some finding the motorcycle to be a great sports machine, while others look to it to make them a rebel. The rebel, tough guy image is enough to make some people want to ride a motorcycle, even though for just the weekend. Whatever the case, the Hollister instance was a huge defining event.

The Norton Featherbed frame was designed by the McCandless brothers in 1950 and had a huge impact on motorcycle geometry, and was copied my many other manufacturers. British motorcycles, in general, were known for superior handling because of the format derived from the Featherbed.

From 1949 to the late 1950s, the British motorcycles gravitated from 500cc parallel twins to 600 and 650cc twins. A decade later they became 750s, and Norton offered an 850 twin (828cc). The engines kept the pre-1950s design and were just enlarged over time in order to keep up with the demand for performance.

The invasion of British motorcycles being imported into the US ended almost as quickly as it began. The manufacturers enlarged the engine sizes to remain competitive but did little else to advance the engineering of their motorcycle brands. They slowly lost their market share, without an attempt to compete in the areas in which there was great demand. For decades, articles and books were written as to why they could ascend to the top of a business category then slowly descend without attempting to compete in markets which they once owned.

The BSA Goldstar singles (500 & 350cc), though dating back to 1938, found their greatest success after the early to late 1950s. They were winners in nearly every category of racing and were sorely missed after production stopped in 1963. To say that the Goldstar became legendary is an understatement; however, BSA looked backwards, rather than to the future, and did not develop a new version of an old successful model.

During this time period there were a number of very significant motorcycles which were built and evolved into seminal motorcycles; The Ducati 125 desmodromic racer designed by Fabio Taglioni (125cc, 1956), the Harley-Davidson Sportster (883cc, 1957), the Yamaha YDS-1 (250cc, 1959), the Triumph Bonneville (650cc, 1959), the Honda Hawk, Super Hawk, and Scrambler (250/305cc, 1961, 1962), and Suzuki RM62 eight-speed racer (50cc, 1962). There could be another twenty bikes put on this list, but these are landmark models, each being very significant in their own way.

Yamaha YDS 1

Notes on the motorcycles listed above: The Ducati established the direction of the company from then until today; the Sportster is the iconic Harley-Davidson; this early Yamaha 250 blew away some British 650s and began a very significant history; the Triumph Bonneville was the king of the early 1960s and is still special today; the Honda 250/305s, especially the 305cc bikes, put Honda on the world map and changed the world's attitude about Japanese motorcycles; the Suzuki 50cc racer won at least five national championships and made Suzuki a serious builder of motorcycles going forward.

1963 Triumph Bonneville, From the author's collection

From the mid-1950s to the end of the time period being discussed, the accessory market was growing exponentially in every direction, from clothing, modifications for specific motorcycles, custom parts, complete frames, and parts to increase engine or suspension performance.

The Honda 50 Cub, first marketed in 1958, continues with few changes and becomes the largest selling vehicle in history, even out-selling the Model T Ford.

Joe Parkhurst launched *Cycle World* magazine in 1962, with one of the main goals being that of giving unbiased reports on motorcycles being tested and giving accurate performance figures, rather than the figures reported by manufacturers. The magazine was publicly criticized by a few other motorcycle magazine editors, but within a few years, the *CW* model became the norm.

In conclusion, until 1963, the motorcycle community had seen drastic changes taking place very quickly. Older motorcycles were dying out, and new technically advanced motorcycles were beginning to appear on the horizon. The two-stroke was becoming a racing engine, rather than one primarily used for utility purposes. The British parallel-twin was on its way out, and the Japanese invasion of motorcycles was just in its beginning stages. Many new brands were coming into America from around the world, as were many new types of specialty motorcycles being offered in the marketplace. Off road racing, especially scrambles, was on the rise, with new really light motorcycles of no more than 250cc and being very competitive. The British single could no longer compete with many of the smaller two-strokes, and 50cc Japanese motorcycles were winning road races at over 100mph. It appeared that huge changes had occurred within the motorcycle community, however, the biggest changes were just around the corner.

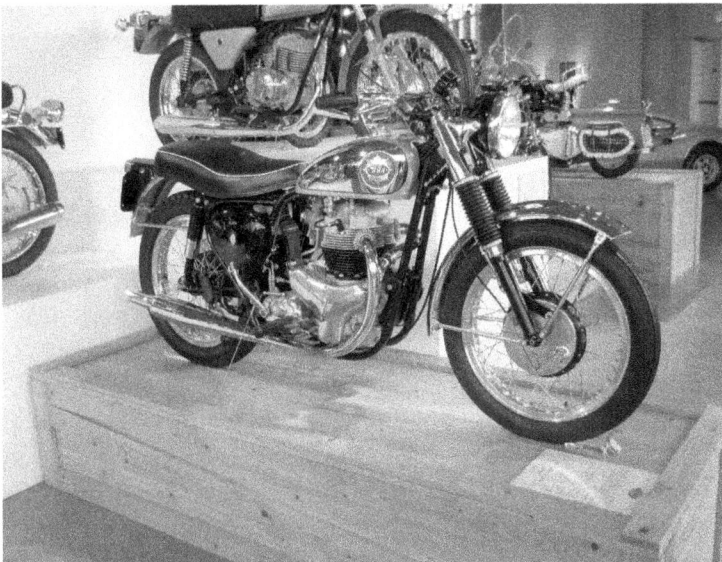

1963 BSA Rocket Gold Star, Courtesy of Barber Vintage Motorsports Museum

Chapter 5

The Motorcycle from Approximately 1963 to 1983

The Japanese Motorcycle Invasion

By the beginning of this time period America had already become the industrial engine of the world. It was also a military, cultural, financial, and political super-power. America was big, wealthy, adventurous, and forward-looking as a nation. Cities had grown big, and many farmers had moved from the country to cities or rapidly growing towns. The population had grown exponentially, and our cities and towns were filled with the children of the WWII generation, who wanted to do new things. The population explosion, which occurred from the early 1950s well into the 1960s, resulted in such a huge growth in the US that anyone could see that there was emerging a huge social shift from a predominantly older population to one made up of young people.

American culture after the 1960s included aggressive music styles, the increase in popularity of televised sports, a new demand for greater social freedoms, along with the power of the growing hippie movement. Furthermore, there were new forms of artistic expression emerging, and a growth in all forms of entertainment was in forward march mode.

American culture was beginning to impact world culture in a big way. In the early 1960s Kar Culture was still big, as was the new hot rod culture. Muscle cars were in their infancy, and the horsepower war was at full speed ahead. The NHRA was just about ten years old, and these new younger Americans had more time and money than ever before to entertain themselves. More young people could now buy cars. Because they had more money and more freedom, and this was to have a major impact in the arena of motorcycle riding, racing, and motorcycling as a hobby.

Motorcycle culture was still growing but was somewhat stagnant. The British motorcycle invasion was subsiding and was having to compete for a market that was getting smaller. Motorcycles were very popular on the West Coast but were slim picking in the huge Midwest area. This was to change in a big way.

British motorcycles were big, leaked oil, were loud, and not good for a beginner rider. Furthermore, the big motorcycles popular in America were intimidating, loud, required lots of maintenance, and were somewhat expensive. Motorcyclists were generally seen as an exclusive group of hardcore people who were not in the mainstream of society. The American motorcyclist was still a niche group except in middle and southern California areas and some areas in the northeastern part of the country. Much of this was to change with the Japanese motorcycle invasion, which was already beginning to occur.

After WWII the Japanese had rebuilt their nation with new factories which were modern, efficient, and able to operate with high levels of volume production. Japanese products of all kinds were beginning to creep into many areas of the US and world markets. The Japanese needed new markets because their mainland was small and lacked the rich natural resources that the United States had. Furthermore, they needed jobs for the masses to keep money flowing into their nation by exports. They wanted a nation which was strong and secure, and places for their highly-skilled engineers and machinists to use their skills. What the Japanese had to offer was a willing workforce who were committed to quality and had already developed fairly efficient production techniques, due to the fact that their factories were new and smaller. Above all, the Japanese were motivated to build a new market for their products to increase the strength of their nation.

American business exhibited many of these qualities as well, but for the Japanese it was an absolute necessity, rather than an option. This is not a criticism of American business, but was a core reason why so many American industries were receding, rather than growing.

There were a number of areas, however, which up until the early 1960s, remained unchanged. One area was that of the American automobile industry. GM, Ford, and Chrysler dominated the American automobile scene. The dozens of smaller manufacturers were almost gone. Packard, Studebaker, American Motors, and numerous smaller companies were either gone or almost extinct. General Motors alone accounted for nearly forty-five percent of the US automobile market. At the time of this writing, GM is barely at seventeen percent of the US market.

The car was truly king, with the motorcycle a very distant second. Harley-Davidson was still the only American motorcycle manufacturer, and their primary "sporty" bike was the Sportster. British motorcycles had changed only incrementally, and most of the British motorcycles were much the same as they were a decade or more earlier. Even though British bikes were still selling well in the US in terms of total market share, the market was just not growing like other markets were. There was trouble looming on the horizon. The lack of development was showing.

1960s Harley-Davidson Sportster, Courtesy of Barber Vintage Motorsports Museum

BSA Lightning, Courtesy of Baxter Cycle

It was not as important to the Harley-Davidson riders, as

they were a more committed group accepting whatever the "Motor Company" produced. Furthermore, the hard-core motorcycle clubs almost universally demanded that their riders rode Harley-Davidson motorcycles. This was good for the Motor Company, as it guaranteed Harley-Davidson consistent sales, but it was bad because it stereotyped the rider and the motorcycle. Harley was a niche unto itself, being almost an independent group with its own standards and somewhat exclusive customer.

The British motorcycle manufacturers didn't have the same protections. Inroads were also being made by the German BMW, numerous Italian companies including Ducati, and the big four Japanese manufacturers. There were other motorcycle companies as well, but their numbers were small and were never significant to the market as a whole.

The majority of motorcycle shops in the 1950s and early 1960s (and certainly before that time as well) were small shops, often housed in older buildings and typically located in the less stylish parts of town. They were generally not places which drew the interest of the general public. Certainly, there were a few nice, clean, and well-organized dealerships, but they were in the minority.

As the 1960s progressed and as Japanese motorcycles were marketed in America, Japanese motorcycle dealers just popped up everywhere. Many of these new dealerships were not operating the same way as traditional motorcycle dealerships had in the past because the sales departments were now much larger than the service departments. However, this will be discussed in more detail later.

By 1970 there were more dealerships which advertised Japanese motorcycles instead of the older brands, even though many still carried the older motorcycle brands. The Honda sign or Yamaha sign would be bigger than the Norton or Matchless sign. The new larger Japanese-based dealers began to mimic automobile dealerships in size and looks.

Up until the end of the 1960s the larger Japanese motorcycles were not accepted by the typical big motorcycle riders as equals, but that was to change by the 1970s. By the end of the 1970s there was no question that the larger displacement Japanese motorcycles were to be respected, as they were typically much faster, more reliable, technically advanced, and were now ridden by the new generation of serious riders. Above all, they were outselling the former brands by double-digit figures and were now winning in most of the national races.

By 1973, the Japanese motorcycle had overwhelmed the

motorcycle community and was seen as superior in most of the areas that motorcycles would generally be compared. The British and American brands of motorcycles were primarily followed by an older school of people who looked back to the former patterns of the motorcycle community from the previous decade.

In 1955 there were around 450,000 motorcycles registered in the US, and by 1962 the number had risen to around 650,000. By 1970 the number had risen to over 2.8 million motorcycles being registered in the US. Between 1965 and 1985 there was an increase of around 400% in the motorcycle industry in America. This huge jump in sales and activity has been referred to as the "Japanese motorcycle invasion." These numbers reflect the huge jump in motorcycle sales. To complete the picture, however, sales peaked in 1970 and remained in the 1.5 million to close to 2 million motorcycles sold yearly mark until the mid-1970s, then sales plummeted afterwards. The reasons for this decline will be discussed in a later chapter.

Let us consider the four dominant brands of Japanese motorcycles and consider why they saw such significant growth patterns.

In 1953 Honda was building over 32,000 motorcycles annually, and by the early 1960s the number grew ten times. By around 1963 Honda was building around 350,000 motorcycles annually, with approximately 135,000 coming to the US. By 1965 the numbers jumped to nearly 465,000 Japanese bikes being delivered to the US, with Honda still being the largest exporter. By 1969 the number had risen to around 800,000 Japanese motorcycles imported to the US. The numbers rise to nearly a million Japanese motorcycles being imported after 1970.

For example, in 1970 Harley-Davidson sold a little under 29,000 motorcycles, all of the British manufacturers sold around 70,000 motorcycles, while the Japanese sold well over 900,000 machines. The year *1970* was the highest point for the British manufacturers, with Triumph being the largest selling British brand. The numbers continued to exceed one million imported machines until the early 1970s.

Honda built light, fast, reliable, and stylish motorcycles which didn't leak oil and were also much cheaper than the British and American competition. For more than any other reason, Honda did well because they were selling very reliable small motorcycles in a market which Europe had skipped over. Honda sold tens of thousands of 50s, 70s, 90s, 100s, 125s, and 150/160cc motorcycles, most of which had electric starters and were reliable and nearly maintenance free.

In 1963 the CB77, the 305cc Superhawk, a sporty bike, was already selling well, but it began to really take off. The 250/305 Scramblers did the same. From 1962 to 1965, Honda sold more motorcycles in the US than all the other Japanese manufacturers combined, times two. People who were buying the smaller motorcycles began moving up to the bigger models. After 1965, Honda was selling around fifty percent of all motorcycles sold in the US.

Honda CB450, From the author's collection

In 1965 Honda released the Black Bomber CB450 which was an exotic bike on paper, to say the least. The original four-speed 450 did not sell well. Most historians state that the first series 450 didn't sell well because of its stodgy looks. I strongly disagree. In 1965, big bike buyers were buying 650cc British machines or even larger Harley-Davidson motorcycles. By this time the 500cc

Honda CB450D, From the author's collection

bikes were much less popular than the 650s, except in racing, and I think those wanting a larger motorcycle didn't see the 450 as a big enough bike. A 450cc motorcycle was an odd size, which would have not necessarily registered as a big motorcycle to the seasoned rider of the day.

Many Honda dealers, especially those in smaller towns, carried more of the smaller bikes, never even carrying a larger 450. People didn't quickly associate Honda with larger motorcycles, and a 450 didn't clearly say, "I am a big bike," to those in the existing motorcycle community. I think the Black Bomber was a transitional machine which opened the door for larger Japanese motorcycles to be accepted going forward.

The 450 was just a duck out of water with little to commend it to the buyers wanting a larger motorcycle. The performance was not exceptional, either, until the second generation 450s came along. Original road tests put the first 450 in the same league as the 500s or single-carbureted 650s. Within a year or two, this was all to change. The 1968 CB/CL 450 were rockets for the day.

When the CB750 was placed on the market in 1969 the motorcycle world was put on notice. The big Japanese motorcycle was here. The CB750 is typically called the first "Superbike." The CB750 was a big success, outselling the Triumph Trident and the BSA Rocket 3 triples combined by a large margin.

Honda CB750, Honda America

While the British and American motorcycle companies built motorcycles which differed very little over time, Honda and the Japanese companies continued advancing in the big motorcycle market. In 1971 they offered a 500cc four, enlarged to 550cc in 1975. They also offered a 350cc four in 1972 ,enlarged to 400cc four in 1975. The 1000cc Gold Wing came out in 1975, and the six cylinder CBX came out in 1979. The CBX made a huge impression on the motorcycle consumer, with its six cylinders, 100 horsepower, and it looked like a custom motorcycle. In 1980 the DOHC 900cc four was introduced, and in 1982 the high-performance V-4 cylinder motorcycles came out. The Magna and Saber were 750s enlarged to 1100s in 1983. Honda also offered a turbocharged bike, the CX500 Turbo, in 1982 and a CX 650 Turbo in 1983. These were just the lead bikes. There were many other models available as well.

The 350cc twins sold by the truckloads from 1968. There were the DOHC 750s after 1979, the 450/500cc traditional parallel twins, the FT500 single, and many other models. By the end of this time period, the Japanese motorcycle manufacturers had produced an incredibly complex string of motorcycles far surpassing whatever choices the motorcycle rider had ever had before this time. Let's look quickly at the other big three Japanese manufacturers.

Yamaha started with small two-stroke commuter bikes until they moved up to a 250cc twin by the early 1960s. In 1967 the 350cc twin came out, followed by the offroad DT 1 (250cc single) in 1968, which was squarely aimed at the Bultaco and Montessa two-stroke singles, which were winning so many offroad races.

By the early 1960s, small two-strokes were outperforming the big British singles and literally transforming many types of competition. In 1970 Yamaha brought out the XS 650 twin, which was a loose copy of and direct threat to the Triumph Bonneville. In 1973 they brought out the TX series. These were 500, 650, and 750 SOHC twins with five-speed transmissions. In 1976, the XS 750 three-cylinder and in 1978, the XS 1100 four were offered in the US. Some thought that these engines were the best of the big Japanese engines.

In 1981 the XJ 550 and 750 bikes came out, as did the first V-twin Virago.

In 1982, the high-performance Secas came out and set the performance standards. I remember the first test on the Yamaha Seca 550. It recorded a quarter mile time of 12.9 seconds, which was very fast for the time. These times were much faster than the other British or American motorcycles could ever expect to attain if in stock condition. The performance envelope was being pushed.

Yamaha was the second largest Japanese exporter of motorcycles from Japan to the US and, like Honda, was offering an increasing array of new motorcycles.

By 1961 Suzuki was building the T 10, a 250cc touring motorcycle. Few Suzukis were imported until after 1965. In 1964 Suzuki offered only a 50, an 80, and a 250cc machine. When the X-6 Hustler was offered it created a stir because it was an extremely fast small bike which could compete with much larger bikes.

They began selling in large numbers in 1966. The X-6 Hustler sold for around $695, making it an inexpensive form of entertainment as well. A Suzuki and BSA dealer told me an interesting story which occurred in 1965. He had received his first Suzuki X-6 and had challenged the dealer next door to a race. The 250cc motorcycle was to compete with a much larger Triumph Bonneville. They were to race just the one block. The smaller Suzuki rider was a past flat track racer and was used to quick starts, while the Triumph rider was just a dealer/enthusiast. The little Suzuki won the race, which was humiliating to the Triumph rider. Certainly, the Triumph would have won a longer race, but the image of a 250 racing past a 650 certainly bolstered interest and sales. This sort of exhibition caused the Japanese motorcycles to fly out the door.

Suzuki X6 Hustler, From the author's collection

The T 500 two-stroke twin was offered in 1968, followed by the two-strokes of 380cc, 550cc, and 750cc sizes. The 750 three-cylinder is often referred to as the Water Buffalo. The four-strokes came in 1977 in 400, 550, and 750 sizes. The GS 1000 series started in 1978, and a special GS1000S motorcycle was offered in 1979 with a partial faring. The "S" bike pushed the performance envelope further than Suzuki had done before. In 1980 the GS 1100 touring bike was offered, and in 1981 the Katana 650, 750, and 1100 series were first offered. These bikes were probably the most advanced sport bikes which were to precede the modern GSX series.

For Kawasaki, the motorcycle division was a small and secondary business for the much larger Kawasaki Heavy Industries Corporation. Kawasaki built few motorcycles until they fully took over Meguro motorcycles in 1962. Meguro was an old line of Japanese motorcycles which had been built since the 1930s.

Kawasaki was a late comer to the US, not being imported until 1963, then only in really small numbers. Up until 1965, they just offered an 85cc bike, a 125, and the SG250 four-stroke single, which was a Meguro with a Kawasaki nameplate. In 1966 they offered a very similar copy of the older BSA A10 twin called the "W" series, but that series of motorcycle never sold well. In 1967 the Samurai 250 and 350s were offered, which were high performance two-stroke twins.

Kawasaki H-1 at the Barber Vintage Motorsports Museum, From the author's collection

The big change took place in 1969 (marketed in 1968 as a 1969 model) when the 500cc Mach I was unveiled to the US market. This was a three-cylinder two-stroke, five-speed motorcycle which was a white hot performer and even recorded faster quarter mile times than the larger Honda CB750. The first Mach I was a super performer but was not a practical bike in that they handled poorly and got really bad gas mileage. The Mach 1 had an almost unusable power band for anything but street racing. None of that made any difference if you were on one of these machines; riders just liked them because they were fast.

The year *1972* brought 250, 350, 500, and 750 triples. These motorcycles were less highly strung but the legend of the H I lived on.

In 1973 Kawasaki unveiled the Z 1, a 900cc four. This was the king of street motorcycles for a number of years. It was the fastest production motorcycle made at the time, no matter what size. They were also very good bikes, and many live on today as very collectible motorcycles.

After 1977 they offered the KZ series, then in 1981 the GPz series. The GPz series motorcycles were very fast, very reliable, and also attractive motorcycles. In 1982 they built the KZ1000R Eddie Lawson model which is still fast when compared to modern motorcycles. They are also very collectible.

Kawasaki built an enviable record of motorcycles, many of which are still running today. After the earliest years when Kawasaki made more utilitarian machines, their motorcycles have been generally been marketed as high performance machines. Kawasaki motorcycles have a strong record of performance and reliability.

All of the Japanese companies copied other manufacturers when building their first motorcycles. The German Adler, DKW, Horex, NSU, and BMWs were common templates. Some British motorcycles were copied as well. Yamaha, Suzuki, and Kawasaki all copied the Adler MB250 two-stroke for their own 250cc twins. Kawasaki and Yamaha, in their larger earlier bikes, copied the British BSA and Triumph motorcycles to a greater or lesser degree.

The Japanese were masters of taking solid designs, tested and built by others, and making them much better. The Japanese were also masters of efficient manufacturing practices, able to quickly design, test, and build new machines.

Above all else, the Japanese needed new markets and increased exports, and the motorcycle was a market to exploit. With a new market, new factories and smaller motorcycles, which did not directly compete with most of the existing competition, the Japanese companies were free to build this new business on volume and price.

Honda was the first large Japanese exporter, and they bypassed the traditional motorcycle businesses from the very beginning. They sent bikes in by the ship-load and gave them to filling stations, hardware stores, motorcycle dealers that would take them, and anyone else interested in selling these early motorcycles. Yamaha and Suzuki were next, with Kawasaki being last to be imported in large numbers. Bridgestone was also an early import but discontinued production by 1967.

At first, the Japanese motorcycles were seen as cheap, but they quickly proved themselves otherwise. By the mid-1960s some dealers began dropping the older and better known brands of motorcycles in order to sell the Japanese brands. It became common for established dealers to move from selling a British brand to selling two or even three Japanese brands of motorcycles.

New dealers were popping up all over the country, and the motorcycles of choice were the Japanese machines. The primary exceptions were the Harley-Davidson brand, which stuck close to the factory, and Triumph motorcycles, which had a significant following. By the end of the 1960s and into the 1970s, the Japanese manufacturers were

outselling all other brands combined by large margins.

Offering reliable, advanced designed, and smaller sized motorcycles was the initial reason for the success of the Japanese motorcycle, however, a more complete list of reasons will be noted below:

Honda advertised to non-traditional mass markets, such as women's magazines, sports magazines, on TV when popular shows were on, and at sports events. Other brands quickly followed suit.

Honda used the phrase *You Meet The Nicest People on a Honda* to bypass the traditional motorcycle crowd as early as 1963; the slogan was received well and bolstered the image of the Japanese motorcycle.

Japanese brands noted the benefits of over 150 mpg scooters, the ease of operation, and reliability as core attributes of their machines. Ads were cute and portrayed middle-class people using their machines for utility purposes. The older image of the motorcyclist as being out of the social norm was bypassed.

Most of the machines were small and inexpensive and high in value for the dollar. Because so many people started riding on Japanese motorcycles, as they desired a new machine, they just moved up the size structure. Japanese companies made larger machines and greater varieties of machines as riders wanted them.

Japanese motorcycles were readily available through many avenues, most of which were not the "old guard" motorcycle shops.

The machines were reliable, clean, required little maintenance, and appeared very modern, unlike much of what was currently available; Japanese motorcycles were new designs, rather than using rehashed old engineering dating from the past.

They sought after new buyers who were not in the traditional motorcycle market and who just wanted something fun and entertaining.

Japanese manufacturers continued to rapidly advance in technology by adding electric starting (many had electric starters from the early days), disc brakes, five- and six-speed transmissions, water-cooling, better suspensions, and built what the people wanted. The Japanese motorcycle was kept in front of the performance demands of the riders and made bikes so reliable that it was a quality associated with their machines.

Japanese motorcycles were always value leaders, appearing to be a good investment and fun.

Possibly above all, the Japanese motorcycle was bright and shiny, didn't leak oil, was not intimidating, was very reliable, and was seen as a bargain. They were readily available to the masses, and the masses bought them.

By 1963 the sales of Japanese motorcycles were already exceeding the sales of British and American motorcycles combined. Even though most of the Japanese motorcycles were small, there was concern by other manufacturers that the Japanese motorcycles would ultimately infringe on their own markets. The builders of larger motorcycles, primarily the British motorcycles, believed that the Japanese would continue to build small motorcycles, leaving the larger ones to them.

By the late 1970s, the superior engineering, performance, and variety of the Japanese motorcycles was stunning. While British and American manufacturers had numerous models, they were basically the same foundations with minor changes. Put on different fenders, a new tank, and you had a new model. With the Japanese motorcycles, the 500s, 650s, 750s, 900s, and 1000+ sized bikes were often completely different machines Other brands just used the same platforms.

What was stunning was the speed in which the Japanese could conceive of, build, market, and update their motorcycles. Because of the extreme development of Japanese motorcycles, most manufacturers were outdated every three to four years. Though impressive, this was to become a negative factor which hurt the business rather than helping it grow. By the end of the 1960s many British older manufacturers were already going out of business.

Vincent had gone out in 1955	
James	1966
Ariel, AJS, & Matchless	1967
Velocette	1971
BSA	1973
Norton & Royal Enfield	1977
(A few 1977 Nortons sold as 1978 model motorcycles.)	
Norton Villiers Triumph	1977
(NVT)	
Aermacchi-Harley-Davidson	1978
Cotton	1980
Triumph	1983
(Low numbers were still built and sold outside the US.)	

There were a number of reasons why the Japanese motorcycle invasion was so destructive to many motorcycle manufacturers from around the world. For Italian and German companies, a limited range of motorcycles, limited national marketing, and the lack of interest in high-volume production kept their brands small. Small factories did not allow for volume production and furthermore, limited production did not allow companies to discount their machines very much.

With the British motorcycles, new models were typically warmed-over older models with only cosmetic changes being the major changes. By the early 1970s the Triumph Bonneville had lost its luster and was no longer a competitive motorcycle. BSA was gone by 1973, and Norton was still updating a 1940s' engine which was overworked and modified beyond its ability to function well. The British brands fared well until the late 1960s but were quickly overwhelmed by the huge influx of fast, reliable, inexpensive, and ever-changing Japanese motorcycles.

The British were caught off guard and were not able to make the sort of adjustments necessary to compete. During the late 1960s the manufacturers, primarily BSA and Triumph (BSA owned Triumph since 1951), did not update their core engineering. The BSA and Triumph three-cylinder bikes used old technology, simply with an added cylinder. With OHV engines, four-speed transmissions, and shoe-type brakes, they were quickly out of league when compared to the Japanese motorcycles.

The first series Triumphs and BSA 750cc triples looked outdated from their inception, and the American buyer shunned them. Americans complained that the Triumph and BSA tanks on the Trident and Rocket 3 looked like toasters. When Triumph put on their "beauty kit" several years after being first introduced, it was too late.

I had read somewhere that within a few years after being unveiled, Honda had sold around 30,000 CB750s to BSA and Triumph's 7,000 three-cylinder machines (combined sales figures for the BSA and Triumph).

Honda ended up selling well over 100,000 CB750s, while the BSA/Triumph three-cylinder motorcycles sold significantly fewer in number, never being close to the sales numbers of the Honda. Even beyond raw sales figures, the British three-cylinder motorcycles were expensive to build and suffered from many warranty claims compared to the less expensive Honda CB, which had many fewer claims and a much larger profit margin. By the time BSA and Triumph could have experienced a needed sales victory, BSA was gone and Triumph was in serious financial trouble. Here are the basic reasons for the failure of the British motorcycle industry:

Factories used outdated equipment and equipment which did not work effectively with no investment plan to update old equipment with new technology.

No new designs were developed which could compete with the Japanese (such as the proposed 350 BSA and Triumph OHC five-speeds). The new models which were envisioned would have cost much more than the comparable Japanese motorcycles to build, yet were no more modern.

High build costs, high warranty costs, and high service requirements were always a setback for the British manufacturers. The Japanese had lower build costs with lower warranty costs. A five-speed Honda OHC 350 twin cost a little less than a British four-speed OHV 250 single. The BSA/Triumph 250s had a terrible reliability record, while the Honda 350s were bulletproof. The British motorcycles were known for requiring extra care, as well as needing ongoing maintenance far beyond what the Japanese bikes generally required.

Some of the upper management of the British motorcycle manufacturers actually thought that buyers "liked" to continually work on their motorcycles. This turned out to be untrue, and when it was found to be an issue, they did not know how to build more reliable machines quickly enough.

Far too few British bikes were made available, and the low levels of production did not allow for mass production. In the late 1960s a showroom might have fifty Japanese motorcycles compared to two or three British bikes being displayed. Dealers of British motorcycles were often unable to get the models which were most marketable, while the Japanese brands were much better at providing what the customers wanted.

British industry leaders were not in touch with what their customers or dealers wanted. For years, Triumph dealers had to change the handlebars that Americans didn't want to ones that they did want, at their own expense.

When machines like the BSA Rocket 3 and Triumph Trident were sent to America, they were so unacceptable in appearance that thousands sat in warehouses. The British companies sent over thousands of motorcycles that wouldn't sell and too few of those that did. Unsold machines had to be greatly discounted in order to sell them, and they often missed the primary motorcycle selling season.

1972 Triumph T150, Courtesy of Yesterday's Antique and Collectible Motorcycles

They made far too few changes far too slowly. People wanted British bikes, but when compared to the Japanese bikes, they were being quickly outdated. By 1970, it was basically over for the larger British companies because they had lost so much ground in just a few years. From being at the top of their game in 1963, by 1967 they were generally seen as old and outdated.

Although 1970 was the highest sales year for British motorcycles, the writing was on the wall. "Too little too late" led to the basic destruction of the industry, with no time, money, or engineering to effectively compete. To simply survive became the goal.

The unions were also not a help. When Triumph was struggling to simply stay in business, the company unions went on strike, further exacerbating the problem.

Too many issues came into vision in too short of a time. The individual brand executives, workers (unions), corporation board members, and the British motorcycle community as a whole retreated into division and blame, rather than to unify and attempt to compete.

The writing on the wall was clear for at least a decade before their fall, but no action was taken until it was just too late to compete. When action was taken, it followed the former destructive patterns which caused the failure of their industry in the first place. A fresh vision and renewed energy was needed, but all that surfaced was an attitude of retreat.

1969 BSA Rocket 3, Courtesy of Yesterday's Antique and Collectible Motorcycles

For most of the British manufacturers, their demise was based on poor upper-management, which had little vision for the future and did not develop modern new machines. In the case of Ariel, the brand did not carry any

mid-sized or smaller machines until close to the end of their production of motorcycles. Their big bike, the Square Four, was heavy, underpowered, and was prone to overheating. The Ariel Leader, a 250cc two-stroke, was not designed for the US market, so sales were minimal, and the machine still had to compete with more advanced and popular Japanese bikes in their own home market. In 1970, after Ariel was out of production, a three-wheeled scooter was built, which had no chance of being a big seller.

The James, Velocette, Royal Enfield, and Cotton brands were low production motorcycles, which were built in low volume factories with no chance of building the sort of volume which could compete with the Japanese brands. Furthermore, they did not have complete lines of machines, so they were relegated to being a niche market motorcycle.

Norton was a low-volume prestigious brand of motorcycle known for racing, which had been incorporated into the Associated Motorcycle Company line of motorcycles. It built very dated machines and did not have the engineering capacity nor money to update and become competitive as a brand. The latter end of this brand will be discussed in greater detail a little later.

AJS and Matchless, the primary Associated Motorcycle Company brands, were imported with success in the early 1950s, but the company never spent much to update their line of motorcycles. They also served a niche market, never seeming to want to supply the sort of volume required to build a viable business going forward. By 1962, they were struggling to maintain their business but never took the steps to compete in a competitive market. Rather than update their engines, they just used the old Norton engines in many of their bikes.

In 2015 I interviewed a man who purchased an AMC motorcycle in 1962 or 1963. He stated to me that the California dealer sold AJS, Matchless, and Norton motorcycles. When he bought the machine, the dealer asked if he wanted the motorcycle to be either an AJS, a Matchless, or a Norton. The dealer would just put on the badge that the customer wanted.

AJS & Matchless, courtesy AJS, Matchless Club of America

Most of the bikes from all three brands were much the same; the tank badges were just changed as needed. The brands did have different models, but volume was so low that it made little difference.

By 1966 AMC was dead. In an attempt to keep jobs for workers and to help sustain the British motorcycle industry, Manganese Bronze was allowed to buy the assets of AMC with a government loan. With the loan came the requirement to build a motorcycle. The new company was called Nor-

ton-Villiers (NV). The Norton brand was picked because it was the most recognized of the three.

Norton Commando, Courtesy of Baxter Cycles

In 1967 the Norton Commando was released on the market. The primary upgrade was a rubber-mounted rear suspension, which made the motorcycle ride much more smoothly, called the isolastic rear suspension. The new Norton went through several changes, including the Commando, the Fastback, and the Interstate. They were all essentially the same motorcycle. The new Norton lasted until 1977, with unsold models becoming 1978 models. Norton-Villiers was soon to become NVT, which stood for Norton, Villiers, Triumph.

The largest historic British company was BSA, which owned the Triumph brand. These were also the dominant British brands sold in the US. BSA advertised in 1959 that they were the largest motorcycle manufacturer in the world. BSA purchased Triumph in 1951, but the two companies operated differently until after 1970. When there was a greater merging of the two brands, it was just in the use of brakes, frames, forks, and other miscellaneous parts. Toward the end, the 250cc singles were used between both brands, as was the 500 BSA single (B 50), which was used on one model of Triumph motorcycle. The 750cc three-cylinder bikes were much the same, except that the BSA version of the engine was canted forward. After BSA was gone, the forward-canted engine was used in the Triumph Trident.

BSA was a big seller in the US until around 1961, then the sales of the brand was in decline until it stopped production in 1973. BSA just didn't update their machines fast enough, and they lost market share until they were essentially dead. In 1962 they unveiled a shorter-stroke 650 twin to replace the previous 650 twin, but the two were, for all intents, much the same. Both were OHV parallel-twins with four-speed transmissions which leaked oil. The most significant change was that the new engine was of "unit construction" design, which was of little real consequence.

In 1971 they attempted to update the larger models of motorcycles, but poor build quality and really outdated designs eliminated the possibility of any real success.

The Triumph motorcycles were to become more popular than the BSA, especially after the early 1960s. Triumph quickly became the most sought after British motorcycle in the US, best known for offroad racing.

The Bonneville was Triumph's bread and butter motorcycle and carried much of the company. Triumph was severely hurt by the frame debacle of 1971-1972 (called the P39 frame), and the money lost crippled the company.

Liquidation of the company had become inevitable, so the government offered the assets to Manganese Bronze because they had done a satisfactory job with AMC and Norton. It was decided to terminate the BSA line of motorcycles and focus on the more lucrative Triumph models. Because of the costs associated with the Meriden factory, where Triumph motorcycles were being built, Manganese Bronze decided to close the factory and build Triumphs where the BSA models had been built. This decision was made in 1973. This caused an uproar with the current employees' union at Meriden (the Triumph factory), and the group took over the factory by locking the doors shut. This sit-in becomes an independent chapter of the history of Triumph lasting from approximately 1973 to 1977.

In 1977 the union group called the "Triumph Co-Op," purchased Triumph from Manganese Bronze. The co-op continued until 1983, but their goals were short-lived because of serious financial issues. There were attempts to sell the company to a number of possible buyers. These included Suzuki, the Hesketh Motorcycle Company, Cagiva, Harley-Davidson, an Indian motorcycle group, or John Bloor, a British investor.

Bloor ended up buying the company and hired Less Harris, a significant figure in the British motorcycle industry, to build Triumph motorcycles under contract. Harris built the Bonneville until 1988, which coincided with the date that Richard Bloor began building a new Triumph factory.

1979 Honda CBX, From the author's collection

Even though the Japanese motorcycle companies had come into the US as outsiders (and by sheer innovation and volume sales, had dominated the American market), there were serious problems which would emerge after the early 1970s. The big four (Honda, Yamaha, Suzuki, and Kawasaki) were still seen as foreign brands, and they had built so many models of different sizes that even the brand enthusiasts were easily confused. New models were offered nearly every year, so the complex lines of machines was further confusing and growing.

1979 Kawasaki KZ1300, Period promotional photo

One of the big issues to many consumers was that the technology had gone beyond their ability to understand or even what they wanted. Motorcycles could be purchased with DOHC engines, two-, three- and four-valve heads, six-speed transmissions, water cooling, 100+ horsepower ratings, and competing models within the same model lineup. A brand might have a 400cc, 550cc, 650cc, 750cc, 900cc, and 1100cc series of motorcycles which looked much the same. Furthermore, there might be a single, a twin, a V-twin, and a four-cylinder model which might compete against each other in similar size groups. Some motorcycles seemed overly complex, such as the Honda V-fours (they looked complex because they were).

The Japanese had won the immediate battle, but the war was far from being over. Going into the 1980s, there were serious troubles for them on the horizon. By the mid-1970s and especially later, the Japanese manufacturers were not able to sell as many bikes as they were used to, so overstocking occurred. Unsold motorcycles were being stockpiled in warehouses, costing millions to store. One article suggested that there were as many as one million Japanese motorcycles being stored at one time.

There were also overstocked models which were becoming outdated by newer models, which were then being greatly reduced in price. This often caused people to not buy the newest incarnation of the model, but to buy on price alone. Some overstocked motorcycles were sold for greatly reduced prices, which cut the profit margins and took away new bike sales.

The big problem was a psychological one. There were huge numbers of motorcycles with a confusing array of models, which was unsettling to the customer. Price wars made it look like people didn't want the bikes, and a glut of new models further confused the issue. Dealers often promoted the sale of newer bikes, as opposed to servicing older models, creating a world of seemingly outdated models. Over time people expected Japanese motorcycles to be sold only if there were price cuts.

There were more issues than these which were impacting the motorcycle business, and especially the Japanese part of the industry. With more and more items being imported from around the world into the US, there was the beginning of a "buy American" sentiment. This certainly worked against the Japanese motorcycle market. The "boomer" generation was also beginning to have children and families. This was impacting the interest in the motorcycle, causing sales to decline. The gasoline embargoes of 1973 and 1974 certainly had a chilling effect as well. During the same time America was experiencing hyper-inflation, which reduced the motivation for a potential buyer to buy a motorcycle because of the high interest rates. Motorcycles were just another thing that was not essential.

For these reasons, motorcycle sales dropped dramatically after around 1973 and remained low into the 1980s.

Motorcycles were still selling, just in reduced numbers. These were generally bad years for the motorcycle community, but especially bad for the Japanese manufacturers.

Sammy Pierce Indian, Courtesy Mecum Auctions

Harley-Davidson was the last remaining US motorcycle manufacturer, apart from Cushman. Indian had gone out of business in 1953. There were a few attempts at resurrecting the Indian name after the mid-1960s. Sammy Pierce, an Indian parts supplier built around fifty complete Indians from parts from 1965 to around 1968.

Floyd Clymer, a past owner of *Cycle* magazine, attempted to build Indians using Italian frames, with either Royal Enfield or Velocette engines. He built at least one Indian motorcycle with a Horex engine, and one with a Norton engine. The motorcycle with the Horex engine still exists. His effort was from around 1963 to the time of his death in 1970. Clymer may not have actually legally owned the Indian name.

Clymer Royal Enfield Indian, courtesy of Barber Vintage Motorsports Museum

After his death, his lawyer, Alan Newman, sold India-made mini-bikes with the Indian logo through the 1970s. Indian was to rise again, and this will be discussed later.

Going into the early 1960s, Harley-Davidson was selling motorcycles at an increasing rate, somewhat parallel with rising motorcycle market in general. In 1963 they sold a little under 10,500 motorcycles, rising to just under 24,000 motorcycles in 1965. In 1967 sales rose to around 27,000 machines. Harley-Davidson remained strong as a business and was making a decent profit, but they did not have the funds to begin a massive investment into new machines. They also did not have the necessary money to restructure their dated factories.

The idea that the company should be connected to a larger corporate structure looked promising, as this would allow for more operating capitol and possibly more managerial resources. This situation led to Harley-Davidson's connection to AMF, American Machine & Foundry.

AMF grew from a small company in 1900 to a large diversified corporation building a wide range of products over the years. AMF had built cigarette machines, baking equipment, bicycles, golf clubs, exercise equipment, boats, and what they are most famous for, bowling alleys, bowling machines, and bowling products.

From 1969 to 1981 AMF owned the Harley-Davidson motorcycle company. From what I understand, Harley-Davidson operated as an independent organization within the AMF corporate structure with a great deal of freedom to operate as they wished. AMF was not a motorcycle company, and they did not have unlimited funds. Because of this, the motorcycle division did not get the needed money to energize their line of motorcycles or to update their factories to the extent that they wished.

As the 1970s ended and the 1980s began, AMF had suffered losses within a number of its core businesses, and the company did not want expenses from the motorcycle division to further draw out needed operating capitol. The idea of selling Harley-Davidson was floated, but no one was interested. A number of individuals, thirteen in total, and mostly people within the Harley-Davidson division, worked on a plan to buy H-D from its parent company.

Vaughn Beals, a then current VP, and Willie G. Davidson, who was directly related to the original Davidsons, were in the group. A deal was made between the new company and AMF. A little over eighty-million dollars was financed, allowing the new company to operate as its own corporation.

Many historians villainize AMF for not revitalizing the company during their years of ownership, but in reality, the merger probably allowed the company to survive.

The issue, which often comes up during the AMF years, was the quality control problems which seemed to have hurt the brand immensely. I frequently have members of the Harley-Davidson community lambast the years that

AMF owned the company. They state that the bikes were the worst that ever carried the Harley-Davidson name. It must have been true, because quite a number of people have attested to the fact that the bikes built between 1970 and 1981 had many problems, which gave a bad name to the brand.

XLCR-1000 Cafe Racer.

1977 Harley-Davidson XCLR Café Racer, Period advertisement

A number of motorcycles did come from this time period which were significant machines. Of most importance was the 1971 FX Super Glide model, which blended standard H-D geometry with a custom look. This model is said to have energized the street custom motorcycle, which is still a trend today. The 1977 XLCR was a H-D Café Racer which didn't sell well but is now really collectible. The 1980 FXWG (Wide Glide) was another popular

custom, and I think, the first belt drive machine. To many motorcyclists so many of the bikes look similar, but to the H-D aficionado the differences are easily recognized.

Sales also jumped in the early AMF years. In 1970 28,841 motorcycles were sold, jumping to 37,620 in 1971. In 1972 almost 60,000 Harley-Davidson motorcycles were sold, moving up to over 75,000 in 1975.

After the late 1970s, sales went downward, like most

motorcycle sales did. In 1978 sales were just over 47,000, going down to 33,321 in 1981. This was the year that the new company separated from AMF. In 1983 sales were at 26,911, which was a return to the lean years of the early to mid-1960s. Harley-Davidson was to see some significant changes as the new decade came into focus.

In review, from 1969 to 1983 there were a number of new motorcycles imported into the United States from at least six continents that did not sell in large numbers. From Spain came Bultaco and Montessa. These brands sold in small numbers and were most popular as offroad racers. From Italy came the following brands: Ducati, Moto Guzzi, Capriolo, Parilla, and Aeromacchi. Aeromacchis were imported by Harley-Davidson. Of the five brands, Ducati was to become the most significant brand.

From Czechoslovakia came CZ and Jawa. Both these brands were imported in small numbers. Of the two, CZ was to continue the longest.

From Japan came the big four; Honda, Yamaha, Suzuki, and Kawasaki. Other brands include Bridgestone, Hodaka, Lilac, Morushio, and Tohatsu. Motorcycles other than the big four sold in small numbers, with Hodaka being the most significant smaller brand.

Hodaka sold motorcycles from around 1964 to the end of the 1970s. The engine was made in Japan, and most of the other engineering was American. With a factory in Oregon, Hodaka is often credited with starting the trail bike craze in America. Hodaka motorcycles sold well, but by the 1970s they could no longer compete with the big four Japanese manufacturers. The Hodaka story is interesting and worth researching.

Hodaka, From the collection of Russ Briggs

From Britain there were Triumph, BSA, Norton, AJS/Matchless (different in badges only), Royal Enfield, Velocette, Cotton, and Panther. There were actually dozens of really low-volume brands imported from Britain, however, Triumph, BSA, and Norton probably represented over eighty-five percent of the machines ever imported to our shores.

Finally, Germany exported BMW, Zundapp, DKW, Horex, Maico, NSU, and Adler motor- cycles. All but BMW are gone, with BMW being the most significant by far.

1982 BMW R100, From the author's collection

Although Japan was the largest exporter of motorcycles to the US during this time period, the above list of brands from other continents represents a more complete picture of what was available in the US up until 1983. Apart from the big four Japanese motorcycle brands and Harley-Davidson; Indian, Triumph, BMW, and Ducati were to become important brands, which we will discuss going forward.

The time period of 1963 to 1983 is one of the most significant time periods in motorcycle history. The British Motorcycle Invasion brings us to the early 1960s, and the Japanese Motorcycle Invasion begins about that time and radically alters the history of the motorcycle forever.

Triumph X-75, From the collection of Russ Briggs

After the late 1960s, the British brands began to fail, and by 1977, were effectively gone, with just a very few still being built or sold. Harley-Davidson shifted from a public-stock company to one owned by AMF. By the beginning of the 1980s, Harley-Davidson was owned by a new group of investors and was well on its way to being reinvented.

During this time period, two-stroke motorcycles came into their own and became race-winning machines as never before. Within a decade, though, environmental standards made two-strokes no longer able to be sold, and they were effectively gone from the marketplace.

Motorcycle sales, which had been slowly rising, took a huge leap from around 1963 to 1973, then fell. It would take another decade to see motorcycle sales begin to rise significantly again.

Finally, because of the fast-paced Japanese engineering, which occurred during these years, technology lept forward, which made most pre-1964 motorcycles look really dated. At the other end of the spectrum, the Japanese motorcycle reached such a high level of development that many motorcycles made during the early 1980s are still more advanced in design than some current brands are decades later. During this time period, the motorcycle came out of the shadows and became mainstream. The motorcycle took a huge step and advanced racing, technology, and the sport of motorcycling in general.

Kawasaki KZ1000R, Period advertisement

Chapter 6

The Motorcycle from around 1983 to 2000

Technology Reigns and Harley-Davidson Begins to Rise

By the early 1980s it seemed as if the Japanese manufacturers owned the American motorcycle market. The Japanese companies continued in their battle against each other to innovate. From air-cooled engines to water-cooled ones, from front disc brakes to double discs in front and a single disc in back. From single overhead cam engines to the DOHC model becoming standard. From five-speed transmissions to many with six-speed transmissions. By the end of the 1980s all the two-strokes were gone, except for a few offroad bikes and a few factory racers.

From around 1983, the super sport motorcycle began to emerge, and by end of the 1980s the sport bike class was a specific class of motorcycles. Honda had the Hurricane series (1987) which became the CBR series (1989), Kawasaki had the GPz series (1982) which became the ZX Ninja series (1987). Suzuki had the Katana series (1982) which became the GSX R series (1986), and Yamaha had the FZ series (1985) which evolved into the FZR series (1988). All four tried turbo-charged models in the early to mid-1980s, but there was no market interest.

The Japanese were advancing in performance and technology beyond what the buying public wanted, except as low-volume specials. From the end of the 1970s to around 1973 motorcycle sales were around a million a year. After the mid-1970s sales began to drop, but the market was still around the three-quarters of a million motorcycles per year mark. In 1980 approximately 710,000 bikes were sold. but by 1990 sales were down to around 303,000 machines. The big drop in sales came after the "Black Monday" stock market drop of 1987. It was not until after 1995 that sales began to rise again, which they did slowly.

When they did rise, it was Harley-Davidson who was the big winner. In 1991 Harley-Davidson sold just under 59,000 motorcycles, but by 1995 sales had risen to just over 105,000 motorcycles. By 1997 numbers rose to around 131,000 motorcycles, and in 2000 Harley-Davidson sales had doubled, selling nearly 205,000 motorcycles. These were impressive numbers, getting close to around one-third of the total US motorcycle market.

After WWII and moving into the 1960s, Harley-Davidson motorcycles were seen as old school designs slow in development and were not known for having many serious innovations. Compared to the Japanese motorcycles, Harley-Davidson seemed to look backwards, rather than forwards. The company survived on lower sales numbers which could not provide the necessary capitol for anything but basic upgrades but was none the less supported by a dedicated buyer. Furthermore, they remained competitive in terms of performance simply because they were large motorcycles.

I can remember back in the mid 1960s several friends and I supported a Honda 305 drag bike. It was stock except for a full race cam and was ridden by an eighty-eight pound rider. It was also geared down so the top speed was about ninety mph. We could beat a standard 883 Sportster in the quarter-mile if it were not a competition model or one which had been modified. The Honda motorcycle was a third the size but faster over 1,320 feet.

Up until the end of the 1960s Harley-Davidson motorcycles seemed to be frozen in time. For reasons noted in the last chapter, Harley-Davidson became a part of AMF. During the AMF years, Harley-Davidson motorcycles were known for poor quality construction and were often unreliable. They also leaked oil and required frequent maintenance.

When the investment group of thirteen bought the brand from AMF, the first goal was to make better motorcycles which reflected higher standards of quality. The first big positive development was in 1984, when the upgraded Evolution motor was released. It was constructed of better metals, finer tolerances, and better castings. It also didn't leak oil, and it looked modern. The Evolution motor also continued the V-twin tradition. It was much more reliable than previous engines had been.

Harley-Davidson with Evolution Motor, From the author's collection

Around the same time, Harley-Davidson started using belt drives, instead of chains, and in 1985 added a five-speed transmission. The result was a better engine which produced more power, ran cooler, and lasted much longer on a generally more modern motorcycle. The road to recovery had begun in a big way and, most of all, met with the expectations of their customer base.

Harley-Davidson created a simple to understand model lineup going into the 1980s. Up until the 1980s there were three basic model groups. The model lines included the Sportsters, followed by the FX cruiser models, then the FL touring models. The FL models had larger front wheels, while the FX models had smaller front tires.

After 1984, the Soft Tail series was incorporated into the model lineup. The Soft Tail series has a hidden shock, making the bike look like an older "hard-tail" motorcycle (a hard-tail motorcycle has no rear springs). A Soft Tail model was designated with a ST in the model code.

From 1984, the basic lines were the Sportsters, the Dyna series, the Soft Tail series, then the touring bikes. There were numerous models within each designation; however, the basic lineup was simple and easy to understand. More than fifteen models could be made with two basic engines and three frames. The models typically continued year after year and special models were occasionally added but they didn't change the basic lineup.

There were occasionally new models which were oftentimes unusually popular, such as the Fatboy added in 1990, which was an FL model. Another popular model, the Badboy, was added in 1995. The Evolution motor continued for around fifteen years until the Twin Cam 88 was introduced in 1999.

How could Harley-Davidson move from being a struggling company to one which became a dominant company

within a decade? Note the following:

First, Harley-Davidson designed and built a better engine; that being the Evolution. The new motor was consistent with the history of the company and was much more reliable than the past engines.

Harley-Davidson copied the best of modern assembly line design, incorporating efficiency, quality production techniques, and reduced manufacturing costs. I have visited the (now closed) Kansas City Assembly Plant a number of times, and it was a modern, clean, and efficient factory, which could compete with the best.

The company connected with their past history and heritage and worked to determine what their customer base wanted, then they built those bikes. Even though the company did not want to be closely aligned with the one-percent motorcycle crowd, they accepted the fact that this was a significant customer base.

The company promoted their motorcycles as high quality, American made, union built, and a part of American history.

Harley-Davidson encouraged dealers to sponsor HOG (Harley Owner Group) clubs which built community and camaraderie.

Harley-Davidson worked hard to build a business on repeat customers. They requested that dealers not work on older machines so people would invest in new motorcycles.

They built product lines which promote the prestige of their name. Many American motorcycle riders wanted a motorcycle they could recognize as American and one which appeared to be high in quality.

They positioned their products as machines for the rebel, purist, or perfectionist. The Harley-Davidson was advertised as a freedom machine for the American.

They also marketed their motorcycles as holding a higher value for longer. Ads that stated something to the effect, "don't you wish your bike had the Harley-Davidson tank badge when you go to sell it" were very effective. As an excessive volume of Japanese motorcycles had saturated the marketplace they appeared to be cheap, while Harley-Davidson was made to look like a more prestigious product.

By positioning themselves as a premium builder of American motorcycles and connecting emotionally with their buyers, the brand began to grow in the marketplace.

By making their motorcycles appear to be very masculine and by promoting the idea of intrinsic value, Harley-Davidson built their business beyond what it had ever been before.

A major part of the history of Harley-Davidson has been the connection of the brand with the anti-social or rebel crowd. Harley-Davidson did not create this connection but has benefited greatly from it. Many a young man wanting to appear to be a "tough guy" or look like a one-precent gang member has purchased a Harley-Davidson simply because of the image it may give him.

One Eye Brian KC, With permission of One Eye Brian

As One Eyed Brian, of Deadeye Choppers in Claycomo, Missouri, noted, the motorcycle crowd is largely driven by ego. Big, loud, tough-looking motorcycles provide all the macho attitude most men could ever want.

I am also sure that wise financial practices were also a benefit to the growth of the company. Sales continued to climb, and by the end of the century, Harley-Davidson had taken roughly half the American large-displacement motorcycle market.

Note the sales figures from between 1950 and 2000. In 1950 around 17,000 Harley-Davidson motorcycles were sold, in 1960 around 15,800 motorcycles were sold, and during 1970 approximately 28,900 motorcycles were sold. In 1980 around 48,200 motorcycles were sold, in 1990 59,200 motorcycles were sold, and in 2000 around 204,592 motorcycles were sold. This remarkable growth continued into the next century.

An interesting development toward the end of this time period was what has been called the "chopper bubble." With the rise of Harley-Davidson sales and the premium prices of their new motorcycles, custom builders began building complete motorcycles and selling them at prices which were higher, but were somewhat competitive with new Harley-Davidson motorcycles—especially when most buyers were typically purchasing expensive accessories. Among the American motorcycle enthusiasts custom shops had been growing over the years which were doing all sorts of custom work. There were also several companies building American motorcycle parts and, later on, complete knock-off engines.

The largest of these was a company named S&S. S&S goes back to 1958, when the motorcycle accessory businesses were beginning to emerge. S&S was a company building less expensive American V-twin engine parts, which were often times better and more reliable than the original factory parts the manufacturer would claim.

There were actually a number of manufacturers who did the same thing, Ultima started in 1971, TP Engineering started in the mid-1980s, and a number of other parts and engine builders began before 1995 as well. At some point in time, these builders realized that they were making all the parts needed to build complete engines and motorcycles, so they did.

During the early 1990s, a few of these custom builders began making complete motorcycles, typically using S&S engines, branding them, and getting Department of Transportation VIN numbers. Surgical Steel started in 1989, West Coast Choppers started in 1992, Bourget started in 1993, Big Dog started in 1994, and American Iron Horse started in 1995. Titan and Pure Steel also started in 1995. Confederate started in 1996, Panzer and California Customs started in 1997, and Orange County Choppers and Cannondale both started in 1999.

There were actually dozens of other little manufacturers operating all over the country starting in the same manner. I have sales literature for many of these small manufacturers. Kansas City had Big Inch Choppers, made by KC Creations. With a brand name, numerous dealers, and being listed in the used motorcycle books that were used to asses value, they were officially new motorcycle manufacturers.

This chopper bubble lasted from around 1995 to around 2005, though some existed before 1995 and a few after 2005. There are a few still in business, though production numbers are probably very low. One manufacturer noted that they built no more than a hundred motorcycles per year.

Within that decade, there was a significant category of these specialty machines being built. Some called these machines simply "kit" bikes. Just like a traditional builder, they would have basic models with options. Most of these motor-

cycles were very expensive, and all were essentially customs. I doubt that any two were alike.

As the movement began slowly, it also ended slowly. Most went out of business; however, some have continued as custom motorcycle fabricators. One of the problems the movement created was this: when one of these custom machines was entered into a motorcycle show, should it be entered as a stock or custom motorcycle?

It could be assumed that Harley-Davidson started its CVO (Custom Vehicle Operations) department in 1999 to gain back some of these sales. Whatever the case, the CVO models have expanded over the years. Custom builders of complete motorcycles have been greatly reduced in numbers, and many individual buyers are still spending huge sums of money to customize their motorcycles.

I have had a number of motorcycle dealers tell me that these customs have not held their value and are often purchased for a fraction of the original price. Perhaps decades down the road they will be valuable as vintage customs from a previous era? This was an interesting development in the motorcycle community back at the turn of the last century.

Between 1983 and 2000, the Japanese manufacturers did

not rest. Honda's Gold Wing was first produced in 1975 and grew into a full touring motorcycle. By 1981 the Gold Wing had a full faring. This was the model that was to come. Before that time, Vetter fairings had become popular and were sold by the thousands. The Japanese manufacturers realized the popularity of these kits and their value and began putting partial fairings on a few sport models. By the end of the decade, fairings in numerous forms were common.

1985 Honda Gold Wing, From the author's collection

Honda offered the CX500 Turbo in 1982 and the CX650 Turbo in 1984; both had fairings. No one had been asking for turbo motorcycles; they didn't sell well and it was over quickly. It took several years to sell the unsold CX500s and 650 turbo motorcycles.

In 1982 Honda also brought out the first modern pro-link rear suspension. The 1983 CB1100F was not only a beautiful motorcycle, but a fast and reliable one which set a standard for other manufacturers. In 1984 Honda brought out the V-4 engine series in 500, 700, and 1100cc sizes, which have continued in some form for over the last thirty years. I read where Honda had hoped to make the V-4 engine design a trademark of their motorcycle line, but when the design was copied by other manufacturers, the plan was dropped.

1980s Honda VF (V-four), From the author's collection

In 1986 two VFR Interceptors were offered, a 700cc and a

750cc version. The smaller version was sold to meet government tariff limits, and the 750 for those wanting to race. The VFR series was to become one of Honda's most legendary and award-winning motorcycles.

In 1987 the Hurricane 600 and 1000 were featured as very high-performance motorcycles and were early examples of what was to become the "Super Sport Bike." The V-4 VFRs dating from 1984 were the first true Honda sport bikes, followed by the Hurricanes in 1987, which became the CBR series in 1991.

A model Honda offered in 1992 was the ST1100 touring bike. The ST was to become a cult bike among many riders. The CBR900RR from 1992 caused a revolution in creating a high-horsepower motorcycle which was light and small. It was the model used for sport bikes of all brands from that time on. The RC 30 was offered in 1990 as a low-volume sport bike, which was generally purchased and collected, rather than ridden as a daily rider. The Honda Super Blackbird CBR1100 was first built in 1996 and for several years was the fastest production motorcycle. It had a top speed of approximately 180 mph. A derivative of the Gold Wing was the Valkyrie of 1997. This was a huge motorcycle which was quite a performer because of the flat-six engine and reduced weight.

Going backwards a bit, Honda began building its V-twin cruiser line in 1985 with the Shadow series. The demand for V-twin motorcycles was growing, though Honda's version of the V-twin machines were water-cooled and had three valves per cylinder. By the early 1980s water cooling was the norm' and many motorcycles were getting six-speed transmissions.

Yamaha started the Venture touring series in 1983 as more and more riders hit the road. The Venture was Gold Wing-like but never became a big seller. In 1985 Yamaha started the FZ performance bike series. They also introduced the first series V-Max. The V-Max started the naked power bike category which was not copied immediately but is now a well recognized category.

In 1987 the FZ700 Super Sport and FZR were introduced. Both started a long history of very well-built superbikes. 1994 brought the YZF 750, a full super sport motor cycle, followed by the YZR 750 in 1996. The FZ series of 1987 became the lineage of the Yamaha sport bikes.

Yamaha Virago, From the author's collection

Like the other Japanese brands, Yamaha started their V-twin series in 1986 through the Virago models. Yamaha's last two-stroke was the RZ350 of 1986, which was very fast and was a refined motorcycle as well. They have also become very collectible.

In 1991 Yamaha offered only nine models. In 1996 Yamaha started the Royal Star cruiser series. The big Royal Stars had V-4 engines of 1300cc and were decked out in vintage looking trim. The 1999 RZF R6 (600cc) raised some eyebrows when its red line was claimed to be over 15,000 rpms. Yamaha was building some of the most potent sport bikes by the end of the century.

Suzuki started the four-stroke GS series in 1977 which was to continue into the mid-1980s, ending with the GS500 in the early 2000s. The 1982 the Katana GS started the move towards super sport bikes. The first Katana was a 1000cc motorcycle looking very fast, and it was. In 1983 three Katanas were offered, a 650, a 750, and the 1000, which was later enlarged to 1100cc. In 1984, only

Suzuki Katana, From the author's collection

three models were offered because of the unsold older motorcycles. The 1986 G550ES continued the direction toward a full super sport machine, but the full on racers were the new GSXR machines. The GSXRs were available in 750s and 1100cc machines. The Intruder V-twins were first offered in 1986, staring their cruiser motorcycle line. The 1991 GSX1100 naked bike was a new model, which was by then becoming a new niche. Similar to the Honda CBR900RR, the 1994 Suzuki GSXR750 lost around twenty-four pounds, making it a more serious super sport bike, and was now as fast as many of the liter sport bikes.

The Hayabusa, first offered in 1999, was a 1300cc monster and became the performance standard by which all future performance bikes would be judged. The performance of the Hayabusa continued to be legendary, and it was a model feared by lesser machines. Of all the Suzuki models, the GSXR series motorcycles have been a potent series, winning more than their share of race day events.

Kawasaki discontinued their two-strokes by 1978. It was the 1968 500cc H1 which really put Kawasaki on the map. The brand has usually been known for performance machines, and their first series of four-strokes were just that. The KZ four-stroke series started in 1975 and continued until 1986 in some form. The 1983 GPZ super sport series became an extension of the KZ line and was available in 305cc, 550cc, 750cc, and 1100cc versions. They were known for extreme reliability and longevity.

In 1984 they offered the first series KL 600 dual-sport, which was an early model of a bike category which was to become very popular decades later.

Kawasaki KLR650, From the author's collection

In 1984 Kawasaki also offered their first Ninja series motorcycle. It was a very fast 900cc semi-fared sport machine. In 1985 the 900 Eliminator was offered, which was a serious street racer. The Eliminator series was one of the fastest street racers for about a decade.

1986 brought the big Voyager touring bike as well as a 600cc Eliminator to be sold alongside the 900. 1987 brought the Vulcan series V-twins. Kawasaki was the last Japanese manufacturer to create a line of V-twin cruisers.

In 1988 the ZX10 was offered. It was a mix of sport bike and high-performance machine. The new ZX10 replaced the former 1000R Ninja. The ZX10 became the ZX11 in 1991, and the 1994 ZX9R was the sport bike to beat for several years.

In 1999 the VN1500 Vulcan was made to look very much like a Harley-Davidson, and from a distance, few could tell. The Drifter series had valance-type fenders like the vintage Indian motorcycles. I have seen many Drifters with Indian logos on the tank.

In 2000 Kawasaki offered the stripped down ZX-7 naked bike, which was stylish and very usable. It was also a great buy.

The vintage looking W650 was also offered in 2000. The W was a motorcycle which looked back to the days when British parallel twins ruled the road. The W series bikes were offered in the US until 2001 but continued to be made for other markets around the world for at least another decade and a half. The W series never sold well in the US. Kawasaki has always sold the fewest motor-cycles of any of the Japanese brands in the US, but certainly not because of any deficit. Kawasakis have typically been very good looking, well built, and very reliable motorcycles, with the largest ZX bikes typically being some of the fastest motorcycles made on the planet. At the time of this writing, the ZX14R may be the fastest factory motorcycle made, if the new H1 and H1R limited edition models are not included.

One of the significant developments with Japanese motorcycles since the late 1980s to the end of the 1990s was a greater symmetry in model lines. Each would have a small commuter model, a series of V-twin cruisers, several sport models, several super sport models in 600 or 750, and 1000cc (or 1100cc) sizes. They would occasionally have a "naked" bike or series of standard-styled machines. All would also have a touring bike, with the Honda Gold Wing being one of the most significant models.

All four had a turbo model bike during the early to mid-1980s. Honda had the 1982 CX500T, followed by the 1983 CX650T; both are mentioned above. Yamaha had the XJ650 Turbo in 1982, and Suzuki had the GS650 Turbo in 1983. Kawasaki had the GPz750 Turbo in 1984, which was considered to be the fastest of all the turbo-assisted motorcycles of that time.

None of the turbo motorcycles sold well in their day and were seen as expensive. Reviewers of that time felt that they did not give the performance that could not otherwise be found in other less expensive models. They just represented over the top engineering, rather than being a good value. Most buyers were concerned about the maintenance costs if a turbo were to fail.

The four Japanese manufacturers together continued to represent the largest market share of motorcycles sold in the US until the early 2000s. Honda continued as the largest of the four, Yamaha was a close second, Suzuki was generally third, and Kawasaki was a distant fourth in sales numbers.

Italian manufacturers entered the US market after WWII but those bikes were imported only in very small numbers. I spoke with a dealer operating in the early 1970s selling Ducati, Moto Guzzi, and MV brands. He noted that one year he was the largest-selling Ducati dealer in his region. It was funny, because he had sold only "two" Ducatis that year, and the other brands, were sold in lower volumes. Ducati was the largest of the Italian companies to export to the US, but import numbers were really small until the introduction of the Monster series in 1993.

During the early 1970s Ducati built around 3,500 motorcycles yearly, and by the early 1980s production was just a little over 5,000 motorcycles. These numbers represent total production numbers, not US sales figures.

Ducati's production numbers were in the 4,000 unit range in 1986, growing to nearly 16,500 in 1995. By 2000, production grew to over 37,000 motorcycles. Again, these are production numbers, not import or sales numbers.

The Ducati Monster was one of the largest individual production segments manufactured by Ducati. I cannot verify the accuracy of these figures, but they no doubt reflect production and sales. The point is this: Ducati started small and grew slowly, but as the brand moved toward the end of the 20th century, production grew exponentially.

As the Monster was a huge success, so have been the V-twin sport bikes. The 1988 851 Superbike was to create a serious market for Ducati sport bikes, setting a direction very important for the future of the company.

Ducati 851, From the author's collection

The 1990 through 1994 900 dual-sport was an important bike because it proceeded what was to become a huge market segment a little more than a decade later.

The 1992 Superlight was to guide where the Japanese sport bikes were going to go in the near future, and it also helped create the image of Ducati as a prestigious and serious brand. In the twenty-first century, sales have been on the rise as the brand really leaps forward as a prestige motorcycle. Since 2016 the Scrambler series has become a huge part of Ducati sales.

Another manufacturer to surface during the early 1980s was through the work of Erik Buell. Buell got connected with motorcycles in his teens and had a gift for engineering. Buell was, in fact, an engineer for Harley-Davidson at one time. He raced a Yamaha TZ750 two-stroke and later a unique V-4 two-stroke made by the defunct British company, Barton.

Buell started a motorcycle company in 1983 under his name, first selling specialty race bikes. Two-stroke racing engines were hard to come by, and their development even more problematic. He then built a racing-type motorcycle using the Harley-Davidson XR1000 engine. The Buell RR1000 was very aerodynamic and could be built at a reasonable cost.

Buell S-1

In 1993 Harley-Davidson acquired forty-nine percent of the company and by 2003 owned it all. Buell built a number of sport models using Harley-Davidson engines. His work culminated in a genuine competitive model using a Rotax engine. The Thunderbolt was built in the late 1980s, followed by the Lightning in 1996. In 1997 the Cyclone was unveiled. This model had a Rotax engine and was first offered in 2011. Harley-Davidson was to liquidate the Buell division within a decade. What a loss of a company which had been so progressive.

Triumph went out of business in 1983, but a few Bonneville models continued to be built under contract through Less Harris, a Triumph parts manufacturer. John Bloor, a land developer, had purchased the name and the rights to produce the motorcycle that same year. Bloor kept several of the previous Triumph engineers on his staff and designed a

new series of motorcycles using a modular engine, which could be altered by adding cylinders. The first model was the Trophy series, followed by the Daytona series starting in the mid 1990s.

Triumph sold motorcycles in other markets but was unable to sell in the US because of insurance requirements. Once the insurance requirements were met, Triumph expanded in the US market on a continual basis after 1995.

The T595 (955cc) was the first attempt at a super sport model in 1997, and because of problems, it was not as successful as it could have been. The TT600 was a full-on sports model first offered in 2000 and was successful but was not as fast as its Japanese counterparts.

Triumph T595, From the author's collection

It was not until the new Bonneville was added to the

lineup in 2000 that Triumph began to grow significantly. Triumph was to become a company building some of the most reliable motorcycles—at one time having fewer than one percent of new machines sold having any sort of problem. As we will see in the next chapter, Triumph is continuing to grow in an impressive manner, building exciting models which meet the demands of the American market. Triumph is an example of a defunct brand returning to the market in a big way by not looking back, but forward.

Another interesting story during this time period is that of the modern Excelsior-Henderson motorcycle. Excelsior and Henderson go way back as very prestigious brands. Excelsior was built from 1908 to 1931 and Henderson was built from 1912 to 1931. Ignas Schwinn, the bicycle maker, purchased the Excelsior brand in 1911 and the Henderson brand in 1918 to create Excelsior-Henderson motorcycles. Schwinn discontinued production in 1931 because of the Great Depression of 1929-1930. The Excelsior-Henderson was a prestigious brand which made the sort of impact on the motorcycle community similar to that of the Indian motorcycle.

The name itself held a certain status in the history of the American motorcycle. It is no wonder that when someone wanted to resurrect an older brand that the name seemed worthy of bringing back.

Sometime back in 1993, as the story goes, Daniel Hanlon had ordered a new Harley-Davidson motorcycle and was put on a list which might have taken up to two years of waiting. He thought, if people are willing to wait two years to get an American V-twin motorcycle, there is certainly room for another brand.

Another story is that Hanlon and several other people were at the Sturgis Rally in south Dakota sometime back in the early 1980s and saw that most of the motorcycles were Harley-Davidsons. With this being the case, again, there was at that time plenty of room for another brand of American V-twin motorcycle. Either or both stories could be true.

About that time, Daniel Hanlon began conceptualizing a new American motorcycle. He chose to use the Excelsior-Henderson name. He went about collecting money to build the motorcycle and was rumored to have collected around $100,000,000 from hundreds of investors. The factory was built, and motorcycles were manufactured in 1999 and 2000, before running out of money.

In 1999 1,161 motorcycles were built, and in 2000 720 machines rolled off the assembly line. The machine was an SOHC 1386cc V-twin with traditional looks, except for odd front fork springs. The story goes that there was a commitment from many investors to continue production, but the risk of further loss from some of the larger investors stopped the finance process. Whatever the case, funding became the nail which closed the coffin.

The Excelsior-Henderson had potential as a motorcycle brand if the financial part of the equation had been different. Apart from the odd looking forks, the motorcycle was very nice looking and appeared to be of high-quality construction.

From stories which have circulated, the engine suffered excessive mechanical failures because of poor construction procedures related to the company that was hired to assemble them. The design was solid, the assembly was not.

1999 Excelsior Henderson. Manufacturer's promotional photo

Some years ago, I was attending a motorcycle event in another state and was looking at the parked motorcycles which had been ridden to the event. I came upon a group of

at least half a dozen new model Excelsior-Hendersons parked together. This was more than a rare site. One of the jackets on one of the motorcycles listed an Excelsior-Henderson Club. I couldn't find any of the riders, but it was the largest group of these motorcycles I have ever come across together.

Without question, it takes a lot of money to fund a new motorcycle company. From time to time there will be a rumor that there will be another attempt at bringing the motorcycle back, hopefully this will be the case with a better ending. In 2017 there were rumors that a large company in India was interested in buying the name.

Boss Hoss, From the author's collection

Several other oddities worth mentioning are the Boss Hoss, a large motorcycle built since 1990 using large Chevrolet V-8 engines. From what I have read, they use a single-speed automatic transmission. They are huge bikes, have huge engines, and are high-priced. Few are built yearly. I had a friend that owned one. His motorcycle had a 350 cubic-inch Chevy engine. They would be, no doubt, hard to handle and are very heavy, but certainly are an eye catcher. The Boss Hoss certainly emulates the American mindset.

Another interesting oddity is the Rohr motorcycle, which dates back to the mid-1990s. The first Rohr motorcycle offered was in 2000. The company had a two-stroke, a mid-sized sport bike, and a muscle bike based on a turbo-charged Harley-Davidson V-Rod engine. I doubt that many were ever built, and I have never seen one.

Another interesting motorcycle was the Ridley. The Ridley was a two-thirds-size cruiser-styled motorcycle marketed as having an automatic transmission. The engine was a small V-twin of around 750cc, conceived of by Clay Ridley and first offered in 1999. They had also gone by the wayside sometime around 2010. The Ridley was a motorcycle often ridden by women and was produced in low volumes. They did develop a small dealership network selling the brand.

The German BMW has a rich history of quality and innovation. Always known as well-engineered, well-built, and high-end motorcycle, the company has shown continual growth in US sales. After

WWII BMW motorcycles were imported in low numbers and never reached volume sales figures until more recent times.

The big news from BMW came in 1983 with the K100 series of in-line fours, which were 1,000cc in capacity. The two-valve series ran from 1983 to 1989, followed by the four-valve series from 1989 to 1992. A smaller version of the same series, the three-cylinder 750s, were sold from 1985 to 1996. From what I understand, BMW was planning on replacing the boxer with this in-line engine, but demand for the boxer engine was great enough to change BMW's course.

BMW had been a brand which was more in a niche market than being a mainstream line of motorcycles. Because of this, finding and holding their market was critical to them.

Since the late 1970s and going forward into the 1980s the BMW brand was suffering from a drop in sales, just like most of the other manufacturers were. This was a more significant issue with them, because their sales numbers were lower than most other manufacturers to begin with. According to Preston in his book, *BMW Motorcycles: The Complete Story*, he notes that in 1990 BMW worldwide sales were around 26,000 machines and Germany was their largest market. Having an estimated three-percent of the US market. That would be somewhere around 9,000 machines being sold in the US—a small figure.

BMW was not in a position to compete with other brands on an equal footing because they were typically very different in design and tended to be more expensive motorcycles. They wanted something really unique.

The answer came in the newly designed G/S series of 1979. The G/S motorcycles were dual-sport machines, heavy duty, and able to travel the world. The first G/S series was built between 1980 and 1987 and sold well. BMW sold more than 22,000 of these machines alone.

The big G/S was to become a successful racer in the Dakar competition, which is a 6,000+ mile journey through rough terrain and areas with few or no roads. It is an event that has been held for several decades in Argentina and in various South American countries.

BMW motorcycles were the machines used in the television series *Long Way Down* and *Long Way Round*, a really great series worth watching. The BMW brand was to see much more growth and was to come into its own as it moved into the twenty-first century.

In 1983 there were approximately 735,000 motorcycles sold in the US. By 1990, the numbers had decreased nearly sixty percent to a little over 303,000 motorcycles. There was little growth going forward, and by 1995, new motorcycle sales were around 310,000 units sold in the US. By 2000, sales had more than doubled and were in the 710,000 unit range. Moving into the twenty-first century, sales were to see huge increases for nearly a decade, then they began to fall again. We will chart what has occurred in the world of motorcycling since 2000 in the next chapter.

From 1983 to 2000, the Japanese motorcycle went from experiencing huge growth in the US market to having to suffer huge drops in sales. The sales of Japanese motorcycles did remain strong in other countries.

As could be expected, the Japanese brands continued advancing in design and technology at a blistering pace. Engines went from air-cooling to liquid-cooling, suspensions were greatly improved, and almost all braking systems moved to multiple disc units. Faster motorcycles were produced as the decade grew, culminating in what we call the "Sport Bike" segment. Some of the super sport bikes from the second half of the 1990s were so advanced that they could compare with many of the fastest motorcycles which would be built over twenty years later.

The Honda Gold Wing matured into the most advanced touring motorcycle available. Some models began having partial fairings in the 1980s, culminating in fully-faired bikes by the end of the 1990s. The Japanese motorcycle reached a level of technology and sophistication never reached before in mass-produced motorcycle production. However, that was not all that the motorcycle community wanted.

Harley-Davidson motorcycles had gone from a low-volume producer of traditional vintage-styled motorcycles, and the last US manufacturer standing, to one with which many Americans could identify. The company shifted from poorly made motorcycles, known for being unreliable, to more modern, bright and shiny, reliable machines. With simpler and easy to understand model lineup, comfortable cruiser-styled bikes, and machines which were much more reliable than during the AMF years, sales began to rise.

Harley-Davidson also began to cater to their market segment and found out that there were tens of thousands of motorcycle riders who really wanted to ride and buy American. As Harley-Davidson motorcycles grew substantially in sales, a culture developed which supported their brand. Through events and activities centered on the brand, greater acceptance and approval could be found if you rode a Harley. What is referred to as "the biker lifestyle" became a dominant force pulling many into the Harley-Davidson community. The image became the dominant force, rather than the love of the motorcycle. Time will tell if Indian motorcycles can tap into this love of American motorcycles.

Victory V92C, Manufacturer's promotional photo

From the end of the 1990s, there was a move toward custom V-twin American motorcycles. I made reference to the Chopper Bubble, however, the movement was more than just chopper-styled motorcycles. It included bobbers (typically stripped bikes with the front and back tires being the same size) and simply modified custom motorcycles. The motorcycles were usually very expensive and very custom in design. The cost of the machines would have put the motorcycles in a limited market and would have kept the machines from ever selling in large numbers.

The future was looking good for brands like Ducati, Triumph, BMW, and Indian; however each would have to find their niche. Brands like Buell and Victory were to ultimately fail. The twenty-first century would follow much of what had occurred during the years we have been discussing, with just more incremental design evolution. In the next chapter, we will look at the motorcycle in the twenty-first century.

Gilroy Indian, From the author's collection

Chapter 7

Motorcycling Since 2000

A Motorcycle Renaissance Begins

In 2000 motorcycle sales were a little above 700,000 units sold in the US until 2005, when sales had grown to just over one million units being sold. From this high of over a million motorcycles sold, which had not occurred since the 1970s, sales began to drop around 90,000 motorcycles per year until 2008, when sales were down to around 880,000 units. By 2009 there was a plunge in sales to around 510,000 motorcycles sold, which was a huge drop. This coincided with the stock market drop of 2008, precipitating the Great Recession. For the next eight years, the growth in the economy was the lowest it had been since the 1930s, and this trend was certainly reflected in US motorcycle sales. Motorcycle sales in 2010 were approximately 435,000 and by 2015 had grown to right at 500,000 units sold. These were small gains, but at least they were going in the right direction.

In 2016 the economy began to grow at four times the

previous rate, and by 2017 there appeared to be a two-and-a-half- to three-percent growth in motorcycle sales. Time will tell if sales growth can continue.

From around 1995 to around 2006, The Bureau of Transportation Statistics stated that motorcycle registration in the US had grown seventy-five percent. In 2011, by another source, there were approximately 7.7 million motorcycles registered in the US, 800,000 being in California alone.

I would guess that, even though motorcycle sales are down, but also because bikes last longer than they did several decades ago, more older machines are still on the road. Sales of motorcycles over 750cc were up around fifty-four percent and sport type bikes have just grown incrementally.

The vast majority of motorcycle riders and owners also remain male. Other resources stated that while ninety-five percent of rider/owners were men, articles about women riders typically claim that around ten percent of riders are women. Back in the 1960s and 1970s a female rider was rare and they are still rare today, however, just less so.

According to the Brandon Marketing Group, the average rider has been riding for twenty-six years. The age of riders has also been on the increase. Back in 1985 the typical rider was around twenty-seven, and by 2003 that number had risen to the mid- to upper forties. It is as though the same guys were still riding. By 2015 the average age had risen to forty-eight, except for Harley-Davidson riders, which was in the low fifties.

I hear on a regular basis of the need for motorcycle manufacturers to build motorcycles for the next generation of riders. If riders continue to get older, this may not be a huge issue. If young people begin to buy motorcycles in large numbers, as they did in the 1960s and 1970s, a new template will have to be developed around their riding preferences.

To begin a discussion on the development of the motorcycle after the start of the new century is somewhat arbitrary because the bikes after 2000 were much the same as those that were being manufactured before. By that I mean that most of the changes are beneath the surface and are technical in nature, rather than in identifiable external design factors. I am not one to attempt to guess where the sport will be in several decades but want to look at the trends since the beginning of the twenty-first century.

Having read numerous articles written in the distant past about what the future was to look like going forward, I can say that all of them have been very wrong. I read a chapter from a 1930s' book about what the automobile was going to look like in the 1980s, and the cars of that decade were supposed to look like spaceships. Now, thirty-five years since the 1980s, the automobile still does not look like a rocket ship.

In reality, many American motorcycles of the 1940s don't look that much different from some 1980s motorcycles if you are viewing them from fifty feet away. The greatest change from a 1970s motorcycle to one forty-five years later (around 2015) is not necessarily in appearance, but is mostly in technology. With the Japanese motorcycle, they don't necessarily look like spaceships they just go like them.

In this chapter, I will consider a number of trends which have occurred since 2000, and I will discuss some of the most significant changes which have been developing. Without question, there has been a huge growth in some parts of the motorcycle community since the turn of the twenty-first century. These changes are far more significant than just sales numbers. Sales numbers are down significantly from forty plus years ago, but sport activity is much the same.

With great strides in technology taking place, many new specialty bikes are now being offered. Since 2000, there has been a huge growth in the motorcycle touring market, as well as growth in the dual-sport market, and there has been growth in the adventure bike segment of the market as well.

A two-tiered super sport market has also evolved. The major brands have their basic super sport models, plus an additional model with track parts. Yamaha has the R 1 and the R 1 M, Honda has the CBR1000RR and the more specialized CBR1000RR SP, Suzuki has the GSXR1000 with the pricier GSXR1000R model.

Ducati has, for example, the Panigale 1299 Superbike, with both a 1299S and 1299R version. In all of these examples, the M, SP, R, or S versions will be three to five thousand dollars more than the basic model, except in the case of the Ducati. With the Ducati, the Panigale R is substantially more in price and even includes an entirely different engine. These additions create a much wider range of specialized model offerings.

Another example is with the Kawasaki cruisers. Models on the same platform include the 900 Classic, the 900 Custom, and the 900 Classic LT. Consider the Yamaha Bolt, the SCR, and the XSR, all which look very much alike and are within 50cc of being the same size.

Possibly the best example would be the BMW R 9-T series, which includes a Scrambler, a Racer, a model that is called the "Urban," and a model called the "Pure." All of these are on the same platform but are very different in appearance and purpose.

There has also been a growth in vintage motorcycle shows and auctions. There were certainly these events before, but as the new century has proceeded there has been significant growth in the numbers of events.

Bonhams is one of the older auction houses, but new groups, like J.Woods, started

motorcycle auctions around 1998. Other large auction houses, like Mecum, did not start auctioning vintage motorcycles until around 2015. Now there are close to a dozen big vintage auctions every year. There is, without a doubt, a motorcycle renaissance going on.

First, let's look at the dominant motorcycle manufacturers and review how they have changed over the past decade and a half.

One of the big stories, which began after 2000, was the rise of the new Indian motorcycle. Let me briefly review Indian's past history, noting that this is still a generalized overview.

Indian Chief, From the author's collection

The original Indian was manufactured from 1901 to 1953. After 1953 Brockhouse Engineering took over management until Associated Motorcycles, the well-known British motorcycle company, assumed management until 1962. Sammy Pierce and then Floyd Clymer, the one-time owner of *Cycle* magazine, built a variety of Indian motorcycles in an attempt to revive the brand. They delivered up until 1970, at which time Clymer's lawyer sold Italian scooters under the name. Clymer died in 1970.

There was an in-line four Indian built in Europe from at least 1992 to sometime around 2007, called the Berlin Indian or the Dakota Indian, but it was never sold in the US.

There were investors who bought the name and production rights to the brand in 1998 and built Indians until 2003. This series is often referred to as the Gilroy Indian, because that was the city in California in which the factory was located. From what I understand, the Gilroy Indian group was actually doing well; they just didn't have enough operating capital to continue.

Another investment company, the Stellican group, purchased the rights to building Indians from the Gilroy group in 2006, and they lasted until 2011, when they sold the brand to Polaris Industries. Polaris re-engineered the motorcycle

and reintroduced a new Indian in 2013, and in 2017 Polaris discontinued the Victory brand. I do believe that between 2011 and 2012 they sold all the Stellican Indians which had not found buyers.

The Chief has been the primary model in several different configurations, and in 2015 an Indian Scout was offered. The first Scout was a 1200cc machine, then in 2016 a less expensive 1000cc version was offered. From what I can extrapolate, the sales have been very good. Virtually all of the reviews on the Indian motorcycles have likewise been complimentary.

Time will tell as to how Polaris will integrate the discontinued Victory brand into Indian products. There is no doubt that there has been a significant investment into the technology for future products which will move from the defunct Victory brand to the Indian brand. Indian has been truly one of the great resurrection stories of motorcycling, and I hope the best for the company.

In 2000 Harley-Davidson offered the Twin Cam "B" motor. The *B* stands for a new counter-balancer added to some models. This makes the engine run much more smoothly at idle, and at higher speeds as well. In 2001 the Motor Company began offering fuel-injection on some models. Within a few years, all models were fuel-injected. In 2002 the V-Rod was introduced. This model had a high-performance V-twin engine, which was modern in every category. There was a rumor that the V-Rod would be taken out of production in 2015, but later a dealer noted it would continue through 2017.

Harley-Davidson V-Rod, From the author's collection

Harley-Davidson began installing six-speed transmissions in 2006, allowing for lower engine rpms at highway speeds.

In 2000 Harley-Davidson opened a museum in Milwaukee, Wisconsin, which displays motorcycles from the company's past. In 2008 the Motor Company bought MV Augusta, an Italian company known for racing back in the 1960s and 1970s. MV was then sold in 2010. Harley-Davidson engines have also been getting larger.

The old standard, going back for a long time, was the 80 cubic-inch Evolution, which was replaced by the Twin Cam 88 in 1999. A 95 cubic-inch motor was offered in some models in 2000, with a 96 cubic-inch motor being offered in 2007. From 2003 a 103 cubic-inch big twin was available, and a few years later a 110 cubic-inch engine was offered. The big news for 2017 was the introduction of the Milwaukee Eight motor. This new engine has four-valve heads, as opposed to two. The Milwaukee

Eight is offered in a 107 and 114 cubic-inch variations.

Harley-Davidson moves very slowly, and this has been good for them. To most observers, a 2017 Harley-Davidson looks much like the ones which were built three or four decades ago. I doubt that this will change going forward, as the company has built a market on modern vintage-looking motorcycles. General news sources have noted that Harley-Davidson sales have been down for the past three years, which is the same time in which the new Indian has been on the market. Time will tell if this trend will continue.

As is their nature, the Japanese brands have continued to develop new motorcycles at a fast pace and with new levels of refinement. In 2001 Honda unveiled the newest incarnation of the Gold Wing touring bike, which has seen just incremental changes over the past over fifteen years. It continues to be one of the best long-distance road bikes available. The changes from 2012 were minor updates, with rumors of a new front suspension in the works. A new series of Gold Wings was unveiled in 2018. This new model even offers an optional automatic transmission.

The older Shadow V-twin series was replaced with the VTX series in 2002 (1800cc) and 2003 (1300cc), with expanded model being available.

The 1800cc series was discontinued in 2008, but the 1300cc series has continued on.

In 2009 a chopper version with the 1300cc engine was offered called the "Fury." A new CBR was offered in 2004, which was a full-liter bike that replaced the previous 954cc superbike. The previous ST1100 sport touring bike, with a V-4 engine, was replaced with a new ST1300 in 2002 and continued in the US until around 2014. The newer ST is still available in other parts of the world. The ST 1300 was first shown as the X-Wing concept motorcycle.

In 2003 Honda offered the Rune, a factory custom derived from the Gold Wing frame and engine. This was probably brought out because of the custom motorcycle craze going on at the time; however, the Rune was a much more refined motorcycle than the typical small motorcycle manufacturers were able to produce.

In 2008 Honda offered the DN-1, a full sized motorcycle with an automatic transmission. They didn't sell well, but they were actually very good motorcycles.

In 2010 Honda brought out the super high-tech VFR1200 V-4 touring sport bike, which was available with a twin-clutch six-speed automatic transmission. The bike received very high ratings as a refined and exotic motorcycle, but there was confusion as to what market it was attempting to reach. Was it intended to be a sport bike? If so, it was too heavy. Was it to be a sport touring bike? If so, it was a bit small. Was it to be a high-tech version of a universal standard machine? If so it was a bit exotic. Whatever the case, it didn't sell well in America, but from what I understand, has done well in Europe. .

After 2012, the NT700 series was offered in several models. It was designed to be built in a sports version, as a standard, as a dual-sport, or as a scooter version. It was to be a universal platform which could be used around the world that offered good gas mileage and reliability.

The vintage-styled Honda CB1100 was first marketed in a few countries in 2010 but didn't come to the US until 2013. The next year, Honda offered the same motorcycle except with a six-speed transmission. In 2017 a further revised model with more of a café racer look was offered.

Honda CB1100, From the author's collection

In 2014 the 125cc Grom, a street-able mini-bike was added to the lineup and was a huge seller. Dealers were not able to keep them in stock in 2015 or 2016.

In 2016 Honda offered a street version of the RC213 race bike, but the cost was far above what most could afford. It was essentially designed for collectors.

Yamaha offered the first series FZ1 from 2001 through 2005 then upgraded it from 2006 and through 2016 as the Fazer. These models were very fast sport bikes but with an aim toward more comfort. The R1 (1,000cc) and R6 (600cc) machines were the super sport bikes which were the true full-on sport models. They have been upgraded nearly every year and have been consistently winners in amateur race classes.

Another long-term model has been the V-Max. First offered in 1985 through 2007, the motorcycle was the first true naked power cruiser. It was fully revised into a 1700cc power cruiser, now sold as a Star, in 2009. Nearly every year there have been consistent rumors that this model will be discontinued.

In 2006 the Stratoliner and Roadliner cruiser models were introduced as large luxury touring or cruiser motorcycles.

In 2013 Yamaha first offered the Bolt, a retro-looking V-twin custom cruiser. It has been a big selling model.

The FJR1300 first started in the 1980s as an 1100cc sport touring bike, received major upgrades in 2014, and is considered to be one of the best motorcycles of its type.

In 2017 several vintage styled sport V-twins were added to the model lineup called "Heritage" models, which look backward and forward as sport cruisers.

The XRS900 in-line three-cylinder bike is also a retro-looking café-styled motorcycle.

Another model that has been in production for some time is the retro SR400 single. It has been sold around the world but was brought back to the US sometime around 2015. What is interesting about this motorcycle is that it is actual-ly an old-spec bike without an electric starter. It is a genuine retro.

Suzuki has been best known for its sport bikes, like the potent Hayabusa and the GSXR series. The V-Strom series of machines are prime examples of great dual-sport motorcycles.

Certainly, they make a more complete line of motorcycles than these three models, however, these models have been significant motorcycles and often have been considered to be some of the best in their prospective classes over the years.

Suzuki Hayabusa, Manufacturer's promotional photo

The Hayabusa dates back to 1999 and continues into the twenty-first century as one of the fastest production sport bikes available. The first series dates from 1999 to 2007 and were rated around 155 horsepower. The machines after 2008 have been updated and rated at close to 200 horsepower. As a fast super sport machine it has consistently been tested as one of the quickest and fastest motorcycles ever made. Always having a tested top speed of above 180 miles per hour and quarter-mile times consistently in the upper nine second bracket. There are very few motorcycles which test consistently as fast.

The V-Strom Suzukis are legendary dual-sport machines which are as reliable as any motorcycle ever made. The 650cc V-Strom engine has been listed as one of the best motorcycle engines ever made. The original bikes dates back to 2004 and were 650cc V-twins. A 1,000cc model was added in 2014.

The Suzuki GSXR 600, 750, and 1,000cc sport bikes have also been considered some of the best super sport motorcycles in their class. Most Japanese brands discontinued their 750cc sport bikes, but Suzuki has continued with its GSXR 750 model since the mid 1980s. The GSX 600 received fuel-injection in 2001 and a complete update in 2006 and another update in 2011. The 750 received a major update in 2011. The liter model was reduced from 1100cc to 1000cc in 2001 and received a complete redesign in 2005 and 2009. Between 2001 and 2006 Suzuki and Kawasaki shared several cruiser models between the two brands.

Kawasaki's cruiser line is known as the Vulcan se-

ries. The 500cc models were made from 1990 to 2009 and the 750cc series from 1984 to 2006. The 800cc series was offered from 1995 to 2006 and the 900cc models from 2006, the 1500cc series from 1987 to 2008 and the 1600cc series from 2002 to 2009. The 1700cc series was offered from 2004 to 2010 and the 2000cc series from 2004 to 2010. The 1500cc Mean Streak, a semi-power cruiser was in the lineup from 2003. Since 2015 Kawasaki has had at least eight models of Vulcan cruisers from 650cc to 1700cc. The newer series have a naked or café look.

The KLR dual-sport series has also been a long-term model dating back to the mid-1980s. Being offered in 250cc and 650cc models, this motorcycle has been a significant influence on this type of motorcycle, which has been gaining in popularity.

Kawasaki ZX12R, Manufacturer's promotional photo

Kawasaki has been best known for its sport bikes. Its ZX series bikes have been some of the most potent sport bikes made. In 2003 Kawasaki diverted from the 600cc class by offering a 636cc Ninja nearly as fast of some of the liter bikes. The ZX10R, ZX11, ZX12R, ZX13, and ZX14R series have likewise been some of the fastest motorcycles made. The ZX14 competes with the Suzuki Hyabusa and often takes the top prize. The 14R is capable of running sub-ten-second quarter-mile times at nearly 150 mph, very fast indeed.

In 2015 Kawasaki offered a limited edition Ninja H2 and H2R super high performance series of motorcycles. There was also an H2 called the "Carbon" which used exotic carbon-fiber parts. All three motorcycles use a centrifugal type supercharger. The H2 is rated at 250 horsepower and the H2R is rated at 310 horsepower. A period magazine test indicated that the H2R produced 329 actual horsepower, phenomenal for a motorcycle which is purchased from a dealer. The R model cannot be licensed for the street.

Kawasakis have been known as highly refined and very reliable motorcycles which gravitate towards performance machines.

As noted before, the Japanese manufacturers have wasted no time in developing highly refined and world-class motorcycles, which have often led the industry in technology and reliability. I doubt that they will let this momentum slide at any time soon.

Triumph Bonneville, From the author's collection

The return of Triumph motorcycles to America in 1995 was a huge step for the Hinckley Triumph group. Triumph may be the oldest continuous lineage of motorcycles in the world, expanding over 116 years as a manufacturer. In the US, they would date from the late 1940s to the early 1980s, then from 1984 to the present time. Triumph America returned to the states in 1994, but the motorcycles were 1995 models.

Triumph's most famous model is the Bonneville, which returned to America in 2000. It was air-cooled until 2016, when the newly revised Bonneville was unveiled.

The Rocket 3, a 2300cc, 140 cubic-inch three-cylinder motorcycle was offered from 2004.

In 2002 a model called the "Bonneville America" was offered as a cruiser version of the Bonneville.

In 2007 another similar model, the Speedmaster, was offered.

In 2002 Triumph had its hundred-year anniversary, and in 2012 they celebrated their 110 year anniversary.

In 2013 Triumph began experiencing significant growth around the world, especially in Europe. There has been healthy growth in American sales as well. In the early 2000s world sales were in the low 30,000 units per year range, but by 2011 numbers had risen to nearly 50,000 motorcycles being sold yearly. American sales are just under the 10,000 unit per year level.

Several years ago (around 2014) Triumph was rated as the motorcycle with fewest warranty problems, lower than even the Japanese motorcycles. That is a significant statement to make. I have interviewed numerous modern Triumph owners, and all have stated that their motorcycles were trouble-free. One man with an early Bonneville America, which he had owned for over thirteen years, stated that he has had no mechanical problems at all. Triumph has been growing the right way as a quality motorcycle. I think the future looks good for this re-energized company.

BMW motorcycles, Germany's world motorcycle, has done well since the turn of the twenty-first century. Sales began to see significant improvement from 2004. In that year, the K series of in-line fours was radically redesigned. The boxer series received a redesign in 2005, and the F and G series were redesigned in 2006. Every model of motorcycle within their lineup has been completely updated.

There was a shift from stodgy touring bikes to sporty, high-performance, and easy to use machines. BMW has included state of the art electronics called the

Can-Bus" system in their motorcycles after 2005. With advanced GPS, electronic ride control, traction control, and fly-by-wire throttle systems, BMW became one of the most advanced motorcycles available for sale.

After the inclusion of the S1000RR sport bike, the absolute fastest sport bike made in 2010, the image of the company has changed. The S1000RR model was offered in 2010, the naked version was offered in 2014, and the S1000XR model was offered in 2016. The XR model is a blend of sport bike with dirt bike influences, similar to what is called a "motard."

BMW 1000RR, From the author's collection

In 2012 the transverse in-line six, the K1600GT, was offered as a premium touring machine. The café racer model, called the "R Nine T," made its debut in 2014.

When the original R Nine T motorcycle was offered, many of the BMW dealerships sold out quickly, and buyers had to wait for the next season.

BMW was known as a high-end, niche, limited market specialty motorcycle which sold in low numbers. By the 1980s, BMW motorcycle sales in the US were almost always under or around 5,000 units per year. BMW was a very low volume manufacturer. By the early 1990s, BMW was still a low volume manufacturer, selling around 4,000 motorcycles per year in the US. After the 2000s, however, sales began to see a spike. By 2010, world sales were in the 98,000+ range, with US sales being around 11,000 machines sold per year. In 2014 world sales numbers had reached close to 123,500 units.

Around 15,000 motorcycles were sold in the US. There is little doubt that these numbers will continue to grow. Sales have continued to climb in 2016 and 2017. BMW has moved from a company building specialty motorcycles to popular main-line machines. The newer products which they have been developing have been received well and have likewise sold well. For example, BMW took the GS series, the first true dual-sport motorcycles, and have continued to update them so that they have not only maintained their market but have built on it. It was reported that BMW has built over 600,000 GS series bikes over the models first thirty years of production. This is a sign of a company that knows how to develop its machines for the marketplace.

KTM is an Austrian-based motorcycle company that has moved from being relatively unknown to being a much higher profile company.

KTM's history can be traced back to the 1951 R100 motorcycle, powered by a Rotax engine. The company remained small until the early 1970s, when they were producing around 10,000 motorcycles per year.

It was John Penton, the well-known American off road racer, who brought the company over to the US. KTM was a small builder of bicycles, scooters, and smaller motor-cycles, typically using engines made by other companies. Penton paid the company to build the motorcycles he wanted, which were to be used primarily for racing. The motorcycles were so successful that KTM wanted to use his name to promote their motorcycles. Penton sold the motorcycles as the US distributor, and this is where KTM and the US motorcycle market intersect.

KTM built Penton motorcycles from 1968 to 1978, at which time the market was so low that the brand was discontinued. KTM first started building the Duke series in 1994, which has become one of their most successful series. The company currently builds motorcycles from 50cc to 1290cc. Most of their motorcycles ride on trellis-type frames and are typically known as race-bred machines.

KTM Duke, Manufacturer's promotional photo

The big story is how this small company, having been bankrupt in 1991, evolved from a junior manufacturer to one which can compete with the best. One article referred to the company as a giant-killer. According to a KTM source, in 2012 the company sold 107,142 motorcycles. In 2014 KTM built approximately 154,800 motorcycles worldwide and had a fourteen-percent increase in sales over the next year This represents almost 181,000 machines in 2015. Quite an impressive record for a four-year period.

KTM exported around 16,000 motorcycles to the US in 2015, with numbers growing yearly. Furthermore, at the time of this writing, KTM owns Husquvarna motorcycles, having purchased the brand in 2012.

This organization exhibits what makes a company grow, by creating really well-engineered motorcycles and making sound financial decisions. KTM builds machines with high build-quality and makes machines which are exciting. Having performance which matches or exceeds its competitors is certainly not a value negative either. This will be a company to watch.

Ducati has become one of the most prestigious motorcycle brands in the US. The brand has also shown continual growth in the twenty-first century. Best known for their truly beautiful sport bikes, their largest sales segment has been with the Monster series. The Diavell series has also

been a great seller in the US since 2011. Since 2015, however, the new Scrambler models have taken the front seat.

In 2006 Ducati sold around 35,300 motorcycles worldwide, and by 2011 world sales jumped to a little over 42,200 motorcycles. The 2015 sales figures were in the 54,800 unit per year range. Sales in the US have continued to experience strong growth of around ten percent per year. The sales of the Monster and Scrambler amount to nearly half of all Ducati sales.

Ducati Panigale 1099, manufacturer's promotional photo

In that US motorcycle sales have been rising at a rate around or under three percent per year for the past several years, Ducati has been well above the sales curve. Ducati has been selling around 15,000 motorcycles in the US since 2014, with numbers growing nearly every year. As Ducati growth figures continue to move upward and their motorcycles have been reaching a larger audience, it will be interesting to see how long this trend can continue. Without question,

Ducati has become one of the most prestigious brands of motorcycles sold in the US.

A few niche brands have started to pick up dealerships but are still very small market brands.

Ural, a vintage Russian BMW, has developed a market, though very small. The India-based Royal Enfield has grown in presence as well.

Royal Enfield was a very old British company which contracted an Indian company to build their 350 and 500cc Bullet singles in India in 1955. They continued doing so after the parent company went bankrupt in 1970. Small numbers were imported to the US after 1995, but after 2014, major changes were made to make the motorcycle more marketable. In 2015 they offered a 535cc Café Racer which is more modern than previous models and very good looking—a true vintage motorcycle.

Another specialty brand is the US-made Motus V-4 sport touring motorcycle. Several American motorcycle enthusiasts conceived of and designed a fully modern sport motorcycle in 2006, which was finally produced in 2015. The idea was to design the engine after half a small-block Chevy engine to create a V-4. The motorcycles are top quality and sound really good. I hope the best for this company.

There are a few other small American manufacturers of two-wheeled machines, such as Rokon, the builders of off road utility machines. The Rokon has been popular with farmers and people who are not typically motorcycle buyers. Rokon has built machines in low numbers since the 1950s.

Since the twenty-first century several major motorcycle brands known in the US have been discontinued. The most notable has been the Buell brand.

Buell 1125R, From the author's collection

Erik Buell started his company in 1983 and, as noted earlier, was brought into the Harley-Davidson fold in 1993. The Motor Company dropped the brand in 2009. Several financial groups, including the India-based company Hero Honda, picked the brand up again. Buell went into liquidation again in 2016. Buell has been down three different times and was able to find a way back from insolvency, so who knows what could happen in the future.

The Victory brand was started by Polaris Industries in 1998 and continued until

2017. When Polaris purchased the Indian brand in 2011 there were questions as to how the two brands would be integrated. It was announced in 2017 that Polaris did not want to finance and develop two separate brands of motorcycles, so the Victory line was dropped.

There have been a number of other manufacturers which have gone by the wayside that were not American brands. The East German company MZ (Motorenwerke Zschopau), later known as MuZ motorcycles, was one of the oldest existing motorcycle brands. MZ was started in 1906 and continued until around 2013.

MZ actually has had a long history of racing successes and innovations, primarily in Europe. The company exported motorcycles into the US in small quantities after WWII and until around 2008. After that date, there were motorcycles sold in the US but in numbers you could count on your hands.

MZ Scorpion, From the author's collection

MZ was never a mass-marketer in the US, always being sold in small numbers. Like many smaller companies, they struggled with their finances and went bankrupt in both 1993 and 2012. MZ did not last much beyond 2013.

MZ used Rotax and Yamaha singles. The brand was best known for its single-cylinder motorcycles which were generally utilitarian in nature. The glory days for MZ in the US was in the 1970s, when the company was selling around 60,000 motorcycles worldwide. The final models sold in the US were the 1000SF sport bike and the Skorpion singles, which used a Yamaha engine.

What occurred in the early years of the motorcycle was hundreds of backyard innovators building simple motorcycles. These builders often used their name as the brand. Nowadays high development and building costs make the venture very expensive. Insurance liability, warranty costs, and the costs of marketing inhibits the new development of a brand. The ability to import a motorcycle brand into the US is also very costly.

A little known Oregon-based motorcycle company was the Moto Czysz, designed by and built by Michael Czysz. Mister Czysz was the American version of John Britton. Czysz used two-stroke and four-stroke engines but is best known for his electric Moto GP motorcycle. The brand was known for its technology but will, no doubt, no longer be developed because of Mr. Czysz's untimely death in May of 2016.

Czysz Electric Racer

This was an example of what can be done with little money but a lot of enthusiasm, commitment, and innovation. The Moto Czysz was a great experiment but was just not feasible as a production motorcycle.

In the last chapter we discussed the "chopper bubble," which occurred sometime between the early to mid-1990s to around 2005. Custom and specialty motorcycles have always been around, and each time period in motorcycle history has featured a new expression of this type of machine. A new development of this nature is occurring in the twenty-first century.

Sometime after the early 2000s, very expensive, custom, low-production, specialty motorcycle brands began to emerge. Most were based on very limited production and sales models. There were four general incarnations of these specialty motorcycles. These motorcycles were generally based on either "super" high-performance motorcycles, through extreme technical innovations of some sort, a vintage pedigree, or exclusiveness from low-volume or a very high price. Some may include several of these categories in one machine.

Under the category of "super high-performance" motorcycles are the Kawasaki H2, H2 Carbon, and H2R. These motorcycles are very limited-edition models, with the R model not being street legal. All are liter in engine size and have very high-horsepower supercharged engines. The H2s claim actual horsepower to be 250, and the R is over 310 horsepower. The H2 was listed at $28,000, the H2 Carbon at $31,000, and the R at $55,000. A road test of the H2 indicated that it would go from 0-100 in 4.96 seconds, 0-150 in 9.41 seconds, and 0-180 in 16.04 seconds (*Cycle World*, September 2015). Another article suggested that the R version could reach the 250 mph barrier. These are pretty fast figures. For this level of performance, the price is not excessive.

Kawasaki H2R, Manufacturer's promotional photo

Honda has offered a limited-edition of their GP race bike, less the exotic engine drive train and estimated $300,000 transmission. It is called the RC213V and is priced at $184,000. This motorcycle is more of a show bike than actual race bike and has a mere 100 horsepower engine. Although not a high horsepower machine, the factory racer can be tuned to well over 250 horsepower, depending on what is required by the owner. The price alone will make it a limited-edition motorcycle. The motorcycle is a showcase of performance and technology, with high horsepower kits being offered in other countries. A dealer told me that the purchaser of a RC213V will get the bike delivered in its own trailer with a personal set up crew.

Honda RC213V, Courtesy Honda Racing

The reborn British Norton Motorcycle Company is offering the V4SS and RR models. The SS has a claimed weight of 395 pounds, and the engine delivers a claimed 200+ horsepower from a 1200cc V-4. The SS has a carbon-fiber body, while the RR has a chrome-plated finish. It is a real beauty, with only 200 SSs being offered for sale at $34,800 and the RR at $54,700—a real specialty motorcycle with a long lineage of racing motorcycles.

Norton V4, Courtesy Norton Motorcycles

Another British company, Spirit, is making the GP Sport R model, a superlight 750cc triple, based on a modified Triumph 675 three-cylinder engine. The motorcycle claims to have 180 horsepower, and weight is a mere 309 pounds. At $72,000 it is both exclusive and very innovative. A beauty indeed.

Vyrus, Manufacturer's promotional photo

The Italian Vyrus has been a custom builder for several decades, but its 987 C34V sport bike is unique because of its "swingarm, push rod" front suspension. The Vyrus 987 uses a Ducati 1200cc V-twin engine, which is claimed to produce 211 horsepower. Claimed weight is around 350 pounds, and it is a custom-built bike from a do-

Spirit GP R, Manufacturer's promotional photo

nor bike. Price is a little over $91,000. It does not look like a typical sport bike, but what a way to recycle a motorcycle.

These specialty performance motorcycles all claim high horsepower, low weight, and are filled with advanced technologies. A few brands have been around for decades, like the Italian LCR brand. With the LCR the sales numbers are growing, and prices are going way up.

The second list of examples tout "technical innovations" as their primary forte. As with the previous list, technical prowess was certainly important, but this list places usability at a greater premium. The Honda RC213V is an example of a motorcycle that could be in any of the three specialty categories: high performance, advanced technology, or the category of being exclusive. The first example that will be specifically used is the American-made Motus. The Motus is a V-4 sport touring motorcycle that is 1650cc in size. Claimed horsepower is 165, and prices are in the $32,000 to $38,000 range, depending on the model chosen. Motus claims their goal was to build a first-rate American motorcycle that is sophisticated at every level. They wanted to build an American motorcycle for American touring riders with classic lines. The engine is called the "Baby

Block." The motorcycle looks like a number of sport touring motorcycles currently available but is thirty to forty percent higher in price. It is fully modern, advanced in technology, and pricey. Time will tell if the buyer is willing to pay the price.

Confederate, manufacturer's promotional photo

Confederate Motorcycle company builds quirky but truly unique motorcycles. Their first series of custom motorcycles date from 1999 to 2007 and was called the "Hellcat." There were three versions of the Hellcat up until 2015. Other models included the Wraith, built from 2007 to 2009; the Fighter, from 2009 to 2011; and the Combat Fighter, until 2015. Most of the motorcycles used modified Harley-Davidson engines, and the newest model uses the S&S X Wedge engine. They were called "industrial and mechanical" in design, and, in my opinion, more artsy than revolutionary. From what I could derive, there were approximately 750

Hellcats built from 1996 to 2013, so production numbers are small. The newest model was the X13 two-speedster, priced at $65,000. Having looked closely at their basic models at the Barber Vintage Festival several years ago, they do look very industrial and appear to not be comfortable motorcycles to ride. Prices are from $65,000 to over $120,000. These motorcycle may actually become very collectible machines in half a century.

There is an increasing number of reborn specialty "vintage motorcycles" using historic brand names—Ariel, AJS, Brough Superior, Francis-Barnett, Crocker, Hesketh, Horex,

Hesketh X Wedge, courtesy of Hesketh Motorcycles

Matchless, Norton, Rickman-Matisse, Royal Enfield, and Vincent, to name a few. From what I have heard, there is also a new Cushman Scooter company producing new scooters. Some of these brands may not be imported to America, like the Francis-Barnett or Rickmans were. The buyer will have to bring the motorcycle to America himself. The German Horex will be imported in very small numbers, and motorcycles like the British Ariel, Brough Superior, and Hesketh, may be imported on-demand only. Brands like the Royal Enfield are currently being imported with an attempt at making them more mainstream brands. The Vincent name has been used for many years through the Egli group and appears to be currently built on-demand. A California resident and Vincent enthusiast, Bernard Li, built modern Vincent motorcycles between 2002 and 2008, which was the year of his death. Li's Vincent used a Honda RC51 engine and sold for over $50,000 dollars. They were called "Roush Vincents" and are very rare. Ten of the twelve revived brands listed above were British in origin. This indicates the interest in these old names and the value placed on these specific brands. Nearly all of these motorcycles are very expensive, except the Royal Enfield and Norton Commandos (except the V-4 models).

Egli Vincent, From the author's collection

The last general category is the "custom or exclusive" motorcycle category. These motorcycles are meant to be exclusive models marketed as prestige-oriented machines. They are not necessarily better, faster, or technically advanced, just expensive, exclusive, or custom. There are currently at least several dozen custom chopper/bobber builders who have been around for years. The difference between these manufacturers and those who built the customs during the

"chopper bubble" is that they do not sell them as a brand with a VIN number. They just build low-volume custom motorcycles on-demand. These companies will not be discussed because they represent a specialty market which has been around since the 1960s. They also tend to be regional in nature and generally survive as service and parts depots as well. There is no doubt that many of the people and companies who built small brands of custom motorcycle twenty years ago currently survive as specialty motorcycle fabricators. Since around 2000, there have been many modern specialty bikes made available in low numbers.

At the top of the list would be the Harley-Davidson CVO models. The Custom Vehicle Operation models are modified standard motorcycles with a thirty-percent price tag premium added to the top. The CVOs generally include a limited number of specific models, have a larger engine, will have a few special billet parts, and always have special paint. A CVO is the top of the line motorcycle with all the options. The CVO is offered as a prestige model to show off the owners success.

Another example of an exclusive motorcycle is the KRGT-1 billet motorcycle, made by Arch. Priced at a little over $78,000, this motorcycle was the brain child of actor Keanu Reeves of Hollywood fame. The main idea is that the motorcycle appears very custom and has a sort of café racer look. Another goal is to make the motorcycles comfortable, like a feet-forward cruiser. The owner can get the best of three

Reeves KRGT

worlds, that of being an exclusive custom, having usable high performance, and a motorcycle that can be ridden and enjoyed. The engine is an S&S 124 cubic-inch (2032cc) unit with a six-speed transmission. The motorcycle is also designed to be modern, safe, and functional. The motorcycle is a true custom and is essentially handmade. The KRGT-1 is, without a doubt, a custom and prestige motorcycle that could fit into at least three of the categories noted above.

The Ipothesys V-12 Café Racer designed in Italy is a truly beautiful motorcycle. Priced around $45,000, it is built from a Moto Guzzi transverse V-twin motorcycle. The idea was to transform an already beautiful motorcycle into a unique art object. The motorcycle is a modern classic

that stands out as a custom, a unique motorcycle, and one which is exclusive. The Italians definitely have an eye for beauty.

Ipothesys V12 Café Racer, Courtesy Ipothesys Motorcycles

An extreme example of the limited production custom motorcycle would be the Ecosse FE Ti XX, of which only ten were said to be built. Priced at $300,000 in 2011, the motorcycle is the epitome of exclusiveness. With an OHV V-twin engine, however, it is certainly not breaking any design boundaries. With the exotic metals used in its construction and, no doubt, being totally hand-built, the price is justified primarily by its exclusiveness.

Ecosse FE Ti XX, Courtesy of Ecosse Motorworks

There are many other specialty motorcycles that will fit into one or several of these categories and reflect the motorcycle renaissance going on in the twenty-first century. Check out the Lotus C-01 Superbike, the MTT Turban Superbike, the Icon Sheen 1400 Superbike priced at $175,000, or the Ducati Testa Stretta NCR Macchi Nera priced at $225,000. Possibly the most expensive motorcycle ever made available for sale was the Ecosse Spirit ES 1, priced at $3,600,000. For more unique motorcycles check out the 410 cubic-inch Gunbus, priced at $350,000, or one of the unique Millyard motorcycles. Millyard is best known for his Viper V10, his four-cylinder vintage Kawasaki 850 two-stroke, and the huge Flying Millyard, a 5,000cc V-twin motorcycle. The list goes on, but what is certain is that when creativity, art, technology, and the motorcycle meet, some really interesting machines are created.

5000cc Flying Millyard, Courtesy of Allen Millyard

Since the twenty-first century, motorcycles have been sold in more specific categories than in the past. Certainly, there have always been different size, model, and type categories, but of late, these market segments have become more refined and defined. The general lineup will typically be:

Touring
Bagger
Sport Touring
Cruiser
Power Cruiser
Super Sport
Sport
Naked/Vintage
Adventure
Dual-Sport
Off-Road (on- and off-road models and/or motocross)

Honda Gold Wing GL1800, From the author's collection

A touring motorcycle will almost always be a large motorcycle designed for long-distance highway use. A bagger will be a large motorcycle with built in bags and/or additional storage space. Baggers are almost always touring motorcycles.

Yamaha FJR1300, From the author's collection

A cruiser is a feet-forward motorcycle, typically a V-twin. The cruiser is designed for looks, comfort, and sometimes touring.

Harley-Davidson Road King, From the author's collection

Sport touring machines are a blend of sport and touring motorcycles. The Yamaha FJ series or Honda ST series are typical examples.

Suzuki Boulevard, From the author's collection

The power cruiser is a high-horsepower cruiser, like the Yamaha V-Max.

Moto Guzzi V7, Manufacturer's promotional photo

Yamaha V-Max, From the author's collection

Super sport motorcycles are almost always in 1000cc and 600cc capacities. The Suzuki Hyabusa and Kawasaki XZ1400R are exceptions. Sport models are lower-horsepower sport bikes and often do not have fairings.

Honda CBR1000, form the author's collection

Naked or vintage motorcycles typically have no fairing and are often designed to look like motorcycles of earlier times. The café racer look has become more common.

Adventure motorcycles are typically larger motorcycles used for long-distance travel, like the BMW GS series.

The dual-sport motorcycles are typically like the scramblers of the 1960s and '70s, though better-suited for off-road work than thieir predecessors were. There can be an adventure/dual-sport blend in bikes, like the Honda Africa Twin. They are motorcycles designed for occasional off-road use and are also potential long-distance machines as well. The original BMW GS series and the older scramblers were the inspiration for these models.

Off-road motorcycles are designed to be light and used in off-road settings, which may include racing. There is another general category called

Honda Africa Twin, Manufacturer's promotional photo

the "motard." Motard racing includes three surfaces on which the rider must compete. These include hard road surfaces, dirt track surfaces, and semi-rough terrain surfaces. Some brands mix an off-road model with some qualities found in a true motard machine.

2016 KTM 450SX, Courtesy KTM

As noted before, most of these categories existed before going back at least thirty years. The difference is that lines of demarcation are more clear and manufacturers generally market their products within these categories in more intentional ways. The exception is when a brand does not cover many categories or builds motorcycles within a specific category. As the sport continues, more varieties will be developed and will generally stem from a previous type of motorcycle.

Just a comment about electric motorcycles. The concept of an electric motorcycle goes back to the pre-1900 period but never materialized because of weight and potential travel distance. These continue to be the big hurdles, which limit the range of the electric motorcycle. Through the decades, electric motorcycles have been tested but have yet to become financially viable. Since the late 1980s, there has been an increase in research, but they were primarily novelties. Since the early twenty-first century, there have been a number of companies offering electric motorcycles, but none have yet to catch on in a big way. I have only seen one electric motorcycle on the street, ever.

The primary brands have been Zero, the Polaris Empulse, the Yamaha PES (street) and PED (off-road) models, the Alta, the Harley-Davidson Live Wire, and the BMW eRR. I have also come across a number of little companies that are experimenting with electric vehicles, but little can be found out about the companies. Most of these motorcycles are experimental models and not yet for sale to the public. Most of the tests note that travel distances are in the under-150 mile range, which means the rider would typically be limited to seventy-five miles one way. Until there is a demand for electric motorcycles, products will be limited and experimental in nature only. Having worked for an

automobile auction house at one time, I had interviewed a number of new and used car dealers and found that they saw no demand from the public for electric cars. They did not buy electric cars, nor saw a market for them. The big complaint was that the batteries can be recharged only a few hundred times, and after that they need to be replaced. Batteries can also only last for a limited number of years until they require replacement. This is apart from the number of times they have been re-charged. After an estimated ten or so years and 300/400 times of being recharged, they require replacement, which makes the vehicle no longer financially marketable. A ten-year old car needing a battery replacement costing $5,000 dollars or more (at the minimum), in fact, has no viable market. The same would be true with a motorcycle. A $15,000 electric motorcycle becoming ten year old, then needing a battery replacement costing over $2,000, would not be cost-effective. There would be little market for the machine, unless the demands of the consumer changed. Beyond that, recycling the batteries is also very expensive and cost prohibitive. Until a universal battery that could be used in either cars or motorcycles is made available, replacement costs would be exceptionally high. Furthermore, batteries would need to be able to be changed or charged very quickly and would need to last about double the current lifespan in order for the product to be viable. I am not wanting to appear as though I am opposed to the electric motorcycle; I just don't see much interest level in the US yet. Perhaps the battery-powered vehicle will have its day, but that time has not yet come. I could envision that a purely utilitarian electric motorcycle, designed for primarily urban use, and a machine with mostly universal parts (especially the batteries), could become desirable and practical.

There are some basic changes within the motorcycle community that can be generally charted as being more significant since 2000. Note the following:

The motorcycle continues to evolved incrementally.

Motorcycle engines are generally getting larger. (This is true, even though there is a renewed interest in smaller motorcycles.)

More individual motorcycle models are being made available. Over 500 different models of motorcycles were available to the consumer in the American market after 2014.

New forms of electronics are being offered on more mo- torcycles, especially since 2005.

ABS brakes are becoming more common and are being offered on more motorcycles.

Dual-sport motorcycles have been around for decades, but after 2010, the growth of this market has become huge.

Horsepower ratings have exploded, with 150+ figures becoming more common. Numerous bikes claim 200 horsepower figures.

There are more electric motorcycles on the market, but sales have not yet caught on.

More motorcycles have been designed and built for the world market, rather than specific regional markets.

Since 2012, smaller motorcycles are more in vogue, especially in the 300cc categor: Honda CBR300 and F models, Kawasaki 300, BMW 310 R, Yamaha YZF 3, KTM 390.

Honda GB500, From the author's collection

There continues to be a market for motorcycles that have been influenced by vintage models since the Honda GB500 of 1989/1990: the Kawasaki W 650, Honda CB1100,

Yamaha SR400, Moto Guzzi S9, Ducati Monster, Harley-Davidson Sportster 48 and Roadster, Triumph Bonneville, or the new Norton Commando 961. The Kawasaki Drifter series and Indian Chief certainly look to the past as well. Vintage retro is a huge draw.

There has been a growth in the vintage motorcycle segment, with the interest in collecting, restoring, and showing old motorcycles being on the rise. This is true especially in the Japanese motorcycle category.

The impact of Amazon, eBay, and the general Internet business has grown immensely and has included parts, accessories, some services, insurance, and even motorcycle sales, new, used, and vintage.

There has been an increase in electronic developments, like GPS systems, drive by wire, heated seats and handgrips, stereo systems, et cetera.

The comments noted above generally outline the changes in the motorcycle since 2000. I am sure that I have certainly missed something but think that my list is at least fairly complete. Without a doubt, there have been significant changes in the sport of motorcycling since 2000. Most of the changes have been in growing technology, more so than with external appearances. Engine sizes and horsepower are on

the rise. Everything is now fuel-injected. Advanced electronics and GPS are everywhere. The US is no longer a major market. Over fifteen million motorcycles were manufactured around the world in 2016, with the US buying fewer than 500,000 of them. The century had started with healthy motorcycle sales, but after 2008 sales had fallen to around a half-million. In 2005 sales were over a million units, double what they have been recently! The age of the average rider has increased to the fifties, and there is little indication that younger people are getting into the sport. It is estimated that there are around thirty motorcycle manufacturers around the world that are not seen in America, located primarily in China, India, and Taiwan. There is a wider variety of models available than ever before. Specialty and limited edition motorcycles are on the rise, and finally, retro-styled motorcycles have come into the marketplace much more strongly since 2014.

As far as the future of the motorcycle in America, my hunch is that the changes will continue to be incremental as they have for the past over seventy years. Unless more young people come to the sport, motorcycling will become the activity of middle-age and older Americans.

Chapter 8

The Motorcycles That Have Defined the Sport

Icons of the Industry

This chapter will cover a few of the most significant motorcycles throughout the history of the sport. These are motorcycles that have either led through innovation and design, have greatly increased the popularity of a motorcycle, or impacted important developments of the motorcycle going forward. I want to make a disqualifier regarding the machines which I have chosen to represent this part of motorcycle development. Every knowl-edgeable motorcycle historian or enthusiast will have different machines that they would pick and put in their own list. I have attempted to pick only the most significant machines that represent some form of important impact within the history of the motorcycle in America. Hundreds of motorcycles could be chosen that would be great examples. The motorcycles in this list are simply the ones that I have chosen. There could be endless arguments as to which bikes best represent the most important machines, but not all can be represented in such a short list. Someday, I will put together a more comprehensive list of machines, which would more completely satisfy the subject of this topic. Let me note the criteria which I have used to determine what bikes should be on this list.

Motorcycles which have greatly influenced motorcycle development in general.

Motorcycle developments which have led to the popularity of the motorcycle.

A motorcycle which was copied by many other manufacturers.

A particular motorcycle or specific development within a specific motorcycle that started a future trend in the sport that has been seen as significant over time.

Motorcycles which have been inspirational within the motorcycle community.

A motorcycle that has stood far above most of its peers as a really good example of a machine.

I will begin with a header noting the specific motorcycle or circumstance that was important to the development of the motorcycle, then I will list why I chose the particular machine as an example.

Hildebrand & Wolfmuller

Hildebrand & Wolfmuller, Courtesy Barber Vintage Motorsports Museum

The first mass-produced motorcycle, though built in very small quantities compared to modern motorcycles today, was the Hildebrand & Wolfmuller.

The 1894 Hildebrand & Wolfmuller four-stroke twin was the first manufactured and marketed motorcycle available to the general public. The first prototype H&W was a steam vehicle, which was built several years before the internal-combustion model was designed. The rear wheel was driven by locomotive-type connecting rods. Primarily built in Germany, some sources also list Paris, France, as a potential factory location. The machine was a 1490cc flat-twin that was water-cooled and produced around two-and-a-half horsepower. Without a dynamometer output that would only be an educat-

ed guess. Most articles state that around 2,000 were built, though some sources state that many more were built. Whatever the case, few exist today, and the few which have been sold at market have brought astronomical prices.

Having read dozens of articles about the H&W, they were found to be unreliable and temperamental to operate. This would certainly be understandable, considering the limits of technology of that day. One article noted that so many were returned to the factory the company went bankrupt. It would have been unlikely that any machine built prior to 1900 would be reliable and easy to operate. The Hildebrand & Wolfmuller was a ground-breaking machine well in front of the transportation market and worthy of recognition.

The de Dion-Buton Engine

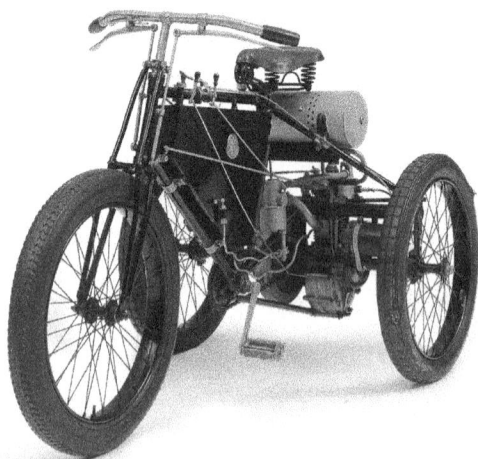

De Dion-Buton 3-Wheeler

The de Dion-Buton engine had the greatest impact on motorcycle production and development than any other early engine built at that time, and led to the start of dozens of individual motorcycle brands prior to 1905.

The de Dion-Buton company was also a leader in early automotive development, and their core engine design was so solid that many simply copied it. Count de Dion sold the rights to build his engine to other companies under contract, but many just copied the basic plan without paying the royalties due the company. Because they were foreign companies, funds could not easily be collected. Furthermore, one company would copy the basic design, then another company would copy the one who copied the original design. This made it hard for de Dion to collect royalties.

The 1897 de Dion-Buton single-cylinder engine, which originally powered a three-wheeled trike, was the design which was the backbone of hundreds of motorcycle brands thereafter. The design was simple, reliable, and light. Count de Dion and his brother-in-law, Georges Buton, began their collaboration in the early 1880s and worked with both steam and internal-combustion engines.

Their plan was to build whatever vehicles could be most marketable. The bikes were sold first, then automobiles were built and sold as early as 1899. As Count de Dion marketed his three-wheelers, cars, and engines, they were early innovators who were not only respected but were very successful. They were actually best known for their early cars. The little 133cc four-stroke engine was especially popular with the builders of two-wheeled vehicles because of the light weight, low build costs, and basic reliability. Within a decade, it was the most copied internal-combustion engine used on motorcycles. Even though there were many engines built after this early unit, the little De Dion-Buton was the blueprint that became the standard.

Engines on Bicycle Frames

The first brands of motorcycles manufactured for public sale began after 1900 and were marketed as engines on a bicycle frame. Most were sold primarily through bicycle dealers or small machine-type shops. This new industry of self-powered vehicles included either two, three, or four wheels and was so new that early growth was minimal and was generally regional in nature. It was around 1908, or possibly earlier, that growth began to occur in more mar-

Indian Camelback, Courtesy of Barber Vintage Motorsports Museum

ketable directions, and development did not slow down as progress was made going forward. Even as late as 1910, there were some who thought that the horse would make a comeback, but they were wrong.

The first motorcycle manufacturers were geared for selling a product, rather than building a brand. What I mean by that statement is this: the market for trucks, cars, or motorcycles was so new that there were no clearly identifiable market groups. There were electric taxicabs in New York City, and a few large cities were beginning to use electric-, steam-, or gasoline-powered trucks, but as a rule, self-propelled vehicles were very new and not standardized. To be accurate, there were a few companies that were developing product lines for specific tasks, but this was a very new business and was, therefore, generally undeveloped. Later, brand building certainly did occur. At first, self-powered vehicles were just the rage in larger cities until interest grew outward to rural areas. Early companies popped up, then disappeared just as quickly as they began. The Indian Motorcycle Company is an example of one of the earliest companies to innovate and succeed in their endeavors as a company, building a specific product for a specific customer.

I will not revisit the history of Indian Motorcycles, but the Indian Motorcycle Company produced the first generally successful mass-produced motorcycle, which was the template for dozens of other motorcycle companies to copy. There were earlier brands, like the Orient and Marks, which were built and sold, but their machines sold in dozens, while the Indian sold by the hundreds. Rather than build a dedicated factory for his motorcycles, which he did later, he contracted the Aurora Automatic Machine Company to build most of the vital parts needed to produce his earliest machines. Many companies copied the Indian blueprints through the Aurora company, which apparently sold many Indian-designed parts to an array of other manufacturers. Most of those who copied Indian failed to develop a stable business and were short lived. George Hendee, having built a very successful bicycle racing career and bicycle manufacturing business, wanted to add to his fortunes by adding this new technology to his product line. He was able to build success upon success by using his bicycle dealers to sell his motorcycles. He also set up independent motorcycle dealers as well. By entering the market early, using his name recognition, by building a good product, and by building a dealership network, Indian succeeded early as a motorcycle business.

The point is this: Indian was building a market for their machines and did not seem too terribly concerned about protecting their parts designs. Patent protection was to become a much greater issue later as more machines were built to compete with each other. By 1913, Indian was building over 32,000 motorcycles yearly and became the largest motorcycle manufacturer in the world. The Indian Camelback became the leader in sales, racing, technology, and name recognition. These qualities have made the Indian motorcycle the best, the earliest, and the most copied of the early machines.

1901 Werner

er 1901

The 1901 Werner motorcycle was one of the most innovative motorcycles in the early years of the industry. The Werner brothers, Michel and Eugene, were early builders and innovators in the new motorcycle industry. They were originally from Russia and operated in both England and France. Their first machine was the 1897 Motorcyclette, which used the front wheel as the driving wheel. They were one of the first to build a dedicated motorcycle frame, rather than using a bicycle frame. In the frame designed for their new 1901 motorcycle, they moved the engine to the base of the frame, where it essentially has remained to this day. This could be called the first "cradle" frame. They also revised the de Dion-Buton engine for their own motorcycle use, wanting to produce all necessary parts in-house. Both Werner brothers had died before 1910 and had left a significant mark on the development of the motorcycle. The Werner was a state-of-the-art motorcycle, being the first, or one of the very earliest motorcycles, to reflect the standard form to come. The cradle frame, possibly the first twist-grip throttle, their commitment to build a reliable and trouble-free motorcycle (for their day), and their total commitment to forward thinking innovation, all make their 1901 motorcycle a ground-breaker, which led, rather than followed, other manufacturers.

1904 FN

FN Inline 4, Courtesy of Yesterday's Antique and Classic Motorcycles

The 1904 FN in-line four was a shaft-driven motorcycle that inspired the next generation of motorcycle builders.

FN, a company located in Belgium, was an innovator for decades. The in-line four-cylinder motorcycle started as a 360cc bike but was enlarged over the years to a 750. It also started as a single-speed machine but was upgraded to a two-speed, then three-speed motorcycle. Known for power and smoothness, the in-line engine was the first of its type. The FN was, no doubt, a significant influence on American manufacturers. As a very advanced motorcycle for its day, the FN was the fastest production motorcycle for years. The four-cylinder model was produced into the early 1920s and was a very influential machine. It is interesting that the basic format, four cylinders with shaft drive, became the standard three-quarters of a century later (except that the UJMs [*Universal Japanese Motorcycles*] used transverse four-cylinder engines).

The Flying Merkel

The Flying Merkel of the mid-teens was advanced in technology, performance, and looks.

Joseph Merkel began as a railroad engineer and ended as a motorcycle designer. His motorcycles were high-end machines that were as advanced as motorcycles got by the mid-teens. Merkel used ball bearings in his engines, as opposed to flat sleeves. He was one of the first to use an OHV engine, and he used an advanced spring front fork, which proceeded the telescopic fork of the late 1940s. He also designed a rear spring system far in advance of other manufacturers. He used the frame for an exhaust system on some bikes and also used oil in the frame on other models. He was the first to use a loop frame and his throttle engine oiler

Flying Merkel, From the author's collection

preceeded that of Harley-Davidson or Indian. Known as fast bikes, Flying Merkle machines were winners on the race tracks of the day as well. Using bright orange colors, they were easily identified. The Merkel was a superbike of the day, having a great influence on motorcycle development. Even the gasoline tank bending over the engine has been a significant image being copied for nearly a century.

Military Motorcycles

The motorcycle was first used by the military in the First World War in 1917. Prior to WWI, horses were primarily used for leading convoys, dispatching purposes, transporting freight, medical use, ammunition support, and general transportation purposes.

Prior to 1910, the US military had no policy to purchase motor vehicles for war use. By early 1914, however, the US Army had an estimated thirty-five trucks, twenty-seven cars, and three ambulances.

Indian 841 Military, From author's Indian History

From 1914 to 1918 the numbers grew to well over 50,000 vehicles. The WWI period brought motor vehicles to the forefront, and motorcycles were certainly included as being vitally important. The First World War brought the automobile, truck, tank, and motorcycle into the military to stay. The use of the horse was diminished and, by WWII, was almost gone. The motorcycle was seen as a good alternative for a number of reasons: First, the motorcycle could be stored in a much smaller area than the horse with almost no care being required. Horses required space, stables, food, farriers, and veterinarians. Furthermore, when a person rode a horse they were high in the air and an easy target. Horses would also not sit still for long periods of time, while a motorcycle could just be stopped and stored. In 1917 the motorcycle was still relatively unrefined but offered many advantages compared to the horse. The motorcycle, proved valuable during the war and by WWII, there was no question as to the value of the military motorcycle. In a sense, the motorcycle was tested in WWI and proved a worthy replacement for the horse. Furthermore, the same fuel could be used for the motorcycle, the truck, for generators, and for the tank. The best of motorcycle design was used for military motorcycles, with Indian and Harley-Davidson motorcycles being the primary machines being used for American military purposes. From other sources, Excelsior and Henderson motorcycles were also used but in much smaller numbers. Although by 1917 the automobile was growing significantly in sales far beyond that of the motorcycle, nevertheless, the motorcycle had found its place. The motorcycle was also used by other countries in larger numbers than in the American military. England used Triumph motorcycles, Panthers, Scotts, BSAs, Royal Enfield motorcycles, Matchless motorcycles, and Sunbeam motorcycles. They used other manufacturers in smaller numbers as well. Sweden actually used the FN four-cylinder motorcycle in their military.

Ner-A-Car

Ner-A-Car, period advertisement

The 1920s Ner-A-Car was an innovative machine crossing motorcycle, scooter, and utility vehicle lines.

The Ner-A-Car was built between 1921 and 1927. Around 10,000 were estimated to be manufactured. Designed by Carl A. Neracher in 1918, many referred to the vehicle as "nearly-a-car." The large front fender of the Ner-A-Car actually looked like a car fender. It may well be the first feet-forward motorcycle that allowed the driver to sit cruiser-style. His goal was to build a very usable, reliable, and comfortable mode of transportation that could be used by the masses. Neracher claimed that the vehicle could cruise at thirty-five mph and get a hundred miles per gallon of gasoline. The body was pressed steel, the brakes were hub type, and the steering was operated through a pivot-type center hub. Ner-A-Car motorcycles were produced in both the US and England. The US version used a small two-stroke engine, while the English version used a slightly larger 285cc two-stroke. The final versions used a 350cc Blackborne engine. Most sold in England because of the demand for utility transportation. Weighing around 175 pounds and costing around $225, it was actually only about a third less than the least expensive Ford Model T. The Ner-A-Car is important because it was an early attempt at building a very usable means of transportation, which was different from the typical motorcycle of the day. The Ner-A-Car looks very much like the modern scooter and was probably the first attempt at marketing a vehicle that was a mix between several different forms of transportation. The vehicle was the first to use metal stamping. The large front fender was designed to protect the rider from flying debris and it was possibly the first true feet-forward motorcycle.

1949 Harley-Davidson Hydra-Glide

1949 Harley-Davidson Hydra-Glide

The 1949 Harley-Davidson Hydra-Glide, named after the hydraulic front forks, established the large V-twin American motorcycle as the standard for appearance and design going forward. By the end of the 1940s Harley-Davidson was selling many more motorcycles than Indian.

Harley-Davidson saw their sales increase after WWII, while Indian began to drop from the picture. By 1953 Indian was gone, and the difference between the British motorcycles and American motorcycles was clear. The Hydra-Glide set the standard for looks and technology for American motorcycles for the next three decades. The profile of a current Harley-Davidson clearly appears similar to the 1949 Hydra-Glide. The resemblance is undeniable. The big V-twin is still the machine of choice for many American riders. The panhead engine was first available in 1948 but was made standard on the Hydra-Glide. The 1949 Hydra-Glide is an important motorcycle because it set the standard for American-built motorcycles going forward. Even today, the modern V-twin cruiser looks back at the image of the first Hydra-Glide. This bike is one of the most important motorcycle icons in the history of the American motorcycle.

DKW125

DKW125, H-D Hummer, Yamaha YA-1, and Others

The German DKW125 has been one of the most copied motorcycles of all time. Its basic design was so solid that it has served as a utility motorcycle, a military machine, a race bike, and a sales leader for many brands.

First designed in 1939, the little utilitarian 125cc single was a popular motorcycle because it was simple to build, was reliable, and was sturdy. The little 125 ran efficiently and was inexpensive. These are the same reasons why it was copied, apart from the fact that German technologies were freely given out as WWII reparations. Small factories could copy the design inexpensively, and the motorcycles were generally cheap to build. The simplicity of the design also made the machine generally reliable. Note the numerous copies of the RT125 made from around the world:

The list below is not complete, but versions of the little motorcycle could be seen into the mid-1960s. Although an ancient design for today, the little DKW was at one time the most copied motorcycle ever designed. What a compliment. Today, the early 1970s' Honda CB100 OHC single has become one of the most copied engines. China has built an industry on this basic engine design, making numerous variations of the same motor available around the world.

Royal Enfield Flying Flea
Yamaha YA-1
MMZ RT125
BSA Bantam
Harley-Davidson Hummer
Jawa 125
NSU 125
**Minck & Moskva M1 & K125
 (both Russian)**
Kawasaki 125
MiVal 125

The Vincents

1950s Vincent Black Shadow, From the author's collection

The Vincent Rapide and Black Shadow are two of the most well-known and respected motorcycles of all time. Having won many speed records of decades ago, as well as having a profile which cannot be confused with any other motorcycle, the Vincent continues to hold a legendary position within the vintage motorcycle community.

Previously known as the HRD (Howard R. Davies), the big V-twin was built to be the best and fastest motorcycle of its day. In 1948 the Black Shadow was considered to be the fastest production motorcycle. Phil Vincent purchased the bankrupt HRD company in the late 1920s and spent the next twenty-five years developing the brand. The famous engine began as a single-cylinder unit, and when an additional cylinder was added, the most famous V-twin version of the Vincent was born. From the post-WWII era to 1955, when production was discontinued, the Vincent was one of the most prestigious and identifiable brands. Vincent used the HRD name until he visited America and saw that his name was close to the H-D logo. He immediately switched from the former name to the Vincent name so there would be no confusion about the brands. Sometime towards the end of Indian motorcycles production run, the Indian company considered building a Vincent-powered Chief. This move may have saved both Indian and Vincent. The Vincent has become one of the most legendary motorcycles of all time, with its status growing rather than diminishing.

Triumph Bonneville

1969 Triumph Bonneville, From the author's collection

The Triumph Bonneville represented the ultimate sport motorcycle in its day, being known for its performance, looks and status as a popular and serious motorcycle.

The 1938 Triumph Speed Twin altered the British motorcycle industry by creating a fast, light, and low cost of production motorcycle. The Speed Twin was also reliable and powerful for its day. Within a dozen years after the introduction of the Speed Twin nearly every major British manufacturing company had made its copy of the basic engine. The big British motorcycle companies became known for their parallel-twin engines, just like the American manufacturers had become known for their V-twin engines. After being imported into the US after WWII (there were a few imported prior to that but not in large numbers), Americans clamored for a larger engine.

In 1953 Triumph created the 650 Tiger from the 500cc twin by increasing the bore and stroke. Just as the 500cc Triumph was a great race bike, the 650cc version did much better. The 650 version did well on the Bonneville Salt Flats, achieving speeds of 192 mph in 1955, 214 in 1956, and 224 in 1962. These high-speed motorcycles were fitted with an aerodynamic body. Because of this notoriety, Triumph named the twin carburetor version of the motorcycle the "Bonneville."

In 1963 the unit construction version was offered, and in the early 1970s the engine size was increased to 750cc and a five-speed transmission was also added.

The original 650 Bon-

nevilles were manufactured from 1959 to 1983. After suffering serious financial problems, to say the least, the Bonneville went back into production from 1985 to 1988. A completely new Bonneville was introduced in 2001. In 2016 a revised Bonneville in either 900cc or 1200cc versions, which was liquid cooled, was introduced. The 2016 version was designed to look much more like the 1960s' version of the Bonneville engine. This is a simple overview of the Bonneville's history, but as the reader can see, the Triumph Bonneville has a long and rich history. The Triumph Bonneville was a prestigious mount in its day and if you rode one it signaled that you were a serious rider. The Bonneville was also considered to be one of the most beautiful motorcycles ever made and was copied by many other companies. The Bonneville look has continued even today in some motorcycles.

Early Hondas

Honda motorcycles came to America in 1959 and offered primarily small machines. The 305cc Dreams, Super Hawks, and Scramblers were the largest motorcycles Honda made until 1965, when the CB450 was first made available. Of these three mod-

els, the Super Hawk became legendary as a super fast, race-ready, inexpensive, and durable motorcycle. The Super Hawk impressed the American rider with its looks and performance, and opened the door for the larger Japanese motorcycle in America.

Honda 250/305 Scrambler, Courtesy of Vintage and Custom Motorcycle Enthusiasts

The Super Hawk was available between 1961 and 1968 as a SOHC 305cc parallel-twin. Honda also offered a 250cc version called the "Hawk," but few of those were sold in the US. The Super Hawk was as fast as many 500cc British motorcycles, and as fast as a few 650s. The Super Hawk could run through the quarter-mile in the low eighty mph range and in the mid-sixteen second bracket. A well-tuned one could reach a genuine 100mph. This was fast for a 300cc machine in the early 1960s. They were also very reliable, didn't leak oil, and were generally not cantankerous. With electric starting and good brakes, they were stellar performers. Many did not like the fact that they were from Japan, but there were none that could successfully argue that they were not good machines, not fast, or not a great value. The Super Hawk and Scrambler versions of the 305s were very popular, selling what was available nearly as fast as Honda could produce them. They upped the ante on motorcycle design and called the bluff on brands that wanted to sell the same machines year after year. The Honda 305s left a mark on motorcycling, forcing other manufacturers to either make big changes or get out of the way. Many motorcycle companies went out of business within a decade after the Japanese motorcycles were brought to America. Other manufacturers were just forced to build better motorcycles in order to remain competitive. In this sense, that of raising the bar, Honda had one of the greatest impacts on the entire industry as a whole, which continues on even today.

Honda CB750

1969 Honda CB750, From the author's collection

The Honda CB750 was named the "Bike of the Century" by more than one source and is generally considered to be the first genuine superbike. Many writers make a line between pre- and post-CB750; the motorcycle was that influential.

The 1969 Honda CB750 was not the fastest motorcycle made, the largest motorcycle being built, or the most expensive motorcycle available to the public. It was, however, close to all those qualities at a lower price, while being much more refined than nearly anything else made at that time. The CB750 was a fast, well-made, attractive, very competitively priced motorcycle that could be considered the first truly modern motorcycle available to the general public in volume. With an in-line four-cylinder engine (which didn't leak oil), single overhead-camshaft engine, having a five-speed transmission, and very high build quality, the big Honda was several steps ahead of its competitors. I am currently aware of numerous CB750s being over forty-five years old and never requiring an engine overhaul or requiring significant maintenance work. Honda got it right with the CB750. Probably the greatest compliment that can be paid to the CB750 is that it was thoroughly modern, well-built, and offered a comfortable ride. A CB750 can keep up with the best, even today. The big Honda was truly a marvel in its day and deserves every accolade given to it. It truly deserves its place as a very important motorcycle within the history of the sport. The influence and impact of the big CB cannot be underestimated.

Harley-Davidson Superglide, From the author's collection

The 1971 Harley-Davidson FX Super Glide began as a factory custom, which continues as a trend in motorcycle manufacturing even today.

Many Harley-Davidson enthusiasts criticize the AMF years, which occurred from 1969 to 1981, but two very significant motorcycles came from this period. The 1971 FX Super Glide and the 1977 XLCR Café Racer were motorcycles that were designed and sold during the time that AMF owned the company. Willie G. Davidson designed them both, as he did the 1990 Fat Boy. Mister Davidson connected the Sportster series with the Big Twin series by mating the Sportster front end with the Big Twin frame and engine. The idea came from what customizers do; that is to mix and blend bikes and parts to achieve the desired look. The original version of the bike had a fiberglass boat-tail body that was not popular, but the bike appealed to the core customer of Harley-Davidson motorcycles and was a huge success. The FX stood for "factory experimental," but the parts were primarily parts-bin items, being readily available. This simple idea was already in the bloodstream of the Harley-Davidson enthusiast, but now they didn't have to own several motorcycles to build one. The custom was now on the showroom floor. The Triumph Hurricane X-75 is another example of an early factory custom, which was even more radical than the

Harley-Davidson FX. Because it was built in 1973 and was not a model designed by the factory (or even with factory approval), the Triumph can- not take this spot. Interesting- ly, the original motorcycle was actually supposed to be a BSA. The big Harley-Davidson FX set the path.

Yamaha RDs

Yamaha YDS3, From the author's collection

The Yamaha RD se- ries of two-strokes were world-changing and were race winners, often beating motorcycles twice their size.

Yamaha developed their first two-stroke twin in 1957, which was the YD-1. The two-strokes were developed over the decades, evolving into the YDS series, the YR series, the R series, the RD series, and finally the RZ series. The best known and best-selling models were the RD series, which included bikes of 60cc, 100cc, 125cc, 250cc, 350cc, and 400cc siz- es. The final editions were the RZ350s, 400s, and 500s, which were super fast bikes. The RZ400s and RZ500s were not officially exported to the US, but I have seen a few of them over the years.

The first RD was offered in 1973, and the series ended in 1979. The RZ series, being derived from the RD series, were built from 1984 until around 1992. They were only available in the US between 1984 and 1986. The last two- stroke Yamaha imported into the US was in 1986. Yamaha offered the first oil-injection system, sometimes called the "auto lube" in 1964, and by the late 1960s all their two-stroke motorcycles had the system. What made the RD and RZ Yamahas so important was their sturdy and reliable performance. The Yamaha two-stroke twins owned the Daytona 200 from 1972 to 1984 on bikes often half the size of their competitors. From the 1957 YD twin to the later RZ series twins, these two-stroke Yamahas spanned almost three decades as formidable motorcycles well-deserving of their significant place in motorcycle history.

1981 BMW R80 GS

1985 BMW R80 GS, Manufacturer's promotional photo, courtesy BMW

The next very significant motorcycle worth its place in the category being discussed is the 1981 BMW R80 GS series dual-sport motorcycle. This motorcycle started an entirely new sales category and new type of race. The influence of the GS series cannot be underestimated.

At the tail end of the 1970s, BMW was struggling with how to invigorate its line of motorcycles. The Japanese had been flooding the market with dozens of overriding models, the British manufacturers were all but gone, Italian motorcycles were selling in low quantities, and Harley-Davidson had its own niche market of loyal consumers. BMW needed something now that did not require millions of dollars of development only to find out that they had missed the mark. The solution was found in an experimental bike built by a BMW R&D man who had already been working on a unique solution to an ongoing motorcycle problem. What about a go-anywhere motorcycle that was big enough for extensive touring and could be used for serious off-road use. It would have to be a motorcycle that was ideal for very long-distance travel in underdeveloped areas and would also have to carry a large payload of travel gear, parts, and supplies. This would include a bike that was even large enough to carry two passengers, if necessary, on poor roads for thousands of miles. People had been doing what was listed above, but no one made the specific motorcycle to do so. Enter the big BMW GS, which at the time had no rivals. A few thought the idea was foolhardy, but from its inception to early 2017, over 600,000 GS bikes have been sold. There is no doubt that the BMW GS series started the adventure motorcycle segment and has remained a leader in its class.

Britten V1000

Britten 1000, Courtesy of Barber Vintage Motorsports Museum

The Britten V1000, built by the legendary John Britten, is an example of what a dedicated enthusiast with limited assets but incredible creative insight and abilities can do when committed to his dream.

The 1992 Britten V1000 was not only a world beater in terms of professional road racing ability, but was a machine with so many innovations that Britten's solutions impacted much larger motorcycle companies. He influenced much larger racing departments who had much larger budgets by blank sheet creativity. Many big motorcycle companies have been unable to create any real innovations of any significance at all, even though they had huge R&D departments with multi-million dollar budgets. John Britten did so much with so little that he must be seen as a modern motorcycle engineering genius. From the Carbon/Kevlar chassis, the stressed-member engine, the double wishbone front suspension, the adjustable swingarm rear suspension, and exotic solutions to many other problems, John Britten built a motorcycle more exotic than most made by the big companies.

He placed the radiator under the rider's seat, used carbon-fiber fasteners, which were stronger and lighter than exotic metals, and initiated engine data logging, which is done by every manufacturer today. The V1000 earned over twenty-eight first place wins at prestigious tracks, like Daytona, Brands Hatch, and Thruxton. The motorcycle was competitive, which was incredible, as his shop was small and his budget miniscule compared to his competition. Britten was known as the "backyard visionary" and did what thousands of motorcycle enthusiasts have tried to do over the decades: build a machine their way and win the respect of the world. John Britten died in 1995 at the young age of forty-five of an incurable form of cancer. He will be forever remembered as a man who did so much in a short amount of time, leaving his mark on a sport in which only a miniscule few can successfully be compared.

Ducati Monster

The Ducati Monster was a huge success for the parent company, having an influence far beyond its own brand. The

Monster looked back to the
motorcycle as an engine in a
frame, and it looked forward to
what the core of the motorcycle

has always been. The Monster,
above all, has stirred the inner
emotions of the motorcycle enthusiast.

Ducati Monster, From the author's collection

The modern Ducati has
been a picture of beauty in
motion. The Italians have always had an eye for design.
The modern Ducati has em-
ulated the qualities of style,
performance, simplicity, and
exclusivity. According to Ian
Faloon, author of *The Ducati
Monster Bible*, the designer of
the bike was Miguel Galluzzi in
1991. As the story goes, Galluzzi had stripped down a Ducati
888 Superbike for himself, and
when some of the Ducati high-
er-ups saw the bike, they demanded that a production version of the motorcycle should
be made immediately. The first
model was the M900 in 1992,
and the motorcycle has been
a big seller for decades. The
model quickly became Ducati's

best selling model and, at times,
represented nearly half of their
total production. Between
1992 and 2017, nearly a quarter of a million Monsters have
been sold. The model has also
been built with quite a number
of different engine designs and
in different engine sizes. Ducati has built a 400 (primarily for
Japan), a 600, 620, 695, 750,
900, 916, 996, 1000, 1100, and
a 1200cc model. The motorcycle has such a simple, classic,
and elemental look. The bike
never seems to age; it is just
what a motorcycle should look
like. There is no doubt that
the Monster will be around
for a while. In my opinion, the
Ducati Monster was the catalyst for the modern naked bike
movement, as well as the street

café racer look. The Monster was also the bike which encouraged the "trellis" frame motorcycle. The motorcycle has "the look," and speaks to the emotions of most motorcyclists. The Monster blends the classic with the modern. The Ducati Monster seems to be larger than the sum of its parts.

Suzuki Hayabusa

Suzuki Hayabusa, From the author's collection

The Suzuki Hayabusa began as a superbike from the superbike movement at the end of the 1970s. The ultra high-performance motorcycle has impacted most of the motorcycle community and led to a horsepower war, which has been going on for several decades. Many brands pretended to make a fast bike, but the Hayabusa separated the wanna-bees from the real contenders.

In 1999 Suzuki offered a special version of their super sport model and called it the "Hayabusa." The Japanese word refers to a type of falcon that swoops down on its prey. The Hayabusa had a longer wheelbase for safe high-speed travel, was aerodynamically designed for speed, and was geared for acceleration and top speed, rather than cornering ability. Though not a true sport bike in terms of having a well rounded personality, it is certainly a straight-line performer. The model quickly became popular and was copied by other manufacturers. Most companies stopped attempting to compete, because the level of performance was beyond what anyone would ever need, and who would ever need to ride beyond 150 mph? The first generation Hayabusa had a claimed 173 horsepower, the second generation claimed 190 horsepower, and the newest models claim 200 horsepower. The first generation Hayabusa, when tested, could reach over 190 mph, which caused a problem because it was capable of going almost three times most of the legal speed limit maximums. One tester claimed a stock machine would reach 204 mph in the early years. Complaints led to motorcycle manufacturers agreeing to a maximum of 186 mph for any street vehicle; this standard has generally stood for years. The Hayabusa was declared to be the fastest production motorcycle made in the world and has only been challenged by Kawasaki with their ZX12R and ZX14R superbikes. Other bikes, like the Honda XXX Blackbird, the BMW K1300R, and the Yamaha FJR1300ES, have been very fast but not to the level of the big Hayabusa or Kawasaki. The big Suzuki broke ground by being faster in top speed than many full-race factory bikes of only a few years back. Furthermore, quarter-mile times have been shown to be nearly as fast double-A fuel drag cars of several decades ago. A Ha-

yabusa with a skilled rider can easily run in the sub-ten second quarter mile bracket, with a trap speed of around 150 mph. The Hayabusa was a groundbreaker in performance and technology yet could still be used as a comfortable around town bike or touring motorcycle. It was truly a marvel, mixing shattering performance with durability and daily usability.

These twenty motorcycles have had a profound impact on the sport of motorcycling. There could easily be many more and many different motorcycles added to the list. In all fairness, there are so many categories over so many decades and over so many continents that it is hard to make a definitive list on which most motorcycle historians would agree. I suppose if the list included several hundred machines, there would be more agreement. The most significant issues have been the inclusion of practical technology, sales potential, usability, reliability, and ongoing design influence. For example, the little DKW125, as noted above, was copied by so many companies, and some even claim that the modern teardrop gas tank had its origins in this little bike. The Triumph Bonneville had a great influence within popular motorcycle culture from the early 1960s to the 1970s, but the original Speed Twin preceded it by being copied by most of Britain's motorcycle companies. The American V-twin engine was copied by the British during the 1930s, but the design was traded for the parallel-twin by the 1940s. The origin of the V-twin actually goes back to the 1890s, when Mercedes Benz made the first V-twin engine to be used as a boat motor. Most Americans connect Harley-Davidson with the V-twin engine, however, there were at least eight other V-twins which preceded the first Harley-Davidson V-twin. Actually, the V-twin became popular as a motorcycle engine because it was an easy and inexpensive way to add power. Just add another cylinder and double the power.

I am working on a more complete and more detailed list of significant motorcycles. In the next list I will more clearly define genuine firsts and original developments within specific categories. Hopefully, someday I will publish my findings in another book. Until then, the list found in this chapter reflect the significant developments of the motorcycle, in my humble opinion.

Chapter 9

The Social Impact of the Motorcycle

How Motorcycles Have Become Part of Culture

This book is primarily a discussion of the development of the motorcycle in the US and the experience of the American motorcycle rider. Certainly, there are many similarities between the European motorcycle experience and those on this side of the ocean, however, there are many unique qualities which define our experience that are very different from those in other parts of the world. We will focus on the motorcycle in America and American culture as it relates to the motorcycle. Listed below are areas of American society that have been impacted in some way over the last century. Most of these topics will be discussed in the categories that are noted below.

- The motorcycle has always been a vehicle of camaraderie.

- The motorcycle is generally connected to the perception of power and speed.

- The motorcycle is a machine that has generally been connected to the advancement of technology.

- The motorcycle has been linked to clubs and associations, well-organized or loosely connected, from its inception.

- After WWII (post 1950s) the growth of the rebel club or one-percent biker gang and the tough guy image, which generally goes along with that connection, exists within and outside many of the motorcycle clubs themselves.

One-Percent Type Club

Motorcycle Club—Vintage

- After the mid-1950s and going forward the motorcycle
  has been connected to entertainment, sports, and racing activities. This is especially true in the area of off-
  road riding. From street scramblers (mid-1960s to the
  mid-1970s) to dedicated off-road bikes (1970s to the
  end of the 1980s) to dual-sport motorcycles (from late
  1980s going forward) and to adventure bikes after the
  early 2000s, the motorcycle has been an avenue of entertainment. The movie *On Any Sunday* from 1971 was
  a huge catalyst, which encouraged people to participate
  in motorcycle activities.

Sport Bikes Racing

- After the mid-1970s motorcycle touring groups have
  grown exponentially.

- After the 1980s there has been significant growth in the
  cruiser market. This includes a growing interest in the
  V-twin motorcycle, with its sound and style.

- Since the twenty-first century, there has been a growing number of fragmented groups of specialized bikes,
  including vintage groups, bike building groups (especially non-H-D groups; the H-D customizers have been
  around for decades), touring groups, and specific type
  or brand-related groups (BMW, Moto Guzzi, sport bikes,
  etc.).

- There has been a rise in the number of valuable collector
  motorcycles being auctioned and an increase in the number of individuals collecting motorcycles. This growth in-

cludes vintage and new motorcycles, which are sold at an increasing number of auctions with increasing numbers of motorcycles of various ages, sizes, and styles being included.

Honda S-90, From the author's collections

- The motorcycle has spawned its own style of clothing, headgear, footwear, jackets, tattoos, and accessories, which seem to have a life within and beyond the motorcycle itself. This style does not require motorcycle ownership.

- There is an etiquette to the universal motorcycle wave.

The following eight numbered paragraphs below will cover most of the topics listed above. Some topics will cover similar material but will attempt to deal with specific new ideas or practices within the motorcycle community. Apart from the inescapable redundancies, each topic will include new information that should be informative. Note the general topics:

I There is been a general and social negativity which surrounds the view of the motorcycle community.

II There are numerous strong stereotypes attached to the motorcycle community.

III The "outlaw" image of the motorcyclist is still alive and well, even though there are actually very few dangerous groups.

IV **The motorcycle community itself has its own sub-social groups that are strong.**

V **The motorcycle and motorcycle community is very much an area that carries with it a great deal of symbolism.**

VI **A list of the primary reasons why people ride motorcycles and how these motivations are centered within the areas of human need is informative.**

VII **A few comments regarding the motorcycle "wave" will be discussed.**

VIII **Preliminary data and notes regarding the social history of the motorcycle in the US, dating back to earlier years, with some concluding information, will be covered.**

Now starting with the first statement overview, note the following:

I Negative Views of the Motorcycling Community

There has been a general social negativity that surrounds the view of the motorcycle community.

Because there are fewer motorcyclists on the roads compared to automobile drivers, the motorcyclists riding poorly and the risk takers influence the general public beyond their general numbers.

Young guys racing on the street and driving their motorcycles in an unsafe manner creates a bad image for the motorcycle.

Furthermore, groups of bikes with riders decked out in leather jackets with patches and colorful bandanas along with what would appear to be club logos create the image that this group might be a gang of some sort. Groups of bikers on loud motorcycles all dressed up simply look aggressive and unfriendly. The designation of a one-percent club, which promotes a big part of this image, will be discussed in the chapter on motorcycle clubs. The motorcycle has long been associated with the rebel or counter-cultural person or group, which ferments the idea that the majority of motorcyclists are roughnecks or troublemakers. Large, darkly-colored menacing motorcycles lined up in front of a bar also strengthens this image. The largest number of motorcycle riders are actually professional people or typical Americans with traditional family connections, rather than people seeking some sort of trouble. The vast number of motorcyclists would hold to traditional values and their lifestyle would not be much different than those of the masses. The stereotype does live on because of the negative images of the motorcyclist as projected by the theatre, television, and the limited public displays of motorcyclists acting badly.

During the late 1960s and into the 1970s there was such a huge growth in the sales of small and colorful Japanese motorcycles that the negative image of the motorcyclist was greatly reduced. With thousands of these small machines being ridden by neighbors and friends, the numbers of friendly riders outnumbered the ones that looked unfriendly. As the smaller motorcycles decreased and larger motorcycles increased, the former negative stereotype returned, though to a lesser degree than

before. When a typical neighbor owned a little Honda or Suzuki designed for in-town use, or a mini-bike was ridden by children in their yard, the public did not associate two wheels with rebellion or danger. It is simply a numbers game.

The fact is many people are drawn to the motorcycle because it does give them an alter-ego, which they want. I have also been told hundreds of times by many motorcyclists over the years that they like the loud muscular sound that their motorcycle emits, and they like the tough guy look. It just builds their esteem. The truth is that motorcycling can be very fun, and the vast number of motorcyclists are good citizens who are a credit to their community. Even the ones who dress up in all the leather garb and do some weekend riding in a group are often times just doing it to break the monotony of their lives. The fact still remains, however, that the public view of the motorcycle tends to be a more negative one.

II Strong Stereotypes

There are numerous strong stereotypes attached to the motorcycle community.

Having been alluded to numerous times before and probably being one of the strongest stereotypes within in the American motorcycle

community is the image of the motorcyclist as a gang member, a rebel, or member of a rebel group of some sort. This is not only a popular image but one some riders want to emulate, even though they are not connected with any club or rebel group at all. Some men and fewer women wanting to appear masculine or intimidating will seek out the outward appearance of the "rebel biker" just to build their self image. Hundreds of dollars will be spent on appearance-related items, such as a leather jacket, biker boots, bandanas, and other visual items just for show. Along the same lines, for some riders dressing in this sub-culture style is important to their identity. Some people may not even own a motorcycle; they just want to have the motorcycle riders' "look." I knew a man a number of years ago who had his biker wardrobe and the correct type of bike painted with the correct tough guy images. The truth was, however, he just rode to places with others like him and stood around acting like a part of what was going on. He put less than fifty miles on his motorcycle during a particular summer, but he sure looked good at the few stops he made, where he parked his bike. This is more typical than what some might expect.

Another common stereotype is the motorcyclist as speed demon or risk taker. By riding a fast bike fast or doing unsafe tricks on the street, a clear image of a guy seeking the adrenaline rush over the value of life is often portrayed. I am familiar with a group of sport bike riders who race around the city at night at over 130 mph, proving to each other that they are that biker. Many feel that the inherent risk of riding a motorcycle alone indicates that the person is more willing to take potential serious risks. Like those who parachute from flying airplanes or like to ride extreme roller coasters, many see the motorcyclist in this same category of being a risk taker.

The motorcyclist is often seen as a loner who travels across the country as a wanderer and portrays himself as a sort of modern day cowboy. Because most motorcyclists recognize each other in a general sense as fellow riders, the loner can cruise around and feel recognized by others, though not really being part of a relational group. The motorcycle culture allows for an outsider to remain unconnected, yet is generally connected to other motorcyclists through his machine. There is a general connection with people that he has no relationship with, especially if they ride a similar type of motorcycle and especially if they ride the same brand. He or she can remain invisible, yet has a bond with others through the motorcycle. The mystery of living a secluded life as one roams the country is an image so powerful that many songs have been written about such a person. The loner, wanderer, or meanderer is an image that some want to project about themselves, even though it is just in appearance only. This is an image which is easily projected by the motorcyclist. Many times while traveling out of town on my motorcycle I would see the biker sitting next to his motorcycle, taking a break at the side of a gas station. When approached and brought into a conversation, the response would be, "I'm just traveling down the road with no particular place to go." Whether or not this may actually be true, within the motorcycle community this is a popular image and one which is desirable.

Solo Touring, above Flaming Gorge, Utah, Courtesy of Michael Fitterling

III Gang Image

As mentioned in (I), the motorcycle gang image is a dominant theme in American motorcycling, but for the actual rebel club there is an identity, culture and hierarchy which is gained by those who participate in it.

I am not wanting to spend a lot of time on the motorcycle gang or its members, but I will cover the one-percent groups in greater detail under the chapter on motorcycle clubs. There is, however, an identity and protection within these organized groups, which to many becomes their social identity. The club member is identified by their colors, their rank within the group, their club name (or branding), or the business they are in, such as drug dealing, theft, prostitution, or stealing and selling parts. In some cases, the club might have at the top of its list that of just protecting their turf or territory. Many will require some sort of initiation to become a full-fledged member of the group. This level of involvement creates its own sub-culture, which is directed by its own history, by-laws, and required activities. There are very few clubs that are actually outlaw groups, but they do exist, and they do represent a place where outcasts or anti-social people can hide. Much has been written about the escapades of these groups, embellishing their crimes or anti social stances. Social media wants to focus on the destructive acts that they claim to have done, with the goal of adding drama to the immaturity, which is implied. All that needs to be said is that in most segments of society there are people who are unable to adjust to life in productive ways but need to justify their actions by some rationale, and the motorcycle club can be an easy cover to do so.

IV Motorcycling Sub-Groups

The motorcycle community itself has its own sub-social groups which can have strong influences.

For many motorcyclists the brand of motorcycle can be a source of their interest or loyalty. It could also be the type of motorcycle they ride, such as sport bike, an exotic or vintage bike, cruiser, or off-road machine, that connects them to a group. Club identification can also be important to some. Harley-Davidson riders are well-known for their sense of community. There are a number of basic reasons people join groups, and this includes motorcycle-related groups. Note the following:

1 **A community allows for camaraderie, friendships, or companionships to develop and to be validated.**

2 **A group can eliminate loneliness and make a person feel connected to others with like-interests.**

3 **Group involvement can connect a person to valuable activities, which can be pursued at a personal or group level.**

4 **Through the development of associations and being involved in activities perceived as worthy, a person can gain greater self-worth and the feeling of having a greater purpose in life.**

5 **A person can develop their personal abilities through group activities.**

6 Through self-development a person can cultivate their ability to lead, which will increase their value and status within their group.

7 Through a group a person can get connected to people who have resources, information, or abilities who can be of personal assistance at some point in time.

These qualities are basic human areas needing affirmation. Far too often, however, motorcycle clubs become confrontational and competitive, rather than just a positive place to get involved. This is also a human nature issue, which has no resolution apart from the seeking to fulfill the emotional need which a person might have.

People join motorcycle-related groups for the same reason they join other social cliques; to be part of something larger than themselves and to give them something with which to identify. To better understand this topic the reader would simply be required to look deeper into the behavioral sciences.

V Loaded with Symbolism

The motorcycle and motorcycle community is very much a group which carries with it a great deal of symbolism.

Chopper

The motorcycle symbolizes a number of powerful images, which can generally be understood in the bullet points listed at the beginning of this chapter. A symbol is simply something represented through something else that will better define the item at hand in a clearly impactful way. A picture of a long-haired, shirtless hippy on a chopper symbolizes rebellion and a rejection of responsibility.

A couple of road racers carving out a corner of a racetrack with the riders hugging the gas tanks symbolizes raw speed, competition, and the desire to win.

The motorcyclist on his bike is often depicted as an individual on his freedom machine or as a means in which to live as an outsider. The motorcycle becomes a way to secure his independence or to prove that he is either a tough guy or a rebel, or if nothing else, a means of becoming a liberated person. Riders may attempt to emulate these symbolic concepts, which are used to flaunt the attitude they want to mimic. It is not uncommon at all for the motorcyclist to copy the image which inspires him, rather than to actually find his passion and work at fulfilling it. In a very general way, the motorcycle experience could relate to Abraham Maslow's Hierarchy of Need chart. Note below:

Self Actualization: The motorcyclist finds his place in society through the sport of motorcycling. He/She has no need for further or additional approval!

Self-esteem: He "masters" his place within the sport through activities and experience. Acceptance is found!

Love: The rider develops friendships which affirm his/her self value with other motorcyclists and becomes secure in an identity within the sport!

Safety: Security through activities and participation creates feelings of safety through group involvement!

Physiological needs: The feeling that core needs are met or available through the sport!

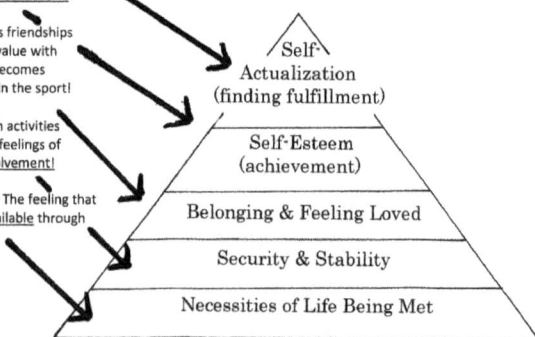

Self-Actualization (finding fulfillment)
Self-Esteem (achievement)
Belonging & Feeling Loved
Security & Stability
Necessities of Life Being Met

The above chart is loosely based on the Abraham Maslow theory coined the "Hierarchy of Need." This is a learning theory which can very generally apply to the motorcycle experience.

This chart is somewhat fanciful and is not intended to be scientific as a serious study, and certainly did not include a great deal of research or reasoned insight. It is simply used as an illustration to show that the individual motorcyclist can move from riding the motorcycle for basic human esteem reasons and then may progress into a more serious commitment to the sport at a more mature level. A new or immature rider might dwell on projecting an outward image to others, which he thinks communicates something he wants others to think about himself. This is a common response by many motorcyclists; that of simply projecting an outward image. A more serious and seasoned rider will find out what he truly enjoys and will develop his activities within that direction. The highest level that the active motorcyclist can reach is that of fulfilling his or her dreams and having an impact on the sport while finding their activities fully rewarding, apart from simply the desire to impress others. There are many examples of this process of riders moving from being a young motorcyclist driven by image and then over time moving from immaturity to self-actualization. An excellent example would be the motorcycle personality Floyd Clymer. Clymer was a one-time motorcycle racer, dealership owner, a motorcycle book writer and publisher, a motorcycle magazine owner, and finally, motorcycle builder. Clymer sold motorcycles as a young man, raced motorcycles as a young adult, owned *Cycle* magazine as a mature adult, and died attempting to bring the Indian brand back to life. Clymer was certainly involved in much more than just motorcycle-related activities throughout his life, yet certainly had a significant impact on the field of motorcycling. Clymer's activities are symbolic of a life given to the things in which he was committed. and his achievements went far beyond those of the vast majority of motorcyclists.

VI Why Ride a Motorcycle?

Here is a list of the primary reasons people ride motorcycles and how these motivations are centered within the areas of human need.

The primary reasons that many people gravitate toward the motorcycle are easy to understand. Probably at the top of the list is the freedom that one feels when riding unencumbered in the open air on a motorcycle. There is a thrill that only the motorcyclist can feel as they glide down the road in the open air and with a feeling of freedom. Many attest to an adrenaline rush that allows for sensations to be experienced that cannot be imitated through any other means. For others, motorcycling almost guarantees that the rider will experience some form of adventure, even if the ride may not be a long one. This is why many riders love to tour on their motorcycles. The highway allows the feeling of freely roaming about to be greatly enhanced. Riding a motorcycle generally requires much more direct attention than driving a car, so many riders enjoy the heightened demand for the need to be concentrated while they navigate their motorcycle. The feeling of engagement is generally much stronger when riding a motorcycle than when driving a car or other types of vehicles. Motorcycle riders generally feel the strain on their senses and experience a stronger desire to be aware of their surroundings. For some, the camaraderie is a driving force, and for others, a group of loud motorcycles making noise in unison gives the feeling of masculinity and virility.

The "pack" mentality makes some motorcyclists feel strong, while the same activity might make another motorcycle rider feel connected. Some motorcycles will encourage a rider to feel as though he or she is outwardly expressing their individuality or identity. For many, the motorcycle is just the party that they have dressed for. The motorcycle, especially when in groups, will make a rider feel "cool" or will feed his or her image and ego needs. For most, however, the feeling of freedom, adventure, or the idea of being connected with others are the driving forces behind riding motorcycles. For others, the motorcycle is seen as just the mirror, which reflects themselves in a way which bolsters their self-esteem. The motorcycle and narcissism can be at times very close.

VII The "Wave"

Motorcycle "Wave"

A few comments on the motorcycle "wave."

As long as I can remember, motorcyclists have generally waved to other passing motorcycles. The wave is a symbolic act of unity. I am sure most of this waving can be simple to understand and is the same as that of a passing Porsche driver (or Corvette or BMW, etc.) waving to another Porsche driver because of the identification they have through their vehicles. I do not deny that there is a distinct psychology to waving, but I am sure that most bikers just wave as an act of gratuity or courtesy. The act of waving is done for a number of reasons; to recognize another motorcyclist:

- **as a form of approval**
- **as a sign of conformity**
- **as a form of acceptance**
- **to acknowledge others like themselves**
- **to show solidarity**
- **as an obligation**
- **as an act of community**
- **as a means of connecting**

When another motorcyclist does not wave, the reason could be:

- **they didn't see your wave**
- **they didn't have time to wave**
- **it might have been unsafe to ride and wave at the same moment**
- **they waved, but you missed it**
- **they nodded, rather than waved**
- **they don't like to wave, so didn't**
- **for some reason, they don't approve of your motorcycle and don't want to acknowledge the type or brand of motorcycle that you ride**
- **they feel that the passing rider is not of their status level and not worthy of a wave**
- **they are currently angry or defiant and want to show it**

Some of these notations are intended to be somewhat humorous, but in reality, a rider should not feel slighted if they do not receive a wave back from other motorcyclists. To wave or not to wave, that is the big question. I have heard many metric riders allege that riders of a certain specific other brand of motorcycle tended to not wave at them or to not return a wave. I really doubt this, because in many cases, it can be really hard to actually know what brand of motorcycle is passing until the opportunity to wave has passed. To not respond to the wave from another motorcyclist is generally seen as contemptible.

There are a number of typical waves. I will note the top ten waves:

- The "peace sign wave," which consists of fingers in a "V" pattern.

- The "James Dean wave," which is the pointer finger pointed downward with the arm flowing backwards in the wind.

- The "disciplined and alert enthusiast wave" is when the finger is pointed erectly upward rather than downward.

- The "open outstretched hand" wave (the just being friendly wave or the obligatory wave).

- The "shaking finger wave" is one indicating subliminal disapproval.

- The "limp hand wave" is when the arm is half-heartedly lifted up but left at shoulder height (I don't have the energy to do more than imitate a wave).

- The "lazy wave" is when the arm is barely lifted up from the riders side.

- The "closed fist" wave (I am aggressive and want you to know it).

- The "salute wave" is generally used by law enforcement people or military people, current or retired.

- The "middle-finger wave" is when the other motorcyclist knows you and has a problem with you.

- When the rider looks directly at you but does not wave he is saying, "You are not worthy of my recognition."

- **The most common form of wave is simply some direct movement of a body appendage that the driver going the opposite direction can observe. The waves noted above are ones intended to communicate a direct message.**

I have been waving for over fifty years, and I typically use the "semi-outstretched hand" wave. If I had to pick my top three, beyond the primary one noted above, I would probably add the "peace-sign wave" and the "lazy wave." Sometimes, I just get tired of waving. If I don't wave, it is because I am unable to wave at that moment or it is possibly unsafe for me to wave at that time. More times than not, if a stream of motorcycles is going by, there might just not be enough time to wave to everyone. In concluding this conversation, motorcyclists have traditionally waved to each other, mostly out of obligation and recognition. Generally speaking, younger riders tend to wave less, and more mature riders tend to wave as a gratuity. In reality, it is more of a habitual reaction than one done with intended meaning.

VIII Notes

Preliminary data and notes regarding the social history of the motorcycle in the US, dating back to earlier years, with some concluding information.

1 **The automobile developed after 1893 (Duryea Brothers); Henry Ford (1896); Oldsmobile 1901; after 1904 many more brands were added in large numbers.**

2 **According to the *KC Star*, KC's first auto show was in 1907, and at that time there were only about 200 cars in the city (note from old article).**

3 **Car sales were always much greater than motorcycle sales in the US, but after 1908 the difference grew exponentially until the 1970s.**

4 **Estimated US car sales vs. estimated US motorcycle sales:**
   1895 ___300 to 0 known
   1899 ___2,500 to 1 (an Orient)
   1900 ___4,200 to 3 (1901 figure)
   1905 ___78,000 to 1,189
   1910 ___113,000 to 9,305
   1913 ___485,000 to 71,000 (highest m/c to car ratio)

1920_____ 1,452,000 (2.5 times increase) to 38,000 (45% drop)

    1930 ___2,347,000 to 27,000 (another 30% drop)

    1950 ___6,500,000 to 20,355 (another 25% drop)

    1970 ___8,400,000 to 1,100,000 (motorcycles = 12% of all new vehicles)

    2000 ___9,000,000 to 710,000

    2014___7,900,000 to 484,000

5 The car was considered a rich man's sport because of the cost of a new automobile compared to the typical family income.

    Car owners typically had a mechanic (like a person watching the stables before the automobile was popular).

    It was common for car owners in the earliest years to give rides to common folks (like an amusement park ride today, the car was a novelty)

    Owners might allow their car to be used by others when they were out of town.

    Cars were really expensive until after 1908 (development of the Model T). Even the Mode T was expensive until mass-production was improved. The first Model T took 33 hours to build, by 1914 it took only 1.5 hours.

6 Initially there was a battle between the car, motorcycle, and the horse.

    Households were set up for horses, so the reduction of horses in a household took a while after the automobile had became popular (the evolution was from having horses and no car to having a car and a horse, then no horse at all).

    Early motorcycles (& cars) were very unreliable, so to many, the horse seemed a better choice.

    The tipping point, especially for the refined person, was that the car was cleaner and more people could ride in such a vehicle. As the practicality of the car was evident, they began to dominate the transportation systems.

    Between 1900 and 1905, the horse was superior to the motorcycle, but quickly the motorcycle became faster, easier to maintain, and required less time (the horse required 24-hour attention).

    The motorcycle was like a mechanical horse; younger

people interested in technology liked the challenge of a machine, rather than that of attending animals.

7 What initially attracted young men to the motorcycle?
They were unique—something new and "modern"
They were loud
They could usually outrun a horse, especially after 1905
They gave a person prestige
They were masculine and not for the timid
They could be started more quickly than saddling a horse
Individualism

8 Even as late as 1905, gasoline-powered machines were so unique that they would be shown at public events. This also stimulated the desire for many to own one, and many small towns never saw a car or motorcycle until after 1908 or even much later.

9 Between 1908 and 1918, the switch between horses and self-powered vehicles was made:
1903—Nearly all buggies or carts were moved by horses; it was an extreme rarity to see cars or motorcycles on the streets.
1905—Less than 10% of all vehicles were self-propelled.
1908—60% of all transportation devices were operated by horses, compared to 40% of all vehicles were gasoline-propelled vehicles.
1910—40% of transportation depended upon the horse, while the remaining 60% of vehicles were gas-powered.
1918—95% of all vehicles, except in small rural towns, were powered by gasoline.
1920—Only old-timers used horses, except in the extreme back woods.

10 Up until around 1905, powered vehicles were seen as a fad, after that people understood they were here to stay.

11 The self-powered vehicle brought huge social change.
The practical limits for a horse-drawn wagon was around 15 miles; under gas power distances grew to over 50 miles or to wherever a person could find gasoline.
The gasoline powered vehicle was an emerging status symbol.
There was greater travel for business and for fun as the automobile/motorcycle grew in sales.

New business developed around petroleum-powered vehicles, such as delivery services, faster mail, more public transportation options, larger areas for salesmen to sell their products, the automotive/motorcycle service industries, and especially within the petroleum industry.

There was an enhanced desire for new innovations.

There was a new desire for speed and various forms of competition.

12 The earliest races were primarily reliability events, such as going up a hill, going across rough country areas or between cities.

1895—Chicago race (vehicles were called moto-cycles, but all had 4 wheels)

1903—first car across US

1913—Cannonball Baker's first cross-country trip

1914—Baker's completed trips, 143 records made during his lifetime

Horse tracks were used for early motorcycle races.

Cannonball Run, Modern Race Recreating Baker's Cross-Country Ride, Publicity photo

13 1905 income: $200 dollars per year to around $400 per year for an upper-income person. A high income would be above $600 per year.

A pre-1905 car would be over $1,500 up to over $2,000.

A pre-1905 motorcycle would generally be under $200 new (I have seen ads for used motorcycles for $85 before 1910).

The first Model Ts were around $800, but by 1914 they went down to around $300 (cheapest Model T: $260 from the middle to the end of Model T production).

By the teens, a motorcycle would cost around 80/90% of a car price, so people bought cars in the US

14 Roads became a significant issue because most were bad, to even being impassable during much of the year.

1909—Less than 10% of roads were paved (most paved roads were around cities).

1910—"Good Roads Convention."

1916—Federal Roads Act (little funding but growing interest).

1921—Federal Highway Act. "Two lane Interstate roads constructed."

1930s—Depression era roads were built.

1944—"National System of Interstate Highways" roads built to smaller communities with the idea of connecting large and small areas.

1956—Federal-Aid Highway Act. The development of the Interstate highway system (not completed until 1990 and a cost of 100 billion dollars).

15 Before 1900 the motorcycle was merely an experiment.

From 1900 to the pre-WWI era the motorcycle was a clearly defined category of new type vehicles, somewhat parallel to the automobile, just fewer of them being around.

From WW I to WW II (around 1917 to 1945) the motorcycle lost its place to the automobile. The motorcycle became a vehicle for the sportsman, individualist, or one wanting more excitement. The mechanic-type liked the motorcycle as something to work on and to develop his mechanical skills. People who preferred the open air or the person wanting less expensive transportation (business or otherwise) also liked the motorcycle. I have had several old-timers say that back in the 1930s motorcycles were rarely seen. (One man said that he saw a motorcycle about twice a year.) The motorcycle community was small and generally closely associated in every region.

After 1945 to the early 1960s motorcycles were the machines of choice for the rebels, racers, the hoodlums, the hot riders, or people seeking excitement.

Since the mid-1960s (after the Japanese invasion) motorcycles became an inexpensive form of entertainment.

Donnell's Show, From the author's collection

16 It was not until after WWII that the motorcycle became a common sight throughout the country. During the early years, motorcycles were more readily found around cities or larger populated areas. Just consider chart #4 above. Consider that when you look at sales figures, these figures do not include the accumulated figures. Note the following (figures from the US Department of Transportation):

Year	Motorcycles Registered in the US	Cars Registered in the US:
1960	574,032	61,671,390
1970	2,824,098	89,243,557
1980	5,693,940	121,600,843
1990	4,259,462	127,885,193
2000	4,346,068	133,621,420

Figures courtesy of www.transportation.org

These figures show the exponential growth of the automobile over those of the motorcycle. In 2000 there were over thirty cars for every motorcycle, and that figure does not include all the other forms of transportation that are found on the road as well. Furthermore, the figures for motorcycles include off-road machines and machines ridden only on an occasional basis.

The motorcycle has a rich history in American culture and, therefore, has had a significant impact on our society. Although stereotypes are generally ingrained into our psyches, I have not seen any big shifts in how most people view the motorcycle. As motorcycles get larger and louder, the public's perceptions of them will become more harsh.

What is certain, however, is that the motorcycle is probably here to stay. The humble horse was at one time the dominant form of transportation. By the teens, he had dwindled in numbers, but certainly still survives today. I suggest that this will also be true of the two-wheeled forms of transportation going forward.

I think the numbers of motorcycles per person may decline over the decades, but the machine will survive for future enjoyment. Just as the horse still has a romantic status, I think the same will be true of the motorcycle in decades to come. As in the past, the motorcycle was much more of a machine for the sports-minded person; there is no evidence that this will change. As society has become more complex, the motorcycle has become less important as a vital means of transportation. The only places in which the motorcycle has remained strong is in the areas of camaraderie, entertainment, and to reflect an image within society. The motorcycle has traveled around the outer edges of society and I don't see that changing.

10

Clubs and Events

Post-1960s Motorcycle Club

Motorcycle clubs date back to the bicycle clubs, which existed before the turn of the past century. The bicycle first became popular in the 1860s, then after the development of the safety bicycle (both wheels being the same size) at the very end of the 1800s, brought another time of significant growth in term of bicycle use.

Bicycle clubs were organized associations of riders which would almost always have elected officers and dues to be paid by members. Clubs were generally more organized than those found today. Many clubs would have an association that was involved with a bicycle business or some local business that supported the sport of bicycling. Clubs would sponsor rides, picnics, competitive events, educational seminars related to the bicycle, dances, and even boxing matches.

In larger towns there might be several clubs that would fight for dominance or prestige over the other clubs.

The reader should understand that during these early years, society was more regimented toward codes, rules of order, respect for position, personal responsibility, protocol, and etiquette. The rights and wrongs were much more clearly defined back in the last century. Clubs would be much more formal than what we are accustomed to today.

Because road development was not nearly as refined as our transportation systems are today and most roads were very poor, clubs worked on bettering the roads in their locality. The Good Roads Move-

ment came from the bicyclist as a means of pressuring authorities at any level to make the construction of better roads a high priority.

As automobile and motorcycle sales grew, the Better Roads Movement shifted to these groups. Actually, the demand for better roads fell heavily on automobile groups because they had more power, money, and much more at stake than other types of businesses.

Within a decade or so, bicycle clubs pretty much disappeared as people wanting to travel shifted to the automobile from the horse and buggy.

Motorcycle clubs originally were just a tag-along with the bicycle clubs until a geographic area had enough motorcycles, then motorcycle groups began to form. One big difference between the bicycle clubs and motorcycle clubs was that the motorcyclists depended much more on their associations with other motorcycle owners for service and mechanical help. Car clubs were more prestige oriented groups looking for social standing and often resembled private men's clubs of the day, while motorcycle groups were more concerned with being associated with other motorcyclists for practical purposes.

One of the earliest motorcycle clubs was the New York Motorcycle Club, originating in 1903. The New York club realized the importance of having motorcycle clubs and universal standards, so key members founded the FAM, or the Federation of American Motorcyclists. One of the founding members was George M. Hendee, who was the key individual responsible for the start of the Indian Motorcycle Company. By 1915, the FAM had over 8,200 members and had set up rules for racing, established legal guidelines, and established guidelines for many other motorcycle-related issues and activities of the day. In 1916 the M&ATA (Motorcycle & Allied Trades Association) was formed as a motorcycle trades organization meant to guide and regulate motorcycle manufacturers.

Because of WWI, most young men were called into military service, causing the FAM to shut down. The FAM dissolution occurred in 1919. After the war and in 1924, the AMA was formed, which stood for the American Motorcycle Association. The AMA has been the primary national motorcycle organization from 1924 until today. A number of FAM members were involved in the early development of the AMA, which grew quickly to become much larger than any other national motorcycle organization. The AMA currently has over 300,000 members, sponsors over 1,200 clubs, sponsors

nearly 4,100 amateur and professional racing events, and publishes the *American Motorcyclist* magazine, which has a circulation of over 250,000 magazines monthly.

KCVJMC (Kansas City Vintage Japanese Motorcycle Club), From the author's collection

Motorcycle clubs began popping up as early as 1903, but it was not until after WWII that there was exponential growth in the numbers of clubs. Between the world wars, many clubs were AMA-chartered, as noted above. In 1936 Sucher noted that there were around 615 AMA clubs in the US. By 1950 there were over 1,600 AMA clubs. Today, there are approximately 3,000 clubs, most of which are not AMA-sanctioned groups.

When the term *club* is used in our common vernacular, it may refer to either organized groups or associations of people. The actual word defined simply refers to an association of people who are engaged in some form of singular cause.

Many motorcycle clubs are associations of people who are engaged in motorcycle-related activities but do not have by-laws, elections, or even elected officers. Many of the sanctioned AMA clubs were organized for local or regional racing events, rather than for general motorcycle-related activities. A number of years ago, I did an independent (semi-scientific) study of motorcycle clubs in America and here are some of my findings:

The number of motorcycle clubs in the US can only be estimated because so many are short-term groups that last less than three years or have a name change, making tracking very hard to do.

Nearly all clubs fall into either "brand"- or "dealer"-based clubs, "activity"-driven clubs, "event"-driven clubs, or clubs based on professional "associations" of some type.

At least fifty percent, and probably more, of all clubs are closed or semi-closed groups.

Most clubs that discontinue activities disband because of conflict between members, experience stagnant growth, or suffer from serious personality differences. Personality differences are more significant than differences in the purpose of the group.

Many clubs stop because one or two people are holding the group together, and once they discontinue leading, the group disbands activities.

Over ninety percent of all clubs have only eight or fewer active members.

Few clubs exceed fifty people, and only a small percent of all clubs have over 100 active members. By active, I mean people who identify specifically with the group, are engaged in club-related business, and regularly engage in club activities.

Most clubs are organized and operate with fewer than ten percent of members being engaged in leadership activities. A club of fifty people will essentially be run by five people doing ninety percent of the work.

Clubs specifically organized as motorcycle "brand" clubs are larger in membership numbers but tend to have a reduced commitment by members. Membership activity tends to be more casual or social. Large membership numbers reflect more of brand ownership than interest in club activities.

The success of riding or touring clubs is most closely related to the popularity of the events which are scheduled.

Successful clubs succeed because of good leadership (or have a strong leader), offer positive and popular goals, have good marketing skills, and are friendly as a group. Many groups are founded on an energetic and popular leader and often will fail because selfish interest or conflict between individuals or goals has entered the group.

Motorcycle club devel-
opment can be outlined in

four basic time periods. Note
the following:

1. **1902-1940s. Stage One** of the development of typical American motorcycle clubs. During this time period clubs were generally more organized than what is common today. Clubs demanded member responsibility, sought membership growth, tended to be civic minded, and had membership fees. A number of articles in pre-1930s motorcycle magazines that discussed club activities seemed to discuss dues collecting as a big part of club responsibilities. The motorcycle club was a social organization for responsible people who wanted to be associated with other enthusiasts in an organized and formal way. The most significant club to start during this time period was the FAM and AMA.

2. **1945-1970s. Stage Two.** Many returning military personnel looked to the motorcycle as a source of excitement and community. Most of the one-percent clubs, to be discussed in greater detail later, were formed between the years noted. Although the rebel and some rebel groups did exist long before the post WWII era, this post WWII time period was the time which these groups came to life and became a distinct segment of the motorcycle community. Touring has always been associated with the motorcycle, but after the early 1960s, touring was on the increase. By the end of this period, long-distance travel by motorcycle was becoming much more popular, though generally done more often in a singular manner by individual riders. There were certainly groups of motorcyclists which went on tours, however, this was a rarity and non-typical. The numbers of AMA groups declined. The most significant clubs to form during this time were the national Triumph motorcycle owners club in 1949, the national BMW motorcycle owners club in 1951, and the AMCA (Antique Motorcycle Club of America) in 1954. Another organization called ABATE (A Brotherhood Against Totalitarian Enactments) began in 1977 from writings which began as early as 1971. ABATE is a national motorcycle club that works through lobbyists to support issues related to the motorcycle.

3. **1970-2000. Stage Three.** During this time period there was a huge growth in non-AMA clubs. The Harley-Davidson

HOG group was formed by the Motor Company during this time period, as were many other groups. Because of the one-percent motorcycle club notoriety, many groups did not want to use the word *club*, because of the negative association that came with the term. They were, in fact, clubs but did not want to be called such because of the negativity of the term. Furthermore, if a group was called a "club," having a logo might create a problem. Many clubs began to form as mostly regional and non-AMA groups. Some of the significant clubs to form during this time was the VJMC (Vintage Japanese Motorcycle Club) in 1977, a new BMW touring club in the late 1970s, the GWRRA (Gold Wing Road Riders Assn.) in 1977, and HOG (Harley's Owners Group) in 1983. The BMW club claims membership numbers to be over 32,000, and the GWRRA claims membership to be over 72,000.

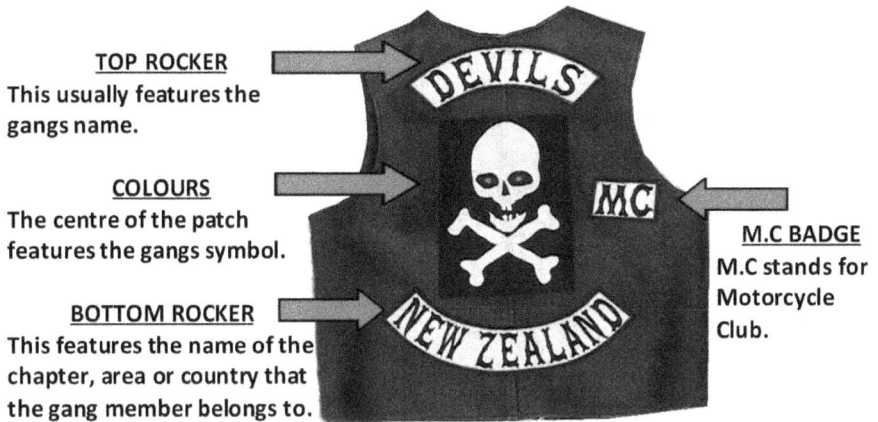

TOP ROCKER
This usually features the gangs name.

COLOURS
The centre of the patch features the gangs symbol.

BOTTOM ROCKER
This features the name of the chapter, area or country that the gang member belongs to.

M.C BADGE
M.C stands for Motorcycle Club.

Motorcycle Club Logo, Courtesy Cam Stokes and gangscene

4. Stage Four. Developments since 2000. Since the turn of the century, there has been an explosion of motorcycle clubs that tend to be more informal than in past years but are driven by enthusiasm and purpose. Typical reasons for a club might be for touring, camping, going to restaurants, or for purely social reasons. Every year a new batch of groups form, and other groups will disband. Touring and riders clubs, vintage clubs, AMCA clubs, brand-oriented clubs. women's clubs, and new chapters of previously organized clubs have formed since 2000. Little new has been initiated, except that in the past de-

**cade, numerous independent motorcycle dealers have
established groups of their customers as "club"-type en-
tities. The club as a marketing and sales arm of a business has been around since the earliest years of the motorcycle. Note the following developments since 2000.
In 2001 the Combat Veterans Motorcycle Association
was formed, in 2005 the Patriot Guard was formed, and
in 2010 Bikes & Trikes was formed. Numerous women's
clubs have also formed.**

The development of the one-percent motorcycle gang has always been a popular topic for many of the same reasons the general public loves movies about crime, violence, drug dealers, and gangsters. Because most people have a latent rebellious side, the thug mentality or tough guy image has a certain attraction. Most people think about doing dangerous things that excite them but would never actually do anything illegal or dangerous. The vast number of motorcyclists would run from any questionable activity. The motorcycle can be a quick connection to feelings of vulnerability, machismo, or risks because of its history and inherent danger.

The motorcycle gang movies of past decades encouraged fear, which connected the individual with the basic primal fear found within the human consciousness. When the motorcycle is connected to the rebel mentality and doing evil things, there is a deep emotional connection, which both draws some individuals toward it but also repels others from it.

Most want to feel the energy of acting out counter-cultural activities but don't act upon the feelings in any way. Many men and women have actually purchased motorcycles to connect themselves with this malevolent image. Becoming a biker connects many to these primal desires.

I mention this issue before going into the history of the motorcycle gang because of the connection it has with the dangerous or destructive side of humanity. This part of motorcycle culture still remains strong. I can remember reading an article in a motorcycle magazine dated before 1919 that suggested that the motorcycle tended to draw people who were thrill-oriented and risk-takers. This idea was prevalent even 100 years ago.

The first really influential motorcycle gang movie was in 1953 called *The Wild One*, featuring Marlin Brando. Although being very innocent compared to the rebel-focused movies of today, it was considered to be a very bad influence on the viewer back in the 1950s.

After the mid-1950s there was a string of movies that focused on the evils of the motorcycle gang: *The Teenage Devil Dolls* of 1955, the *Motorcycle Gang* of 1957, *The Dammed* of 1963, and the *Outlaw Motorcycles* of 1966. All of these movies pictured the motorcycle gang as a bunch of evil and violent people. There were actually dozens of "B" movies that focused on the corrupt and dangerous gangs of motorcycle riders who destroyed innocent girls and devastated small towns. Possibly the most famous motorcycle movie was *Easy Rider*, released in 1969. In the movie, Peter Fonda and Dennis Hopper use money received from a drug sale to travel across the country on choppers. It appealed to the free love, hippie, and no responsibility crowd of the late-1960s and was a huge hit.

I wanted to preface the discussion of the 1947 Hollister, California, AMA Gypsy Tour, the event which inspired the *The Wild One* movie and the general motorcycle gang movement. I have read numerous accounts of the Hollister event and believe that there have been many intentional embellishments that have idolized what happened at that rally, creating a scenario that is somewhat true but largely exaggerated far beyond reality.

1947 Hollister Rally, Period newspaper photo

The purpose could be assumed to be that of creating fear and newspaper headlines. As the story goes, the rally was made up of several thousand rambunctious young men who were motorcyclists. Most were not many years out of the military who went to the Hollister Rally to see the races and to have fun over the weekend. As could be expected, there was a little racing in the streets, drinking, and general revelry going on.

At the event there was a picture taken of a guy sitting on a motorcycle drinking a beer with empty bottles of liquor all around the motorcycle. The picture was staged, and the guy on the bike was not drunk. The man was Gus Deserpa, who had just left work and as he was walking by a bar. He was asked to pose for the picture by a major magazine publisher. The picture was published as though real and went viral. In 1997 he recounted that the event was fake and "phony."

As the greatly exaggerated story was told, the gang of motorcyclists took over the town, and violence ensued. As the excesses of the story spread, AMA officials attempted to protect the sport of motorcycling by noted that ninety-nine percent of all motorcyclists were law-abiding citizens and were, in fact, not a danger to society. Over time, this led to groups wanting to be identified as rebellious or non-mainstream motorcyclists or club members to use the *1%* notation as an identification. This classicifaction was at first meant to be somewhat humorous or sarcastic. Fairly quickly, however, the *one-percent* term stuck, and those wanting to promote their counter-culture identity began wearing a one-percent patch with pride. The Boozefighters had actually organized as a motorcycle club in 1946 and were followed by the Market Street Commandos in 1947. The Commandos became the Hells Angels in 1953. Other major one-percent clubs are the Pagans, who organized in 1959;, the Bandidos, who organized in 1966; and the Mongols, who organized in 1969. These clubs reflect only a small percent of the motorcycling community.

The reality is that the typical outlaw or one-percent club engages in some sort of crime activity at some level. Whether activities are drug trafficking, prostitution, the sale of illegal weapons, or a myriad of other crimes related to their club business, these clubs do not reflect the love of motorcycles but are based on depraved intentions. The typical one-percent or outlaw club follows these general patterns:

Most demand that members ride Harley-Davidson motorcycles.

Almost all members' motorcycles are cruisers.

Memberships are generally progressive. An interested party would move from being outside the group (called an "associate," "friend," or another similar name), to a participant who is active until their membership can be voted on, then finally to a full member status worthy of wearing a patch or jacket.

Clubs will have a logo, colors, and earned patches. Jackets generally have the name of the club at the top above the club logo, then below will be the state and chapter. Additional patches will be attached as earned.

The club color is important and cannot be worn by other clubs. Colors and jackets are protected with honor.

Loyalty is very important, and few could leave a club honorably.

Clubs will generally have an entire inner culture with practices which are closely followed.

A typical person could never accidentally become an outlaw club member. It is not uncommon for some riders to wear clothing which emulates one-percent club membership but are, in fact, not members of a club of that sub-culture at all.

There are a few clubs which are crime-free but appear as outlaw groups. Many active groups do not use the term club *or refer to themselves as clubs because of the one-percent connotation. The term remains so caustic that wholesome groups simply stay away from any activity, look, or connection to any group that appears to be a rebel group.*

Motorcycle events began when the first motorcycle club had a general gathering, however, the large staged events were primarily related to racing until after WWII. A general list of the types of motorcycle events would be the following (from the oldest types to newer types). The oldest events would be local club events, followed by regional racing events, then the original Gypsy Tours. Next would be the rally, the show, the charity event, then the more modern bikefest events.

The oldest large motorcycle event that has been going on as a continuous event would be Laconia Bike Week, dating back to 1923. The event dates back to 1916 but was not recognized until 1923. Laconia, New Hampshire, was the location of early racing and motorcycle gatherings, including early AMA Gypsy Tours. The Gypsy Tours began in the early 1920s and were simply regional motorcycle gatherings, which included picnics, social gatherings, and low-level competition events. Laconia grew from the 1920s until

1965, at which time one-percent gang activity created problems, and the event was greatly reduced in size. After the 1990s, it began to grow again and currently is attended by somewhere between 350,000 and 400,000 people. Laconia is usually held in mid-June. ending on Fathers day.

Daytona Beach, Florida, has hosted an event since 1937 called Daytona Bike Week. The event began with track races and grew until WWII. There were no races between 1942 and 1947 because of the war. After WWII the event has grown into a ten-day event hosting races, bike shows, and dozens of other related events. By 2015, attendance was around 500,000 people. The bike week is usually held in early March of each year.

Sturgis Bike Rally, Sturgis publicity photo

Sturgis, South Dakota, has become the largest single motorcycle event in the US and possibly the largest in the world. From 1938, the year it started, it grew slowly until the 1980s, when the numbers grew exponentially. The event was originally a flat-track race event with around 500 to 700 people in attendance. It had grown to only several thousand people by the 1970s but began to really surge in the 1980s. Today the event can host up to 600,000 people. The event is so large that it actually covers several different towns. It has become a place for manufacturers to show their new stuff and for suppliers of all types to promote their wares. For years it was a one-week event but has grown into nearly two weeks in length. The event has grown in terms of influence, and manufacturers have even named models of motorcycles after it. The Sturgis motorcycle event usually starts on the first week in August but has been slowly getting longer as days have been added in front and after the primary week scheduled.

Myrtle Beach Bike Week started in 1940, and Black Bike Week (at Myrtle Beach) started in 1980. Myrtle Beach, South Carolina, has been the location of a number of motorcycle events for decades. Myrtle Beach Bike Week is sometimes called "Harley-Davidson week." The early season events begin with the Myrtle Beach event in mid-May, then Black Bike Week following that event and ending over Memorial Day weekend. There is also a fall event held in October. The first event generally hosts over 200,000 visitors, while Black Bike Week is the larger of the two events, often times hosting over 350,000 guests. The events include racing, concerts, parties, promotional events, and beach activities.

The ROT (Republic of Texas) Rally was first planned in 1994, but the first actual event occurred in 1995. The event is held in downtown Austin, Texas, and has featured some of the largest currently popular southern-rock bands. Groups which have been featured have been Charlie Daniels, Ted Nugent, Grand Funk, Steppenwolf, and David Allen Coe. The event is primarily a funfest of food, bands, mini-shows, stunt riding, biker build-offs, and other forms of entertainment. Held just after Memorial Day in late May, the four-day event has become the largest motorcycle event in Texas. Around 200,000 people will typically attend the event.

Bikes, Blues, & BBQ—Ozarks, Bikes, Blues, & BBQ publicity photo

Fayetteville, Arkansas, has been the center of an event called "Bikes, Blues, & BBQ" since around 2000. The event is a charity event that grew slowly at first but of late has become enormous. From a few thousand attendees, it grew to an estimated 200,000 in 2004 and currently hosts around 400,000 people. From what I have been told, many come for the festivities who do not ride motorcycles. The event is centered around blues bands and features dozens of groups, big and small, during the event. It is always held during the last week in September, and promoters claim that it has attendees from all fifty states. Apart from raising money for charities, it is primarily an entertainment event, and motorcycles are just the primary means of travel.

The Barber Motorcycle Museum in Birmingham, Alabama, was named the largest motorcycle museum in the world in 2014. The original collection goes back into the 1980s, but the current museum building was not built until 2003. An addition was added in 2016. In 2004 the Barber Vintage Festival event started and has grown into possibly the largest vintage motorcycle event in the US. The event hosted around 70,000 people in 2015 and includes AHRMA races (American Historic Racing Motorcycle Association). The museum has a must-see collection, and the early October Vintage Festival event is well worth the trip. The Barber event is dedicated to the motorcycle, rather than crowds of party-goers.

Barber Vintage Festival, From the author's collection

These seven locations that host events are the cities where the largest US motorcycle events occur. Some of these locations have numerous smaller events in their areas on a regular basis. There are thousands of mid-sized and smaller shows throughout the country, which occur throughout the year. All events focus on either some form of direct entertainment, the display or sale of motorcycles or parts, or some form of racing event or motorcycle-related activity. As the years have progressed, most of the older events have remained strong ,and newer events are emerging and are growing. Events that focus on entertainment will typically be much larger than events that are primarily about the motorcycle. Just as with the exponential growth of car shows since 2000, there has also been a growth of motorcycle-focused events

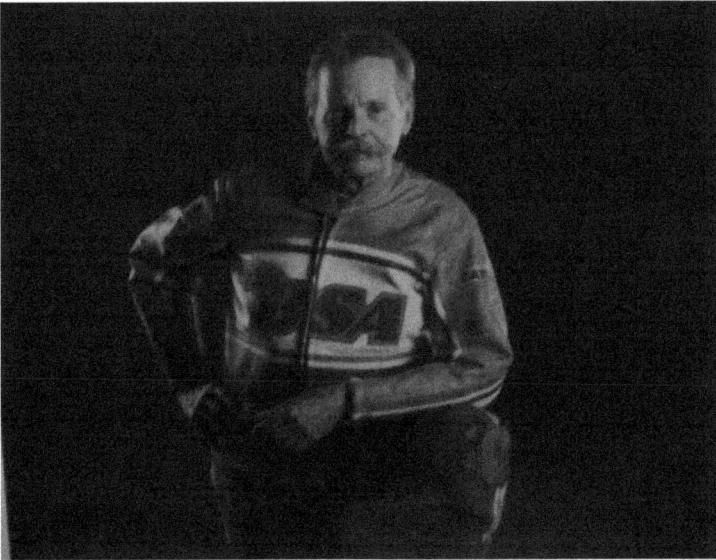

American Historic Motorcycle Racing Association (AHRMA) Racer Stephen Spencer, Courtesy of Stephen Spencer

11

Motorcycle Racing

An Overview of Motorcycle Racing and the Types of Competition

One could guess that the first forms of competition from the most ancient of days were designed to identify or develop the most talented people, to find or develop the best equipment, or could possibly be used as a means of experiencing the adrenaline rush that is enjoyed by being involved in sporting endeavors. These goals certainly fit clearly into the history and development of the motorcycle from its earliest days.

From the beginning of motorcycle history there have been four general and basic types of racing. First, road or track categories of racing. These forms of racing would be on a paved or hard surface roads or tracks. Secondly, a growing list of off-road types of racing. This would include various types of scrambles, flat-track, moto-cross, or super-cross racing. Thirdly, endurance racing, such as the historic trials, dual-sport, or off-road cross-country type racing. Fourthly, there have always been specialty forms of racing, such as hill-climbs, drag racing, the breaking of speed records, vintage racing, and motard racing, where a mix of surfaces and skills is the principal challenge. Certainly, many of the same skills and types of race requirements can be very similar yet be categorized in very different ways. A specific type of race might even be held on a particular track or in a specific area.

Racing typically crosses many boundaries, and so the various types of classifications can be hard to clearly identify and isolate. It is often disputed exactly where a category or type of racing should begin or end. Furthermore, as time progresses, additional types of racing are often introduced in addition to existing types of racing. Most forms of racing programs are continually revised and altered.

This chapter will review the basic types of motorcycle racing platforms within a historical context and will look at their beginnings and how they developed. The complexities of racing cannot be fully explained here because of the vastness of the specific types of races that have been going on historically and how they have evolved over the decades. If you look for an individual book on motorcycle racing, they will

either cover a specific type of race, a particular track(s), or a particular brand or type of race bike. Races within specific countries or some of the great riders over the years can also be valuable topics. The topic is so vast that there are no comprehensive books on the sport. Hopefully, this chapter will provide an overview on the field of racing in general.

The earliest recognized governing body in the US for sponsoring racing events was the FAM (Federation of American Motorcyclists), which existed from around 1904 to 1915. It was discontinued because of the WWI conflict. The AMA (American Motorcycle Association) began 1n 1924 and continues today. The AFM (American Federation of Motorcycles) was started in 1954 and is the oldest road racing club in the US and is the governing body for a number of sanctioned road racing venues. The AFM is licensed through the AMA. The NATC (North American Trials Council) governs trials competition in the US and is also licensed under the AMA. The FIM (Federation of International Motorcycle racing) dates back to 1904 and continues today, however, the organization has undergone a dozen or so revisions. The FIM is the largest international body to govern competition, which includes road racing, moto-cross, trials, enduro, and various track categories. Britain has the ACU (Auto Cycle Union), which originated in 1903 and continues today. The ACU covers every part of motorcycle racing in Britain, including grass track, motocross, enduro, road racing, drag racing, and anything using two wheels. The AHRMA (American Historic Racing Motorcycle Association) sanctions vintage racing in the US. American drag racing is sanctioned by the NHRA (National Hot Rod Association) and superbike racing through MotoAmerica. MotoAmerica also works through the AMA. The oldest active organization that still sponsors motorcycle races is the MCIU (Motorcycle Union of Ireland), with leadership dating back to 1902. There are also dozens of smaller organizations that sponsor and support motorcycle events in various market categories. Smaller racing oversight organizations are often recognized by the larger national associations but function almost separate from them in terms of judging. The numbers continue to grow because of the inherent complexity that exists with an ever-growing number and type of motorcycles being raced. The organizations noted above would probably constitute over ninety percent of all forms of sanctioned motorcycle racing organizations,

however, there are many more smaller groups which operate regionally.

International racing preceded racing in the United States by nearly a decade and was organized by associations a little sooner as well. Because the United States comprised so vast a land area and population numbers were very small in the Midwest region, the market for professional racing was very small, except in specific areas. This was not the case overseas. With towns closer together and a much better road system, race events were larger than American events until the twenties and thirties.

The first recorded road race between motorcycles was unofficially held in Surry, England, as early as 1897, which was an area to become known for motorcycle and auto racing. The famous Brooklands track. which was to be constructed in Surry. was actually the first paved race track built in the world. It was in operation from 1907 and continued until the WWII era. The track was made of unrefined concrete and was bumpy compared to a modern paved tracks.

One of the earliest European races, which was to become known as the Isle of Man TT race, was given that name around 1907, though the races dated as far back as 1904. This sort of track racing didn't come to America until the 1930s, when the Daytona races were first held in the late 1930s. For Europeans, track racing was the premium form of racing and off-road racing was to have to wait much longer to be popular.

The Isle of Man led European manufacturers to be conservative, precise, and to develop riders into being the best that they could possibly be. The British, being inher-ently conservative, were less advanced but much more detail-oriented. They worked hard at getting all that they could out of their engines, tires, brakes, and frames. Every bit of power was squeezed out of the big single-cylinder motorcycles, and every part of the evolving track was considered when adjusting frames, tires, and gearing.

1971 Isle of Man TT. Gunther Bartusch on a 300cc MZ

The British counted on well-balanced machines that did the best with the least changes, while the Germans were the innovators. The British owned much of racing from the 1920s until the very early 1960s by incremental development. They lost ground because of the sheer growth in horsepower by German and Japanese racing machines. Manx and the Manx GP races evolved from the Isle of Man track and were amateur racing events, though highly followed. Manx racing began in 1923 and the GP in 1930. It was not until the early 1960s that the Japanese manufacturers, especially Honda, began to change history in a big way. In 1961 Honda won both the 125 and 250 World Championships, forever changing international racing. Within a decade, all the old names were gone. Today the GP races represent the most advanced motorcycles and the very best riders that have ever been involved in the sport.

Ulster, since the early 1920s, and the Ulster GP, since 1949, have been another high profile road race being held in Ireland. Ulster has been a very historic track, being raced by many of the great racers of old, such as Graham Walker, Stanley Wood, Artie Bell, Les Graham, Geoff Duke, John Surtees, Mike Hailwood, and Phil Reed.

The ISDT (International Six Days Trials), now called the ISDE (Enduro) since 1981, started in England in 1913 and is a premier off-road event. The event has been held around the world, but only once in the US in 1973. This off-road event is a battle for machine, rider endurance, and skill. The distance of generally over 1,200 miles is over mostly rough terrain and little paved roads. It was primarily a European event in the early years but is now an international event. It is clear-

ly a team sport with exacting rules, which can easily disqualify a team. WWII stopped most professional racing until around 1949.

Speedway racing could be found in Europe as early as the late-1920s. Speedway tracks were dirt ovals, with the riders racing full bore with no brakes. The first British speedway races occurred around 1927. It was not until after WWII that off-road motorcycle racing took a huge leap in popularity. Since the early 1950s dozens of types of off-road racing have become popular around the world.

Trials competition was also a European invention. Trials competition were known to exist in a simple form as early as 1910 but did not fully develop until the early 1960s. Some believe that Scotland was the first location for this form of competition, however, there has been active competition in Great Britain, Spain, and the US. America does have Trials competition, but the US was a late-comer to the sport. The NATC (North American Trials Council) was established in 1972. I have heard of a number of regional trials events that operate independently.

Europe's first organized motorcycle races date back to the first of the 1900s and were primarily track races. Dirt track or off-road racing began around 1913. Britain was the primary country for the largest racing venues and also had the most prestigious tracks until the WWII era. After the early 1950s motorcycle racing has exploded around the world.

The first races in the US were on public streets or were on existing horse tracks. They were generally organized locally or were essentially unorganized events. These races began before 1900. There were numerous horse versus motorcycle races that go back to the time of Sylvester Roper and his steam motorcycle at the end of the 1860s. There was a general feeling in the early years that the automobile or motorcycle would never be able to compete with the horse.

The next major type of motorcycle event was the hill-climb, of which events can be dated as far back as 1910. The first hill-climbing events were organized to show how much of an incline a motorcycle could ascend. They were sort of a reliability event. As time moved forward, the hills got tougher, until around the 1970s, after which time, competition became much more severe. The modern hill-climb event would have been an impossibility even thirty years ago. If you look at an event from the 1940s, the hills are still manageable compared to the modern events. It was the increase in horsepower, along with the ability for very light machines to be made which have allowed hill-climbing to evolve into the extreme events that they have become. I might also add that the tires used on serious hill-climbing machines have made a huge difference as well.

Hill-climb

By the early teens, but especially after 1914, dirt tracks became a dominant motorcycle sport. The reader must understand that during the teens and until much later times most American roads were unpaved, so the races were on what were actually typical dirt road surfaces. Dirt roads were all there was. The difference was simply that the track was set aside for racing, rather than for public travel. These early dirt track races were like speedway races, because the motorcycles had no brakes and were operated wide open. Motorcycles were not allowed to have brakes because it was thought that a rider applying their brakes would cause accidents. Furthermore, in the early years the machines had significantly less power than a modern motorcycle, so running wide open was just what was done.

Flat Track Race

As the motorcycles got faster, larger tracks were required. One solution was the use of board tracks. From 1910 until 1929 there were around twenty-four regional board tracks built from California to New Jersey. Board tracks were built using local wood resources and were typically ovals of one to one-and-a-half miles in distance, with the corners being banked. The model for these tracks were the bicycle board tracks, which originated around 1870. The motorcycle required an outdoor track because of the noise, speed, and the fumes. An indoor bicycle track might host several thousand people, while an outdoor motorcycle board track might hold 80,000 people. Many of the board tracks were also used to race cars. In the early years board track racers might go seventy miles per hour, but by the 1930s speeds of over 120 were possible. The tracks themselves, being outdoors, tended to last only a few years. The wood would easily rot or warp. To fully understand why wood was used, the reader needs to understand that paved roads were few and far between.

Vintage Board Track

To build a paved race track would have been financially questionable back in those early days because of the expense and lack of know how.

Wood was cheap, available, and there were many men who knew how to build with wood.

The Indianapolis Speedway was built in 1909 and is considered to be the first paved track built in the US. It was originally built of bricks, then was covered with asphalt in the late 1930s.

The early board tracks caused many tire problems and were not known to be smooth. As the board tracks allowed motorcycles to go faster, it became common

*1911 Excelsior Board Track Racer,
Courtesy of Russ Briggs*

for riders to get badly hurt or to even die. Wood would splinter, and riders could be speared. Many racers actually did die on the track, and deaths also included those in the audience if a motorcycle went off the track. A hole in the track might maim a rider, and a bump might cause a motorcycle to go airborne. The result was the tracks being called "murderdromes." Board track racing was over by the early 1930s.

Large flat track races were known to be held as early as 1911. Locations like the Dodge City, Kansas, track became well-

Dodge City 300, courtesy of Dodge City Daily Globe *and the Kansas City Heritage Center*

attended and famous for battles between manufacturers.

Flat tracks were generally large. The Dodge City track was approximately two-miles around and was first sanctioned by the AMA in 1924. The AMA introduced the Grand National Flat Track races in 1954. The Grand National events offered racing on dirt tracks of mile, half-mile and TT classes. A paved road version of the Grand National was also offered. Both the Riverside and the fa-

mous Ascot race tracks, located in California, were opened in the late 1950s as well. From the mid-1950s there was a huge growth in regional and national racing in America.

Daytona, Florida, became the location of early road racing dating back to the late-1930s. The first races were on sand, then they moved to sand and paved roads. A fully paved track was built sometime during the 1950s. Road racing had its greatest growth after WWII because established tracks were willing to invest money into paving. Daytona includes both road racing and flat track racing.

In the United states, racing followed this general pattern:

- **dirt track**

- **hill-climbing**

- **board track racing**

- **flat track racing/Grand National flat track**

- **scrambles/motocross**

- **desert racing**

- **drag racing**

- **Observed Trials**

- **GP/Moto GP**

- **Motard**

As noted earlier in this chapter, racing centers on a track, which may be either unpaved or paved. Tracks may be on unimproved dirt surfaces or in dirt spaces without a specific track. Special spaces, like steep hills or sandy ditches, may be used. A desert area or salt flats are also used for specific types of racing. Racing can be on a quarter-mile surfaced track or over really rough terrain that could include large rocks. The big endurance races might include dirt, mud, rivers, sand, big hills, and even highway travel in one multi-day event. High speed GT races will have long sections of paved roads, allowing for super-high speeds to be reached. Racing or competition may occur wherever there is a place to pit two or more machines competing against each other or just against a clock.

The history of motorcycle racing has been simply picking a space to compete, establishing some basic rules, having people around who will ensure that the rules are being followed, then seeing who can go the distance the quickest (or in the way that winning is defined) while following the rules. This is why there are so many different types of races and so many differences between races of the same type in different locations. As a race continues over time rules become more complex, and all the various arguments about the nuances of the specific race need to be addressed and adjusted. This is the dance of competition; every competitor pushes the rules in order to win, but without boundaries no win is legitimate or respected.

Manufacturers, parts companies, miscellaneous motorcycle-related businesses, or individuals who just have competition in their bloodstreams race for many of the same core reasons. At the top of the list is the desire to win; to be the best. Winning builds pride, esteem, and the desire to do even better. Showing yourself a winner is important to people wanting to excel. From the earliest years of motorcycle production, companies wanted their name to be the one mentioned in the winners' circle. Secondly, winning

requires developing a product. The British raced big singles long after they were no longer truly viable products. The British singles, like the BSA Goldstar, Norton Manx, Matchless G 80s, and Velocette Venoms, were raced long after the engines were no longer competitive. They did continue to win races because the motorcycles handled well and the riders were refined and competent. As noted before, the British owned much of racing for many decades. More advanced German and Japanese motorcycles struggled at first until their machines and riders were refined, then the older bikes were left far behind.

Modern factory race bikes require a fortune on development and rider salaries in order to win but there is typically

Modern GP Race

some trickle down technology. For parts builders, being a

winner is directly reflected in the quality of their products.

In the early years of motorcycles and racing, there was the idea that to win on Sunday meant a sale on Monday. Winning certainly

Honda RCV211, courtesy of American Honda

can impact sales, and manufacturers certainly were aware of this. Racing does improve the breed, and the various brands need to convince their customers that they are the ones making the improvements. In general, winning in competition speaks well of a motorcycle.

Companies like Penton were dependent on winning, and when they did there was definitely a spike in sales.

Penton Enduro, courtesy of Penton USA

This brief discussion on motorcycle racing is short and is an overview, at best. Racing has been a very important part of the motorcycle community since the very earliest days of the sport. Types and the categories of competition are always growing, with promoters always looking for ways to draw a larger crowd. Racing is either about the ability of the bike, the location of the competition, or the skill of the rider. These factors will never change much. The only factors which will continually change are the rules. Competitive advantage is about using the rules to a team's greatest benefit. This is both good and bad. Good, because it requires development to make a motorcycle better at competing, but bad because of the tendency to overstep boundaries is ever present.

GasGas Trials Bike, Manufacturer's promotional photo

Harley-Davidson XR750 Racer, Courtesy of Russ Briggs

Beta Brand Motard Racer, Stock photo

12

Dates and Developments

A Timeline of Important Dates and Historical Developments Related to the Motorcycle

This section is an incomplete list of motorcycle firsts and includes important dates related to the development and significance of the motorcycle throughout its history.

Many firsts are found to be incorrectly assigned and are often challenged by those who research specific developments. My goal is to simply recognize these developments, and I do not wish argue the various nuances surrounding them. New findings are always being interjected, which are great to consider and are often entertaining to discuss, but are generally not worthy of an argumentative debate. Some items determined to be new are often a revision of something that already existed. An example would be bicycle pedals transitioning into the kick-starter. These dates come from many sources, and I will list them in the reference section of this chapter.

1862—First compression engine.

1876—Otto Cycle built.

1885—Gottlieb Damlier motorcycle (2 training wheels).

1885—Damlier V-twin engine tested (first used as a boat engine).

1887—De Dion-Buton "original" engine built but not perfected.

1889—Damlier V-twin engine built to be sold and marketed.

1892—First pneumatic tire sold to replace solid rubber treads.

1894—Hildebrand & Wolfmuller motorcycle commercially built and sold.

1896—Carl Benz built first "boxer" engine design.

1896—First motor show, which included motorcycles, in London, England.

1896—The first 4-cylinder motorcycle was built by Henry L. Holden by placing two sets of twin-cylinder engines side by side (British).

1899—Orient motorcycle built and claimed to have been sold.

1900—the American Columbia motorcycle was built by Colonel Albert Pope, who was to later build one of the most popular American motorcycles.

1900—George M. Holley builds his first motorcycle. Holley later became famous for his carburetors, which became an early standard.

1901—Matchless, Opel, NSU, Indian, Durkopp motorcycles begin production.

1901—The term *moto-cycle* becomes more common.

1902—Adler, Rover, Triumph, Ariel, Merkel, Norton motorcycles begin production.

1902—Spark plug greatly perfected over glow tube.

1903 Motorcycle Engine, From the author's collection

1903—Mars, Curtiss, Tribune, Thor, Rambler motorcycles go into production.

1903—The magneto is perfected.

1903—First V-twin sold, manufactured by Curtiss.

1903—Harley-Davidson begins developing a motorcycle, first sold in 1904.

1904—First two- & three-speed transmissions emerge; most still used leather belt final-drive systems.

1904—Hand pumps for engine lubrication are offered on some bikes.

1904—Sidecars had originally been designed for use on bicycles, but in this year the first sidecar was attached to a motorcycle. This led to the demise of tricycle-type three-wheelers, because it was easier to just attach a sidecar to an existing motorcycle, rather than engineer and build a special frame and drive-train.

1905—The friction clutch is offered as an attachment to current motorcycles.

1906—Stable foot pegs first emerge and begin to replace bicycle pedals.

1907—Isle of Man TT Race begins (British Isles).

1907—Curtis builds a V-8 motorcycle. The engine was first used for an airplane. and he goes 136.27 mph.

Curtis V-8 Motorcycle, Period photo

1908—Triumph offers a variable-speed transmission.

1909—First hemispherical-head engine used on the Royale Pioneer motorcycle.

1909—First kick-starter offered on the Scott motorcycle (British).

1909—Motorcycle sales go over 10,000 units per year (from around 7,000 in 1908 to just under 15,000 in 1909).

1910—BSA begins building it's first motorcycle.

1910—Over 100 US brands of motorcycles.

1911—Detroit motorcycle brand offers "oil in frame" system.

1911—Henderson offers an in-line 4-cylinder engine, which copies the FN brand.

1911—First motorcycles used for police patrol in California.

1912—Kick-starters are common, and most motorcycle brands begin removing their bicycle pedals.

1913—First rear swingarm offered (Indian, Merkel, and Pope).

1913—First push-rods used for intake & exhaust valves, first water-cooled motorcycle engine built and sold. Water cooling existed before 1900 as an experimental system.

1913—Gasoline was18 cents per gallon.

1913—Motorcycles sales reach around 70,000 units yearly and remains the highest figure until the very end of the 1950s.

1914—The first stop sign was installed and was located in Detroit.

1915—Electric lighting becomes more common and an option on many bikes.

1915—Gasoline rises to 20 cents per gallon.

1920—Harley-Davidsons are sold in 67 countries.

1921—Moto Guzzi goes into production.

1923—Laconia, New Hampshire, Motorcycle Rally begins. Bikes began meeting there in 1916 as an unorganized event.

1923—Max Fritz designs first BMW motorcycle.

First BMW Single, 1924, Courtesy of Yesterday's Antique and Classic Motorcycles

1925—There were only 500,000 miles of surfaced roads in America, compared to over 56 million miles today (not paved roads, but roads with a surface of some type).

1927—Reggie Pink begins importing British motorcycles to the US in small numbers.

1928—First mechanical front brake used. The few front brakes that existed before this time were just a piece of wood or metal pressed against the front tire, and they were rare.

1928—DKW, a German manufacturer, becomes world's largest producer of motorcycles.

1928—Philip Vincent buys the defunct HRD (Howard R. Davies) motorcycle company, which built motorcycles between 1924 and 1928, and builds his own motorcycle, which gets a name change in 1949 to the Vincent.

1928—Texaco has gasoline stations located in 48 states, allowing for greater distances to be traveled. All states were taxing gasoline by this time as well.

1937—Bill Johnson begins importing Ariel and Triumph motorcycles into California.

1932—The first "hard-tail" rear suspension is offered on the Italian Sertum motorcycle.

1936—Triumph car and motorcycle groups split into two separate businesses.

1936—Cushman releases their first scooter.

1937—Daytona Beach races and events begin (Florida).

1937—Edward Turner designs the Triumph Speed Twin, which has a significant influence on the British motorcycle industry.

1938—Sturgis, South Dakota, is the location of motorcycle races, which later becomes one of the largest motorcycle rallies in the world.

1939—BSA copies the Triumph Speed Twin.

1940—Myrtle Beach Motorcycle Rally begins (South Carolina).

1940—First sealed-beam headlight used.

1946—First rubber-mounted engine used on the British Sunbeam.

1947—Sochiro Honda build his first motorcycle.

First Honda Engine on a Bicycle, Courtesy of Barber Vintage Motorsports Museum

243

1949—Norton unveils the Featherbed frame, which is copied by nearly all other British manufacturers within just a few years.

1951—BSA buys the Triumph brand of motorcycles. With BSA and Triumph sales combined, the group claimed to be the world's largest producer of motorcycles.

1952—First Suzuki motorcycle built.

1953—The original line of Indian motorcycles stops production.

1953—The movie *The Wild One* opens and has a significant impact on motorcycling.

1955—Yamaha builds first motorcycle, copied from the DKW125.

1959—Honda begins exporting motorcycles into the US and within four years becomes the largest motorcycle manufacturer in the world.

1959—John Oates starts the 59 Club, which becomes a large worldwide club.

1960—Yamaha begins officially exporting motorcycles into the US.

1960—Between 1960 and 1962 motorcycle sales jump around 33% (from around 60,000 yearly to around 90,000 yearly, a huge jump).

1962—Kawasaki Heavy Industries buys the oldest motorcycle manufacturer in Japan, Meguro, and begins developing its own line of motorcycles.

1962—BSA offers the A10 Rocket Gold Star as a special model in 1962 and 1963. It is considered to be one of the most beautiful British motorcycles ever made. An estimated 1,584 motorcycles were ever built; many today are copies.

1965—Honda builds a 5-cylinder 125cc racer, causing the FIM to not allow small racing motorcycles to have more than two cylinders.

1966—AMC (Associated Motorcycle Corporation) files for receivership, showing how much trouble the British motorcycle industry was in. AMC built AJS, Matchless, James, Francis-Barnett, and Norton.

1967—Norton re-emerges as a brand after Manganese Bronze purchased AMC.

1969—The Honda CB750 was unveiled, and after 2000, becomes recognized as the motorcycle of the century. The CB750 has been called the most significant motorcycle in modern times and outsold the BSA and Triumph three-cylinder motorcycles combined, by nearly four times.

1969—BSA offers the Rocket 3, and Triumph offers the Trident. Both are 3-cylinder motorcycles that just add another cylinder to existing models.

1970—Ducati builds its first V-twin and begins making larger motorcycles.

1970—Yamaha introduces the XS650 twin, the first four-stroke Yamaha motorcycle marketed.

Yamaha XS650, From the author's collection

1970—Yamaha breaks the world speed record at Bonneville, going 251.66 mph using two 350cc two-stroke engines.

1971—The movie *On Any Sunday*, a documentary on motor-cycle racing, greatly increases interest in racing and starts a genuine amateur racing movement.

1973—Ducati builds its first Desmo (desmodromic valve gear).

1973—This year records the highest sales for motorcycles ever. Close to 1.8 million motorcycles were sold in the US that year.

1975—The Honda Gold Wing first offered as a flat-four, and it becomes the premier touring motorcycle.

1975—Yamaha breaks the world speed record at Bonneville, going 265.492 mph.

1983—Eric Buell starts Buell Motorcycles, and the brand ends in 2009.

1984—Yamaha begins using the 5-valves-per-cylinder heads on many models of motorcycles.

1985—Cagiva buys Ducati.

1985—Yamaha unveils the V-Max, which begins the naked muscle bike category.

1988—ABS brakes first offered by BMW.

1990—Triumph unveils its new line of motorcycles to be sold around the world.

1996—Honda unveils the 1100cc Super Black Bird, which can reach 180mph.

Honda Super Blackbird, From the author's collection

1999—Suzuki unveils the Hayabusa, which tops the Honda Super Black Bird by being able to reach approximately 190 mph.

2007—Taiwan, China, and India become the largest producers of motorcycles in the world by a large number.

2008—The Honda Cub reached 60,000,000 in sales around the world.

Honda Cub, Courtesy of Bill Brown

2008—Between 2008 and 2010, motorcycle sales drop nearly 40%. 2008 was the year when the stock market crash

was greater than the one in 1929, which brought the Great Depression.

2009—Ducati patents the first "frameless" motorcycle.

2012—Triumph celebrates its 110th year of production.

2015—Honda reported that the motorcycle division of the company had sold 300,000,000 motorcycles between 1947 and 2015.

13

Final Thoughts

Concluding Comments

The motorcycle has been around for well over a century and has found its own varied following. Actually, two-wheeled transportation is approaching 150 years in existence. In America the motorcycle is primarily an object of leisure. Common uses are for law enforcement, commuting, industrial use, touring, sporting around, and hunting. Small machines are often used as pit bikes or for meandering around camps or events. Probably high on the list is the motorcycle as a "stress-relief" vehicle! The motorcycle is primarily a means of entertainment, and a good one at that. Some claim that the motorcycle has allowed them to maintain their sanity.

There was great hope placed on the new steam-, electric-, and petro-leum-based vehicles of the early 1900s. The idea that "machines" would increase productivity and make life better was an idea that had found its time.

Steam quickly lost out because steam engines worked best with large engines on trains or large farm tractors. When steam power-plants were reduced in size for cars or trucks they were not as efficient. Furthermore, these vehicles needed a continual water supply, so they were dependent on going places where there was water readily available. Steam power also required boilers, pressure tubes, and some form of fuel, which burnt inefficiently. Steam also required a special form of technical expertise, which was more complex than most were comfortable with.

Electric power also had some serious limitations. An electric-powered vehicle was limited by distance. If the batteries were good for fifty miles, the vehicle could only go twenty-five miles until the return trip had to be considered. Charging locations were expensive, and because there were few electric vehicles, it was costly to build charging stations. Furthermore, depending on the type of vehicle and load, the travel distance was not really accurately known. Batteries were also expensive and heavy.

None of these issues were a problem with the internal-combustion engine. Small engines actually worked just as efficiently as big ones, they

were light, and a fuel supply was available through most hardware stores. Gasoline was used as a cleaning agent for pumps, which were becoming common, and as a chemical for starting fires. It was also really cheap. The greatest thing was that a small engine could be placed on a bicycle and would propel the rider down roads much faster than pedaling. The gas-powered bicycle would also go up hills readily and could take the rider to the next town in a short amount of time. Gasoline would also be available in the next town.

As more bicycles were powered by small engines, the business of making motorcycles grew larger and more complex. The engines began to grow in size, and riders began to go farther and faster. The manufacturers began to copy each other, and nearly all the motorcycles made began to function much better. By the teens, dozens of companies, regional and nationally based, began to pop up. A new product had been engineered and was marketable. As motorcycles got better, more people used them.

When the automobile grew in popularity, the sales of cars seriously hurt the fledgling motorcycle business. Because of the sport of motorcycling, there remained a market for the machines, which ultimately found their own niche. The motorcycle found its own market and really came into its own after the 1920s. With more brands from around the world flooding into America, especially after WWII, and with more sizes being made available, the motorcycle was definitely here to stay. The sport of motorcycling became a lifestyle that was seen as sporty, somewhat dangerous, and very masculine in nature.

Early Sidecar, courtesy of Yesterday's Antique and Classic Motorcycles

The tough guy appearance, in terms of being either athletic or promoting a physical image that was seen as socially desirable, became important to many motorcyclists. If these qualities were not high on the list, the motorcycle allowed for the rider to feel free and to get the adrenaline rush of speed and wind in the face. The motorcycle could also allow for the feelings of being a loner or the desire to be a wanderer to be freely experienced. The motorcycle allowed for the identity of the rider to be freely expressed and was not nearly as expensive as doing it in a car. There are many individual reasons why people ride motorcycles, but at the top of the list is the natural sensations which are readily available on two wheels.

As the years have passed there has been quite a legacy that has developed around the motorcycle and its development. The motorcycle can be an inexpensive way to get a thrill, the motorcycle can appeal to the natural need to express an image in an outward way, the motorcycle can be a source of experiencing nature (like horse and rider of old), or the motorcycle can be a means of finding a person's physical limits. Whatever the case, the motorcycle connects many people to the values they see as important or see as significant to their lives.

The largest group within the motorcycle community is the cruiser segment. In America the feet-forward, lounge chair, low-slung motorcycle represents over a third of all motorcycles sold in the US. Some would say the figure is closer to fifty percent. The cruiser fits the American lifestyle.

The big touring and sport touring bikes represent another serious segment of the market. These bikes, the big Harleys, the Gold Wings, or the big BMWs, are all built for the long-distance traveler. Cross-country touring has become very popular in the US. Every summer motorcycles are seen on the highways and traveling the Interstates. It is not uncommon for the men to ride to a location far away, while their wives fly to the location later. Once at the desired location, they go together. There are also women's riding clubs. You guessed it; men are typically not allowed.

The sport bike crowd is definitely made up of the thrill seekers. The typical modern sport bikes really fly. There are many deaths on these bikes, because the riders go far beyond any posted speed limits. This practice sours the image of the sport, and is incredibly dangerous as well. Motorcycle safety is very important for both rider and the other vehicles on the road.

Dual-sport and off-road motorcycles continue to be popular; however, the larger size of many of these motorcycles makes riding them very different than the street scramblers of years past.

Without question, motorcycling is a fun sport. Because of the inherent dangers of riding out in the open, protective body wear is desirable. Safety should be high on the list of importance. When I go riding, I make myself aware of the dangers of riding by reflecting on what could potentially happen while on the street. Even more importantly, I ride as though every driver in a car is a really bad driver who cannot see me. Always make sure you have a safety net around you by having a space to go if a problem occurs. Do not take foolish risks but drive within all the road rules. Learn to be extra careful when the roads are wet or in poor condition. It is advisable to take a certified riding course and, above all, be familiar with the machines that you ride.

Hopefully, this book has given you a better picture of the sport. My goal was to give the reader a usable and simple outline of the history of the motorcycle. Please do some additional research on topics you find interesting. There is some really interesting information out there. I would challenge you to visit some vintage motorcycle events in your area and to visit a motorcycle museum when you can. My hunch is that you will really enjoy the motorcycles. The study of the motorcycle can be a never-ending quest for information. I will almost always have a motorcycle book in-hand, anxious to learn something new. Let this book be a start of your journey into the world of motorcycling

The Author's Triumph Speedmaster, From the author's collection.

14

Resources:

Books

Alexander, Jeffrey W. *An Introductory History, Japan's Motorcycle Wars*. Vancouver B.C: UBC, 2008.

Avery, Deret. *Motorcycles*. Oxfordshire: Caxton, 1988.

Bacon, Roy. *An Illustrated History of the Motorcycle*. London: Promotional Reprint Company, 1995.

Bacon, Roy, Hallworth, Ken. *The British Motorcycle Directory*. Ramsbury: Crowood, 2004.

Brown, Roland. *Classic Motorcycles*. NY: Hermes House, 1999.

Brown, Roland. *History of the Motorcycle*. UK: Parragon, 2004.

Brown, Roland. *The Motorcycle, A Complete Story*. Bath, UK: Paragon, 2004

Carroly, John. *The Motorcycle a Definitive History*. NY: Smithmark, 1997.

Clarke, Massimo. *100 Years of Motorcycles*. NY: Portland House, 1986.

Clymer, Floyd. *A Treasury of Motorcycles of The World*. NY: McGraw Hill, 1965.

DeCet, Mirco. *The Complete History of Classic Motorcycles*. Netherlands: Rebo, 2008.

DeCet, Mirco. *The Illustrated History of the Motorcycle.* St. Paul: MBI, 2002.

Falloon, Ian. *The Ducati Monster Bible.* UK: Veloice, 2011.

Ganneau, Didler, Dumas, Francois-Marie. *A Century of Japanese Motorcycles.* St. Paul: MBI, 2001.

Garson, Paul. *Born To Be Wild.* NY: Simon & Schuster, 2003.

Girdler, Allen. *The Harley-Davidson and Indian Wars.* Minnesota: MBI, 1997.

Hatfield, Jerry, Halberstadt. *Indian Motorcycles.* Wisconsin: MBI, 1996.

Hatfield, Jerry. *Standard Catalogue of American Motorcycles.* Wisconsin: Krause, 2006.

Holmes, Tim, Smith, Rebekka. *Classic Motorcycles.* Canada: PRC, 1986.

Holmstrom, Darwin. *Indian Motorcycles, Americas First Motorcycle Company.* Minnesota: Motor Books, 1996.

Hopwood, Bert. *Whatever Happened to the British Motorcycle Industry?* England: Haynes, 1981.

Hough, Richard, Setright, L.J.K. *A History of the World's Motorcycles.* NY: Harper & Row, 1966.

Howdle, Peter. *Best of British.* Cambridge: PSL. 1979.

Kimes, Beverly. *The Star and the Laurel.* NJ: Mercedez Benz of America, 1986.

Lacombe, Christian. *The Motorcycle.* NY: Grosset & Dunlap, 1974.

Mitchel, Doug. *Harley-Davidson Motorcycles 1903-2003.* Wisconsin: Krause, 2004.

Mitchel, Doug. *Japanese Motorcycles 1959-2007.* Wisconsin. Krause, 2007.

Pavey, Adrian. *100 Years of Japanese Motorcycles.* England: Evenwood, 2000.

Posthumus, Cyril, Holliday, Bob, Ayton, Cyril, Winfield, Mike. *A History of Motorcycling.* London: Orbis, 1979.

Reynolds, Tom. *Wild Ride.* NY: TN Books, 2000.

Sagnier, Thierry. *Bike.* Canada: Fitzhenry & Whitside, 1974.

Schilling, Phil. *The Motorcycle World.* Toronto: Random House, 1974.

Sheehan, Dave. *Superbikes of the 1970s.* Buckinghamshire: Panther, 1988.

Sucher, Harry. *Harley-Davidson: The Milwaukee Marvel.* USA: Haynes, 1992.

Sucher, Harry. *Inside American Motorcycling.* California: Infosport, 1995.

Thompson, Eric, Caddell, Laurie. *From Motorcycle to Superbike.* New Orchard, 1986.

Tragatsch, Edwin. *An Illustrated History of Motorcycles*. NY: Quarto, 1986.

Vanderheuval, Cornelis. *A Pictorial History of Japanese Motorcycles*. Holland: Elmar, 1997.

Walker, Mick. *German Motorcycles*. London: Osprey, 1989.

Walker, Mick. Hamlyn. *History of the Motorcycle*. Great Britain: Reed, 1997.

Walker, Mick. *Italian Motorcycles*. UK: Aston, 1991.

Wright, Stephen. *The American Motorcycle 1896-1914*. US: Megden, 2001.

Websites:

Hiko, Terveisin. "Early Japanese Motorcycles." www.GT-rider. com. Golden Triangle Rider August 2015.

No author noted. "Classic Jap Cycles." www.classicjapcycles.com. Powered by Google, no date published.

No author noted. "Floyd Clymer." www.amamotorcyclemuseum. org.

No author noted. "Hap Alzina." www.amamotorcyclemuseum. org

No author noted. "Sylvestor Roper." www.amamotorcyclemuseum.org.

No author noted. "Honda Motorcycles." www.hondarenaissance. com. March 2015.

No author noted. "Motorcycles Sales Statistics." www.webbikeworld.com. Motorcycle news. July 12, 2015, August 10, 2015, October 18, 2015, December 1, 2015, January 11, 2016, February 9, 2016, March 15, 2016, April 3, 2016, July 24, 2016, September 19, 2016, November 16, 2016, December 28, 2016, February 5, 2017, June 8, 2017, August 3, 2017

www.ingramcontent.com/pod-product-compliance
Lightning Source LLC
Chambersburg PA
CBHW052033090426
42739CB00010B/1886